The Making of
Mămăligă

The Making of Mămăligă

Transimperial Recipes for a Romanian National Dish

Alex Drace-Francis

Central European University Press
Budapest – Vienna – New York

©2022 Alex Drace-Francis

Published in 2022 by
CENTRAL EUROPEAN UNIVERSITY PRESS

Nádor utca 9, H-1051 Budapest, Hungary
Tel: +36–1–327–3138 or 327–3000
E-mail: *ceupress@press.ceu.edu*
Website: *www.ceupress.com*

All rights reserved. No part of this publication may be reproduced, stored in a retrieval system, or transmitted, in any form or by any means, without the permission of the Publisher.

ISBN 978-963-386-583-5 (hardback)
ISBN 978-963-386-584-2 (ebook)
ISBN 978-963-386-624-5 (paperback)

Cover image:
villagers making *balmoș*, a type of mămăligă with cream or whey specific to Transylvania, adjudged to be the largest ever made. Gârda de Sus, Alba county, Romania, 2007. Photo credit: Doru Panaitescu

Library of Congress Cataloging-in-Publication Data

Names: Drace-Francis, Alex, author.
Title: The making of mămăligă : transimperial recipes for a Romanian national dish / Alex Drace-Francis.
Description: Budapest ; Vienna ; New York : Central European University Press, 2022. | Includes bibliographical references and index.
Identifiers: LCCN 2022028310 (print) | LCCN 2022028311 (ebook) | ISBN 9789633865835 (hardback) | ISBN 9789633865842 (ebook)
Subjects: LCSH: Polenta--Romania--History. | Romania--History. | National characteristcs. | Romania--Social life and customs. | Cooking (Corn)--Romania--History. | BISAC: HISTORY / Europe / Eastern | SOCIAL SCIENCE / Agriculture & Food (see also POLITICAL SCIENCE / Public Policy / Agriculture & Food Policy)
Classification: LCC TX360.R8 D73 2022 (print) | LCC TX360.R8 (ebook) | DDC 641.6/567209498--dc23/eng/20220803
LC record available at https://lccn.loc.gov/2022028310
LC ebook record available at https://lccn.loc.gov/2022028311

O Mamaliga, o Malai! Ach du schöne Walachei!
(Oh Mamaliga, Oh Malai! Oh, lovely Wallachia, oh my!)
Danubian German saying

Nu călca mămăliga în picoare mă, că te-a bate la pîntece
(Don't trample mămăligă underfoot, or it will hit you in the stomach)
Romanian saying

Mem., get recipe for this also.
Bram Stoker, *Dracula*

Table of Contents

List of Maps, Graphs, Tables ix

Introduction: The Land is Waiting 1

Chapter 1. From the Caribbean to the Carpathians:
The Coming of Cucuruz, c.1492–1700 13

Chapter 2. Conquerors, Cultivators and Collaborators:
Maize at Empire's Edge, 1700–1774 35

Chapter 3. Climate, Conflict, Contagion and Commerce:
The Triumph of Maize, 1774–1812 49

Chapter 4. Maize, *Raki* or Death: The Revolt of 1821 Reconsidered 71

Chapter 5. Mămăligă 2.0: Maize on the World Market, 1829–1856 85

Chapter 6. Independence, Capitalism, Disease and Revolt;
Or, Why the Mămăligă Exploded, 1856–1907 95

Chapter 7. *Manna valachorum*: Recipes at the Interface 113

Chapter 8. 'The sparrow dreams of cornmeal, and the idle man of a feast day':
Mămăligă as Metaphor 131

Conclusion: The Land is Waiting 141

Appendix: Words and Things 149

Glossary 161

Mămăligography 165

Illustration Credits 195

Acknowledgements 197

Index 201

List of Maps, Graphs, Tables

Map 1: Maize in Southeastern Europe, c.1550–1700 32
Map 2: Empires and Frontiers, c. 1700 33
Map 3: Maize in Wallachia, 1716–1820 47
Map 4: Maize in Moldavia, 1713–1820 48
Map 5: Wallachia during the 1821 revolt 78
Map 6: Average wheat production by county in 1907 111
Map 7: Average maize production by county in 1907 111
Map 8: Words for maize in Romanian 149

Graph 1: Cereals cultivated in Romania, 1862–1905 (hectares) 110
Graph 2: Cereals exported from Romania, 1862–1905 (thousands of tonnes) 110

Table 1: Some place and personal names, c. 1450–1800 158

Introduction
The Land is Waiting

In 2003, Mihai, one of ten children of a poor Roma family living in rural northeastern Romania, obtained a place to study at the Faculty of Theology of the University of Iași, one of the country's most prestigious academic institutions. However, after suffering from both financial difficulties and ethnic discrimination, Mihai returned to the family home for a year. His time away from college, where he participated in the heavy labour of his rural homestead while trying to keep up his studies in dire conditions, forms the main subject of the 2004 documentary film *The Land is Waiting*. As the documentary recounts, Mihai's story had a happy outcome as he was successfully readmitted to university, coming fifth out of twenty-six candidates in the entry exam.[1]

The English title of the film, *The Land is Waiting*, captures the ambiguity of Mihai's situation and what he might expect from life: a future of promise, or a dire existence of agrarian toil. The Romanian title, on the other hand, is *Mămăliga te așteaptă* (Mămăliga Awaits You), after a phrase addressed to Mihai by his mother. This, she tells him, is what his fate will be if he doesn't get back to university. Mămăligă refers to a simple dish of polenta or cornmeal porridge. It's an easy dish to make, and not a hard word to say either, but the cultural meanings are considerably more complex. If Mihai can expect mămăligă, this means he may have basic nourishment and fulfilment of primary needs; but also a possibly shameful, messy or ruinous situation.

The Land is Waiting is just one of many works, whether of documentation or of the imagination, and whether by Romanians or foreign observers, where reference to the dish mămăligă serves as an indicator of status and identity that appears both

---
[1] Calciu (dir.), *The Land is Waiting*.

known and insecure, comforting yet potentially stigmatic. We could also mention, among many examples, the prize-winning 2007 feature film *4 Months, 3 Weeks and 2 Days*, directed by leading Romanian filmmaker Cristian Mungiu. In one scene in this film, the godfather of one of the leading characters, Dima, sits down to dinner with his family and asserts the virtues of traditional thrift and hard work in recalling his youth in the Moldavian countryside, where, growing up in a peasant household, he was able to learn while living off the staple of mămăligă, which his mother would prepare and place in the centre of the family of nine children. Dima's invocation of the virtues of mămăligă is placed in implicit contrast with the fussier food choices of the younger characters. His godson Adi, for example, refuses to eat pork. The scene continues with the older characters discussing their family traditions of making the dish: while Dima recalls that his mother added milk to it, another recommends making it with butter and water. 'We never had butter', replies Dima, before lecturing the young university students who, according to him, have everything given to them on a plate by the government. All this mămăligă talk bores and disgusts the students, who have other things on their minds.[2]

Mungiu's movie drama, which won the coveted Palme d'Or prize at the 2007 Cannes Film Festival, is considered to be part of the New Wave of contemporary Romanian cinema, one of the most innovative branches of the international arts scene.[3] But the invocation of mămăligă as a marker of authenticity and humility goes back much further in the country's cultural memory. As far back as 1849, playwright Costache Caragiali's one-act vaudeville comedy, entitled *Doi coțcari* (Two Swindlers), considered by critics as a pioneering work of realist Romanian theatre, was performed in Bucharest. In this drama too—part of an earlier 'New Wave' of European social performance which swept the country in the nineteenth century—a character references mămăligă as a characteristic of the provincial lower classes. 'When I am your servant', one swindler says to the other,

> people would swear that I lived off mămăligă all my life. A careless gait, idle gaze, clumsy hand movements, a coarse speaking voice. These are all powerful shields against any searching gaze. But were I a boyar: head held high, delicate waistline, mincing gait, agitated hands, small eyes, chirrupy voice; these are the true characteristics of a braggart, of a parvenu who tries to play it big in the provinces.[4]

---

2 Palmer-Mehta and Haliliuc, 'The performance of silence', 123.
3 D. Nasta, *Contemporary Romanian Cinema*.
4 Caragiali, 'Doi coțcari', 271.

Likewise, in the Moldavian play *Surugiul* (The Coach-Driver, 1860), a one-act sketch by Vasile Alecsandri, a leading figure in the creation of modern Romanian literature, the eponymous character makes reference to mămăligă to satirize an unassimilated foreigner in the province, a Greek passenger in his coach, who is so horrified by the prospect of having to eat this dish at a roadside inn that he faints. 'You should have told him about olives, lemons, but not *mamalinga*', remarks another Greek character, disdaining the national dish while also mispronouncing its name.[5]

* * *

Mămăligă, then, has functioned as an indicator of ethnic identity, social status and mores in Romanian narrative drama for well over a century and a half. More generally, it is not just a staple food but a cultural signifier, fitting into the category of 'untranslatables'.[6] The basic ingredients and main variants can be simply described: it is a cake or porridge made by mixing cornmeal into water boiled in a pan or cauldron, followed by vigorous stirring.[7] It is sometimes but not always garnished with milk, butter or soft white cheese. The dish is also known under similar names in parts of Bulgaria, Moldova, Serbia, Ukraine and Poland. In a broader gastronomic geography, the content does not differ radically from Italian *polenta*, Georgian *gomi* or other variants. Dishes very similar to mămăligă are eaten with relish in Mozambique, Mexico and China. At the end of the eighteenth century, a North American variant of mămăligă, known as 'hasty pudding', nearly became the national dish of the newly independent United States.[8] And yet both the dish itself and its cultural associations in Romanian society are often felt to be specific and difficult to convey precisely to outsiders.

A motif- or trope-based approach to mămăligă, looking at its sociocultural meanings, or at its transmission in literature, theatre and folklore, can help outsiders understand its resonance in everyday life.[9] But the story of this dish is more complex and international than such an approach would suggest. Romania has

---

5 Alecsandri, 'Surugiul', 73.
6 Cassin et al., eds. *Dictionary of Untranslatables*. It is a shame that there is no entry for mămăligă in this reference work.
7 Throughout this work I refer to maize rather than corn, which is the standard term for *Zea mays* in the USA and many other countries, to avoid confusion with other contexts where corn may refer to any cereal. However, for ground maize I use 'cornmeal' as the most common term in most varieties of English.
8 Fussell, *Story of Corn*, 255.
9 For this type of approach, see, for example, Belasco and Scranton, eds., *Food Nations*; Wilson, ed. *Food, Drink and Identity in Europe*; Gentilcore, *Pomodoro!*; or, for Balkan case studies: Roth, 'Türkentrank'; Mihăilescu, 'En quête de la sarma'; Detchev, 'Dress, Food, and Boundaries'; Smith and Jusztin, 'Paprika'; Nagy, 'Whose is *Kürtőskalács*?'; Mlekuž, *Burek*; Mlekuž, 'Renaissance of Sausage'; Blaszczyk and

been an independent national state since the nineteenth century, and was consolidated into a larger political unit after 1918. Before that, however, its constituent lands lay at the crossroads of larger empires, Ottoman, Habsburg and Russian. Not only Romanians but many other peoples, including Hungarians, Bulgarians, Serbs, Albanians, Ukrainians, Germans, Greeks, Turks, Jews, Armenians and Roma Gypsies, inhabited these borderlands. The making of mămăligă took place in this eminently transnational and transimperial cauldron over roughly two and a half centuries, from the middle of the seventeenth century to the beginning of the twentieth.[10] In some periods mămăligă boiled steadily on the stove of history, or was even stored quietly on the pantry shelf. At others it was vigorously stirred by war, disease, exploitation and tyranny. It was subject to territorial slicing, and during more than one moment of revolution the dish was in danger of exploding. Sometimes it fed the people, sometimes it was lacking; at others, even its presence caused serious nutritional problems in the form of diseases such as pellagra.

One approach to telling the story of mămăligă would be to argue that the specific unfolding of events and processes in these lands rendered the Romanian maize experience unique. The way historians tell national histories is not too different from the way people tell recipes: mămăligă, like my country, was made in this way and not in another. This perspective should not be scorned: it is entirely true that what happened in a given place did not happen in the same way elsewhere. In what follows I seek to offer new information on how individuals used maize at specific historical conjunctures, on what today constitutes Romanian territory.

At the same time, the development of a carbohydrate-rich but status-poor dish as the staple of a larger agrarian population is a relatively common historical phenomenon across the world in modern times. Analogies, comparisons and contrasts can be made, both with other maize-eating societies such as those of west Africa, east Asia, or the southern states of the US, but also with the spread and deployment of other staple foods such as rice or potatoes, which sustained large subaltern populations in ways both similar to and different from what happened in southeastern Europe.[11] As Alison Frank Johnson has recently argued, environmental and global history approaches can be a productive way of challenging the traditional nation-state-centred approach to historical inquiry. But Frank Johnson also reminds us that 'the potential for environmental history to be placed in a

---

Rohdewald, eds. *From Kebab to Ćevapčići*. Neuburger, *Ingredients of Change* arrived just after this book went to press.
10 Calic, *Great Cauldron*.
11 Latham, *Rice*; Reader, *Potato*.

global context does not render smaller-scale studies of European environments less important.'[12] In this book, as well as emphasizing the influence of global events on the making of mămăligă, I try to give space to the local and regional particularities of the fortunes of maize.

From being largely a preoccupation of amateurs and *curiosi*, the study of food has secured by now a respectable and well-established footing as part of the study of human societies and collective experiences. Scholarly enquiry has moved on from a time when food studies was the reserve either of botanists and agronomists, or of ethnographers and cultural anthropologists, each with their circumscribed institutional settings and technical concerns. Moreover, a relatively successful symbiosis has taken place between 'specialists' and practitioners: settings like the well-attended *Oxford Symposium on Food*, academic book series such as *California Studies in Food and Culture*, or the numerous successful undergraduate courses on food topics, point to a ripening of the field.[13] Particularly in the field of cereal history, James Scott's best-selling *Against the Grain* gives a prominent place to the domestication of grains in explaining the rise of the first known states in the ancient Near East, with their attendant practices of record-keeping, urbanization, taxation, irrigation, and technical innovation, as well as the consequences in terms of disease, death and environmental destruction.[14] Works like Donna Gabaccia's *We Are What We Eat*, concerning the contribution of migrant and subaltern food practices to cuisine in the United States, show that food is not just a biological necessity or a cultural accessory, but a problem whose study can lead to a better understanding of the making of a national identity, including its multiple paradoxes and social inequalities.[15] Rachel Laudan, in *Cuisine and Empire*, shows how food preparation in modern western societies is inextricably bound up with global processes including imperial conquest and the domination by capital of a large part of the world's resources.[16] María Elena García, in *Gastropolitics and the Specter of Race*, shows how a vibrant and fashionable national cuisine such as that of Peru is not just a source of delectation and entertainment but a site where hierarchies and impera-

---

12 Frank Johnson, 'Europe without Borders', 130. See also Polónia, 'Think Globally, Act Locally'; Livesey, *Provincializing Global History*.
13 Flandrin and Montanari, eds. *Histoire de l'alimentation*; Kiple and Ornelas, eds. *Cambridge World History of Food* remain landmarks. Recent overviews in English include Freedman, ed. *Food*; Claflin and Scholliers, eds. *Writing Food History*; Freedman, Chaplin, and Albala, eds. *Food in Time and Place*.
14 Scott, *Against the Grain*.
15 Gabaccia, *We Are What We Eat*.
16 Laudan, *Cuisine and Empire*.

tives of capitalist society are deeply inscribed.[17] And these are just a few examples of inspiring works in global food historiography that might help us to rethink mămăligă. Historians, just like home cooks, are always on the lookout for better ingredients and better recipes.

As far as maize history is concerned, a few works stand out for their attempt to gather information, providing broad surveys and bold hypotheses. Margaret Visser's essay on corn, in her 1986 work *Much Depends on Dinner*, is still worth reading, not just on account of its pioneering status in the field of popular food writing, but also for the powerful points Visser makes regarding the interrelation of cuisine, culture, politics and economics in the modern world's relationship with corn.[18] Mexican ethnologist Arturo Warman's *Corn and Capitalism* is an excellent historical overview of the relation between maize and broader economic and political forces.[19] While concentrating primarily on the Americas, Betty Fussell's *The Story of Corn* is beautifully written and illustrated, rich in information and insights, and makes a good case for the interdisciplinary potential of the topic.[20] There are fine shorter treatments, such as Ellen Messer's chapter on maize in the *Cambridge History of Food*, or the chapter by T. K. Lim in his survey of edible plants.[21] Although focusing particularly on maize in Africa, James McCann's *Maize and Grace* makes consistently penetrating hypotheses and arguments that are useful for the student of the crop's spread and use in other parts of the world.[22] Closer to the region I am concentrating on, the recent volume edited by Luca Mocarelli and Aleksander Panjek on the diffusion of maize in the northern Adriatic and its hinterlands offers valuable comparative insights.[23]

Perhaps surprisingly, given the centrality both of maize to the national diet and of mămăligă to the national identity, historians of Romania have only given desultory attention to this topic. Some sociologists and medics produced brief historical surveys at the beginning of the twentieth century.[24] In short pieces published in 1920 and 1946 respectively, leading national historians Nicolae Iorga and Constantin C. Giurescu preoccupied themselves with the arrival of maize in the Romanian

---

17 García, *Gastropolitics and the Specter of Race*.
18 Visser, *Much Depends on Dinner*, ch. 1.
19 Warman, *Corn and Capitalism*.
20 Fussell, *Story of Corn*, 231.
21 Messer, 'Maize'; Lim, *Edible Plants*, 416–47.
22 McCann, *Maize and Grace*.
23 Mocarelli and Panjek, eds. *Maize to the People!*
24 Felix, '*Zea L.*'; A. Nasta, *Der Maisbau*.

lands.²⁵ It is perhaps interesting to consider their contributions in the respective contexts of the periods after the First and Second World Wars, when reconstruction and potential U.S. aid may have prompted these prominent scholars to reflect on the local fortunes of an American plant. More clearly political was a research boom that occurred in Romania and elsewhere in the 1950s, partly as a result of the influence of developments in the Soviet Union, where Nikita Khrushchev launched his famous 'maize campaign' as a major plank of the country's agricultural policy. Weighty treatises on maize were produced in both Romania and Hungary, as well as in other eastern bloc countries, at least partly under Soviet pressure but also reflecting their own interest in developing the crop.²⁶ Khrushchev was personally disdainful of the Romanians, calling them *mamalyzhniki* ('mămăligă people') and even asserting provocatively during a visit to the country in 1957 that they did not know how to grow maize.²⁷ Irrespective of the impulse behind the research, some of the works published at this time contain valuable historical insights as well as agronomic, ethnographic, botanical and nutritional perspectives.

In 1967, the great French historian Fernand Braudel described maize as a 'gripping character' for a historian, a 'miraculous plant', with 'a unique destiny on a global scale'. Braudel mentioned mămăligă in passing and offered his apologies for not writing more about it, because it fell outside of the chronological scope of his classic study of early modern material culture.²⁸ It is a shame that his suggestion was not taken up by contemporaries or since. From the 1960s to the 1980s, there was an excellent school of agrarian history in Romania, which produced a number of important works particularly on labour relations in the eighteenth and nineteenth centuries.²⁹ This was matched in the fields of sociology and anthropology by outstanding works offering *longue-durée* interpretations of Romanian rural society

---

25 Iorga, 'Vechimea culturii porumbului', in French as Iorga, 'Ancienneté de la culture du maïs'; Giurescu, *Istoria Românilor*, 3–ii, 549–50; Giurescu, 'Plants of American Origin', 269–70; Giurescu, *Probleme controversate*, 123–25.
26 Săvulescu, ed. *Porumbul*; Balassa, *A magyar kukorica*. I have not used but note as testimony to the international research boom at this time: Ionescu-Sisești, *Cultura porumbului*; Surányi and Mándy, *A kukorica*; Olbrycht and Nadwyczawski, *Kukurydza*; Kălbova and Staikov, *Tsarevitsa*; Đorđević, *Kukuruz*.
27 Deletant, *Communist Terror*, 282; again in 1963, according to Hale-Dorrell, *Krushchev's Corn Crusade*, 73. Khrushchev was himself nicknamed *kukuruznik* in his own country: Warman, *Corn and Capitalism*, 199.
28 Braudel, *Civilisation matérielle et capitalisme*, 121, 126.
29 I am thinking of scholars such as Andrei Oțetea, David Prodan, Vasile Mihordea, Ilie Corfus, Maria Matilda Alexandrescu-Dersca Bulgaru, Paul Cernovodeanu, Șerban Papacostea, Florin Constantiniu, Sergiu Columbeanu, Ioana Constantinescu and Georgeta Penelea. See the bibliographical guide in Hitchins, *Romanians*, 321–22.

and economy and their relation to the emerging world market.³⁰ Given the Marxist paradigm within which they worked, the focus of these historians was primarily on the connection between social inequality and the development of large-scale cereal production in the context of international capitalism. Remarkably, however, little specific attention was given to maize, either in terms of nutrition or consumption or in relation to socio-economic particularities surrounding the crop and its cultivation. There is, for instance, no mention of maize at all in Henri Stahl's major study on traditional Romanian village communities. Even works focusing directly on the development of cereal production techniques in the Romanian lands give only limited detail about the crop.³¹ There are a small number of relevant contributions in an interdisciplinary three-volume collection of studies on Romanian agriculture published at the beginning of the 1970s.³²

After 1989, agrarian history fell out of favour in Romania. A valuable exception, which describes the problem as 'a missing link' in the history of southeastern Europe, nevertheless has no special focus on maize.³³ An excellent interpretive overview of Romanian economic development gives attention to the problem at relevant points.³⁴ But only a few short articles published in the last four decades analyse maize separately, generally with a focus on the question of origins.³⁵ As in western historiography, there was a turn away from production towards consumption.³⁶ One outstanding recent volume, *Earthly Delights*, edited by Angela Jianu and Violeta Barbu, can be said to bridge the gap, and makes a major contribution perhaps especially in understanding the links between production, consumption and cultural signification. Jianu and Barbu made a powerful case for studying food as a way of understanding the Balkans as 'a contact zone generated by multiple imperial projects', and their approach was inspirational for me in this and other ways. But here again, while a number of contributors mention maize briefly, there is no sepa-

---

30   Chirot, *Social Change*; Stahl, *Traditional Romanian Village Communities*; Verdery, *Transylvanian Villagers*.
31   Neamțu, *La technique*, 219–22; Corfus, *Agricultura în Țările Române*, 307–8, 316–17; older is Garoflid, *Agricultura veche*, 110–15.
32   Șerban, 'Cîteva date'; Gonța, 'Producția de cereale'; Penelea, 'Considerații'.
33   Dorondel and Șerban, 'A Missing Link'.
34   Murgescu, *România și Europa*, 48–49, 53, 121–25.
35   Demény, 'Introducerea unor plante noi'; Florea, 'Câteva considerații'; Ștefănescu, 'Considerații'.
36   On Romanian food history research in this period see Senciuc, 'Istoriografia românească a alimentației'; Păcurar, 'Suntem ceea ce mâncăm'. Generally on the shift from history of production to history of consumption: Hitchcock, 'Historical Agency'. On the need for an integrated approach: Anderson, *Everyone Eats*, 4.

rate treatment.³⁷ In the field of ethnography, maize seems to have been similarly neglected. While there is much interesting work on the cultural and symbolic aspects of nutrition in Romanian lands, in recent times scholars have tended to privilege bread at the expense of mămăligă.³⁸

Argument

At this stage, we might ask whether the neglect of maize as a topic in Romanian history is not actually justified. Can we really learn from it in the classroom, or should it be consigned to the pantry? During the writing of this book, I was several times haunted by the words of an exiled French count, who, traversing Wallachia at the close of the eighteenth century, remarked of the local population that 'their history would be difficult to research and of no great interest'.³⁹ I can readily attest to the truth of the first part of the count's laconic judgement. Sources on the topic are hard to come by, and derive from a hugely diverse set of published and unpublished materials across many different languages, often in hard-to-access repositories. What if this is true of the results of this research? I would contend that the convoluted story of maize-growing and mămăligă-making in the lands that make up Romania today has significance beyond a dry inventory of facts and mentions. Following it through in detail enables researchers, and I hope readers of this book, to see bigger questions of national, transnational and interimperial history in a new light and in a broader context. There are many ways in which this is true: for now I would like to highlight particularly arguments concerning identity and empire. These have been privileged topics of discussion in many areas of Romanian, European and world historiography: many scholars have offered different takes. In particular, this region has long been perceived as 'interstitial' to the workings of the world's great empires before 1918.⁴⁰ The inhabitants of the borderlands at the intersection of Ottoman, Habsburg and Russian domains have either been neglected in

---

37   Jianu and Barbu, eds. *Earthly Delights*; quote from introduction, 5; summary discussions of maize in the contributions of Aslan, 'Turkish Flavours', 118; Székely, 'Food and Culinary Practices', 183–84; Barbu, '"Emperor's Pantry"', 238–39; and Lazăr, 'Food Trade', 318. Again no separate study but valuable information, some new, in Pîrnău et al., eds. *Alimentație și demografie* (I am very grateful to an anonymous peer reviewer for indicating this title).
38   Nothing on maize in Văduva, *Pași spre sacru*; eadem, *Steps Toward the Sacred*; passing mentions in Vlăduțiu, *Etnografia românească*, 208, 220. Older: Pamfile, *Agricultura la români*, 65–92. On bread see e.g. Mihail, 'Pâinea'; Chivu, *Cultul grâului*; Savin, 'Bread'; Barbu, '"Emperor's Pantry"', 224–36.
39   Salaberry, *Voyage à Constantinople*, 103–4: 'Leur histoire seroit difficile de recueillir et peu intéressante'.
40   Verdery, 'Moments', 58; Marin, *Peasant Violence*, 276; and Cotoi, *Inventing the Social*, 6–7 have all invoked 'interstitiality' in relation to Romanian society in different but stimulating ways.

the general histories of these polities; or, in the national histories of the successor states, portrayed as having fought bravely against them. The story of maize shows that there were complex interconnections between empires and their borderland peoples throughout the late imperial era. The question of ethnic identity has received contrasting interpretations, from a national historiography which has traditionally sought to emphasize continuity, survival and resistance, to a different school which perceives ethnicity as a completely modern construct, arguing that national identity was an unknown category in east-central and southeastern Europe before the nineteenth or even the twentieth centuries. These questions are frequently tackled with reference to political, administrative, intellectual or cultural history; I believe an approach from food history can put the question in a new light.

On the one hand, villagers were often scorned and stereotyped precisely because they ate mămăligă—their emerging identity was in many ways contoured by the cultural assumptions of the powers that governed them about what they ate. On the other, people could profit from maize in different ways: by making money out of it and rising in the social scale, or by living off it away from centres of imperial or regional control. While most producers and consumers were poor, other actors in the maize story had power. What is more, maize changed not only people's diet but the possibilities available to them, what they could and could not do. Princes, boyars, monks, priests, merchants, soldiers, bandits, consuls, administrators and intellectuals as well as innkeepers, beekeepers, shepherds, peasants and even Roma Gypsy slaves were all bound up with maize in one way or another—as were women, who not only grew maize and cooked with it but sometimes bought and sold it in large quantities. In short, maize is not only something to eat but also, to paraphrase French anthropologist Claude Lévi-Strauss, something to think with.[41] Further study of its production and consumption can help us better understand the history of these borderland provinces and the interaction between them in the 'long transition' from empire to nationhood.

In preparing this dish, I have opted for a medium-to-*longue durée* cooking time, covering developments from the mysteries of maize's arrival in the seventeenth century, when Transylvania, Moldavia and Wallachia were tributary provinces on the Ottoman-European borderlands, to the beginning of the twentieth, when Romania, by now an independent kingdom, was the world's largest exporter of maize on the international market, and yet still a poor country dependent on this system. In Chapters 1 to 6, I seek to clarify the bigger historical narrative, but also to pay

---

41   Lévi-Strauss, *Le Totémisme aujourd'hui*.

attention to particular people, practices and incidents. I have attempted to recover details of how maize was grown, harvested, shucked, milled, and cooked, but also how it was taxed, sold, transported and exported across land and sea. In Chapters 7 and 8, I return to cultural representations, giving separate accounts of recipes for mămăligă recorded over the centuries, and of the image of mămăligă in Romanian folklore and popular song. My hope is to achieve a history that is local in its details as well as global in its comparative context.

Chapter 1

From the Caribbean to the Carpathians: The Coming of Cucuruz, c. 1492–1700

'For centuries, endless cornfields have adorned the Romanian landscape', asserts cookery writer Galia Sperber in *The Art of Romanian Cooking*.[1] And yet the history of these fields—and of Romanian national cuisine—is shorter and more eventful than many might imagine. To comprehend the foodways of this region, starting with the question of why it contains maize at all, we must look at the wider geographical picture. Beginning in the Atlantic, we will retrace maize's routes, real or hypothetical, across the Mediterranean, Adriatic and Black Seas; through their African, Asian, Caucasian and Balkan hinterlands; along the Danube and its tributaries; and across the Carpathians and the surrounding plains. A little knowledge of this global story will help us better locate the national one which follows on from it.

From the Atlantic to the Balkans

The chief ingredient of mămăligă, maize, probably originated in southern Mexico: it is believed to be a descendant of a wild grass called teosinte, of which it is the only widely cultivated variety. Just like wheat, barley, oats, rye and millet, maize is a cereal grass. It differs from them not just because of its origin but on account of its size, shape, nutritional and cultivational properties. Larger than other cereals and producing more grain-bearing stalks, each bearing many more and larger grains, it offers up to twice or even three times the nutritional value per cultivated area than wheat, but requires more labour and water. In its modern form, it is a product not just of nature but of culture. Over millennia of American tending, the ear devel-

---

[1] Sperber, *Art of Romanian Cooking*, 132.

oped its unique qualities, consisting of large cobs which grow from the stalk and not from the tip, bearing tightly-bound kernels wrapped in protective husks. Because of this, it does not seed naturally: it requires human intervention to reproduce. For better or for worse, the humans have obliged.

In 1493, when Columbus brought some maize kernels to Europe—one thing, among many attributed to him, that scholars still agree that he was the first to do—maize attracted immediate interest. Samples were sent promptly to the Vatican: maize features in mural paintings executed in Rome as early as 1517. It was also cultivated around Seville. But the broader European diffusion of maize was more gradual. Recent research has argued that maize's spread in Europe proceeded not from Columbus's samples but from later imports of more temperate varieties brought in the 1520s and 1530s.[2]

While the Spanish were invading the Americas and the Portuguese circumnavigating Africa (and taking maize with them), the Ottomans were extending their control over the eastern Mediterranean. How maize travelled from the Atlantic to the Balkans remains, amazingly, an open question, and there is still no clear account of precise dates and routes. Broadly speaking, an older narrative sees maize travelling eastwards in the hands of Venetian or Genoese traders.[3] This seems at first to be the logical and obvious assumption to make. Columbus himself was from Genoa, a city which had extensive and long-standing commercial connections in the eastern Mediterranean and the Black Sea, as did Venice and numerous other Italian cities. Despite Christian-Ottoman conflict, many trade routes remained open during the sixteenth century.

More recently, however, a significant number of scholars have proposed that maize entered the Sultan's domains in Egypt or the Near East.[4] Some of these argue that this happened not through the Mediterranean but via African or Asian routes. A speculative case has even been made for the arrival of maize in Cairo via India, where it had already been introduced by the Portuguese, and from there back across the Indian Ocean and through the Red Sea.[5]

---

2   Brandolini and Brandolini, 'Maize Introduction'; Tenaillon and Charcosset, 'A European Perspective', 224; Mir *et al.* 'Out of America'.
3   Burger, *Vollständige Abhandlung*, 71–73; von Lippmann, 'Zur Geschichte des Mais', 335–36; Montanari, *Culture of Food*, 102–3.
4   Crosby, *Columbian Exchange*, 188–89; Toussaint-Samat, *History of Food*, 157; McNeill, *Mountains*, 89 ('probably'); Pilcher, *Food in World History*, 23–24; Tabak, *Waning*, 256, 262; Mikhail, *Nature and Empire*, 84; Kia, *Daily Life*, 224–25; White, *Climate of Rebellion*, 286 ('probably'); Mandelblatt, 'Foods and Diets', 206; Kołodziejczyk, 'Twisted Ways of Commodities' 444. See also note 40 below.
5   Andrews, 'Diffusion'.

Parsing the actual evidence for these claims remains difficult. Any attempt to identify maize in early sources comes up against the problem of names and what they refer to. In west European languages, maize was frequently referred to as 'Turkish corn' or 'Turkish wheat' (Latin *triticum turcicum* or *frumentum turcicum*, French *blé de Turquie*, Italian *granturco*, *granoturco* or *sorgoturco*, German *Türkischer Weizen* or *Türkisches Korn*, etc.). This terminology is regularly invoked to argue for the spread of maize in Europe and Asia via an Ottoman conduit. However, just as is the case with the American bird we call a turkey, the term 'Turkish' as applied to maize has no basis in empirical observation. This was persuasively demonstrated already in the nineteenth century.[6] In general, evidence from names is indirect and hard to intrepret: topographical terms used for a whole variety of plants and vegetables are notoriously generic. In the west European imagination, 'Turkish' was effectively a synonym for 'exotic': it was a convenient and colourful way to label a familiar but unaccountable plant. What these names in fact testify to is not the role of the Ottomans in the diffusion of maize, but a general reluctance, wilful or otherwise, on the part of Europeans to process the fact of the New World's existence.[7]

It is in many ways understandable that scholars have looked especially to Egypt as a point of maize diffusion. Cairo was famous since antiquity as a grain entrepot in the eastern Mediterranean. Previously an independent sultanate, Egypt was conquered by the Ottomans in 1517, and control over the Cairo trade was crucial in consolidating their economic and military supremacy. The modern Turkish word for maize, *mısır*, means 'Egyptian'. The Greek and south Slavic terms αραβόσιτος and *arapka*, which translate as 'Arabic grain', seem to support the thesis.[8] However, *mısır* was not the first word for maize in Ottoman Turkish, and appears to have entered usage relatively late.[9] Moreover, there is no reason to assume that when Ottomans called maize 'Egyptian', they meant it any more literally than when Europeans did when they called it 'Turkish'. Firmer evidence of

---

6   de Candolle, *Géographie botanique*, ii:944; Hehn, *Wanderings of Plants*, 497.
7   Messedaglia, *Notizie storiche*, 21–28; Finan, 'Maize', 160; Warman, *Corn and Capitalism*, 30–31; Regueiro, 'La flora americana', 208; Lowood, 'New World', 300–2; Klemun, 'Globaler Pflanzentransfer', 207–8.
8   This explanation was also popular in socialist-era scholarship: see e.g. Zaimov, 'Nazvaniyata', 113; Ionescu-Șișești, 'Porumbul', 40; Rădulescu, 'Raporturi lingvistice', 715–16.
9   Tabak, 'Agrarian Fluctuations', 144, states that the Ottomans called maize *dhurra shami* 'Syrian sorghum' (mid-seventeenth century) and *mısır* only later. Bilgin, 'From Artichoke to Corn', 280–1, finds the word used in the Morea (1660s), but not in Anatolia before 1750. For early mentions on the Danube (1696, 1700), see n. 61 and 94 below.

CHAPTER 1

maize's presence in Egypt before 1600 or even in the seventeenth century is remarkable by its absence.[10]

Other scholars have looked for maize, and claimed to find it, in sixteenth-century Anatolia and the Middle East. An alleged sighting on the southern coast of the Black Sea in 1547 rests on a strained interpretation of a word more usually meaning millet.[11] There is a tantalizing, and much cited, mention of 'Turkish corn' in the town of Bir on the banks of the Euphrates river (today Birecik in eastern Turkey) in a travel account compiled in 1574 by the German botanist Leonhart Rauwolf. However, although several modern writers have taken this to be maize,[12] Rauwolf himself glossed it as sesame.[13] Travelling further south and east, Rauwolf also saw 'Indian millet' (*indianische Hirsche*) in various places today located in Lebanon, Israel, Syria and Iraq, but then under Ottoman rule.[14] Again, despite some optimistic modern interpretations, this was not maize either. Rauwolf reported that the locals called it *dora*, an Arabic term most commonly applied to sorghum. Remarkably, his herbarium from his journey, containing 191 of the 200 specimens he collected, is preserved in the Netherlands and has only recently been scientifically analysed. Contrary to previous reports, it includes samples of sesame and sorghum, but not of maize.[15]

Less well known, but in fact more promising, is the testimony of some Venetian travellers in the Ottoman Balkans. In 1550, Venetian envoy Caterin Zen travelled through Thrace on his way to Istanbul, and made a list of cereals which were plentiful in the area, including *formentone*, a common word for maize in modern Italian dialects.[16] This is by no means a certain attestation—in several early sources *formentone* was used to designate buckwheat.[17] We should not completely rule out the

---

10 Older scholarship, given in Richards, *Egypt's Agricultural Development*, 48n.65, is more sceptical, as is, on Morocco, Rosenberger, 'Cultures complémentaires', 487–88, and for Ethiopia, McCann, *Maize and Grace*, 77–82. Genetic analysis by Mir *et al.* 'Out of America', 2679 casts further doubt. Maize in Tunis in 1669: Desjardins and McCarthy, *Milho, makka*, 13.
11 Yediyıldız, *Ordu Kazası sosyal tarihi*, 118–19, accepted by Tabak, *Waning*, 359 n. 86, but questioned by Bilgin, 'From Artichoke to Corn', 280.
12 Dannenfeldt, *Rauwolf*, 254; Crosby, *Columbian Exchange*, 189; Coe, *America's First Cuisines*, 16; Tabak, *Waning*, 360 n. 111.
13 Rauwolf, *Aigentliche beschreibung*, 137: 'ganze äcker vol mit Türkischem Korn / Sesamo'. Turkish corn by no means always meant maize in early sources: on this point see Pascu, 'Le maïs', 459.
14 Rauwolf, *Aigentliche beschreibung*, 184, 198–99, 274, 316; identified as sorghum by Dannenfeldt, *Rauwolf*, 105, 254, but claimed as maize by Crosby, *Columbian Exchange*, 189.
15 Ghorbani *et al.*, 'Botanical and Floristic Composition'.
16 'Gran formento, megli assai et formentoni, orzi, vena et risi in quantità': Zen, *Descrittione* [c. 1550], in Matković, 'Dva talijanska putopisa', 221; cf. Hrabak, *Izvoz žitarica*, 471; Garić Petrović, 'Maize Cultivation', 262. Thanks to Dejan Djokić and Ljubinka Trgovčević for help locating these sources.
17 Pascu, 'Le maïs', 458–60; Abegg-Mengold, *Die Bezeichnungsgeschichte*, 96–100.

possibility that what Zen saw and noted was maize, especially as he listed it alongside other cereals: wheat, millet, barley and oats. However, it would be a unique attestation in the Ottoman Balkan heartlands: scholars have looked carefully for it in other core territories such as Bulgaria, Macedonia or Bosnia, and not found it until considerably later.[18]

There is a potential sighting in 1575 in the Adriatic city of Dubrovnik, where another Venetian envoy, Jacopo Soranzo, noted *sorgoturco*—literally, 'Turkish sorghum'—among the grains consumed.[19] Just like *formentone*, *sorgoturco* is an uncertain term. Even though several slightly later Venetian testimonies explicitly specify that *sorgoturco* refers to maize,[20] it is harder to be sure in early sources that it does not refer to sorghum. Historically, sorghum and maize have often been confused, being quite similar in appearance, especially when the plants are young. We have other evidence that sorghum was present in Dubrovnik at this time, being brought by traders both from the Balkan hinterland (Bosnia) and from north Africa (Alexandria) in the 1550s.[21] While the lack of contextual data means that firm conclusions cannot be drawn here, the development of a more elaborate terminology hints at the more general presence and use of the plant.

The presence of maize in central Europe is somewhat better documented, perhaps more so than is sometimes appreciated. The illustrious herbalist Leonhart Fuchs, who grew up in Bavaria, wrote already in 1542 that it was found 'in all gardens, everywhere'.[22] Maize reached Venice some time in the early sixteenth century. From around 1550, Venetians began not only to observe it but to cultivate it on their *terraferma*.[23] It was known in Bohemia, where it featured in herbals published in Prague in 1562 (in Czech) and 1563 (in German) by the Habsburg court physician Pietro Andrea Mattioli.[24] Maize was also included in a set of seed samples sent to Vienna in 1574 by the Bolognese naturalist Ulisse Aldrovandi.[25] Its cultivation is attested in Carinthia from 1559, in eastern Switzerland from 1571, in Styria from

---

18 See Stoianovich and Haupt, 'Le maïs', 85–89.
19 Soranzo, *Diario del viaggio*, 24: 'la maggior parte vivono con miglio e sorgoturco'.
20 Abegg-Mengold, *Die Bezeichnungsgeschichte*, 29, 40, 92–93.
21 D'Atri, '*Per conservare la città*', 81 (sorghum from Bosnia, 1556), 82 (from Alexandria, 1557), 91.
22 Fuchs, *De historia stirpium*, 824: 'passim, in omnis hortis'.
23 Vantini, 'L'inserimento', 655; McCann, *Maize and Grace*, 63–77.
24 Mattioli, *Herbář*, 130–33; Mattioli, *New Kreüterbuch*, 129. On the German edition and its importance, see Taylor, *Putting Down Roots*, 154–55; but the Czech one is still earlier: see Bohatcová, 'Prager Drucke', 171–2.
25 van Gelder, *Tussen hof en keizerskroon*, 87–88.

1572, and in Gorizia by 1600.²⁶ In none of these regions, however, did it become a staple crop.

One widely-cited theory associates the diffusion of maize in southeastern Europe with the Habsburg Emperor Rudolf II (1576–1612). In particular, Rudolf has been credited with having introduced maize into Croatian lands in 1612, in the Varaždin district of the Habsburg Military Frontier.²⁷ At first sight, this is an attractive proposition. Rudolf was the nephew of Philip II of Spain, and spent eight years of his youth at his uncle's court in Madrid, where he is likely to have heard about the plant. He displayed a strong interest in botany during his reign, even purchasing the herbarium of the aforementioned German traveller Leonhart Rauwolf.²⁸ An ear of maize figures in the allegorical portrait of him as Vertumnus, the Roman god of gardening and plant growth, executed in Prague in 1591 by the court painter Giuseppe Arcimboldo. From 1593 to 1606 he led the Christian powers in the so-called 'Long Turkish War' against the Ottomans, during which time he established extensive links with Balkan Christian leaders, including the Romanian military hero Prince Michael the Brave who even had an audience with him in Prague in March 1601. Historians have often wondered what passed between the two men during this meeting.²⁹ It would be tempting to imagine the famously mercurial Habsburg emperor introducing the Danubian warlord to the plant that would later nourish the Romanian people over the centuries, perhaps slipping a few kernels into Prince Michael's pockets. Fancy aside, while some researchers have suggested that the introduction of maize on the southeastern frontier might have had a military motivation,³⁰ there are no sources to back up such a hypothesis. As we shall see below, the Habsburgs were far from displaying any interest in broader military or economic uses of maize until much later in time. The whole dossier in fact rests on a brief mention in a regimental history compiled in the late nineteenth century, at a time when attributing benevolent deeds to long-dead emperors was an act of piety.³¹

Upon closer examination, then, the 'Habsburg' thesis proves to be no sounder than the 'Ottoman' one. Certainly the date is not tenable, given that Rudolf died in January 1612, having already ceded the title of King of Hungary and Croatia to

---

26 Brunner, 'Frühe Nachrichten'; Eschholz *et al.*, 'Genetic Structure', 76; Panjek, 'Tracing Maize', 88.
27 Vaniček, *Specialgeschichte der Militärgrenze*, i:400, popularized by Stoianovich, 'Le maïs', 1027.
28 Walter, Ghorbani and van Andel, 'Emperor's Herbarium'.
29 E.g. Tracy, *Balkan Wars*, 329–30. On their economic relations, see Căzan, 'Princes roumains'.
30 Schmidt, 'Der Anbau', 79–80, a speculative gloss on Stoianovich, 'Le maïs'.
31 Vaniček, *Specialgeschichte der Militärgrenze*, i:400, citing a manuscript history of the Warasdiner-St. Georger (Gjurgevatz) frontier regiment which I have not been able to trace.

From the Caribbean to the Carpathians

1.1 Emperor Rudolf II as Vertumnus. Portrait by Giuseppe Arcimboldo, Prague, 1591

1.2 Prince Michael the Brave. Portrait by Aegidius Sadeler, Prague, 1601

his younger brother some years previously, and renounced all leadership roles. A similarly widely repeated claim that maize was introduced in 1611 in the town of Požega, Slavonia, around 150 kilometres further southeast of Varaždin, is also questionable, seeming to rest on little more than a tentatively reported tradition in a popular agricultural manual from the early twentieth century.[32] Požega did become a prominent locus of maize cultivation but only much later, around 1700.[33]

In short, reliable attestations of maize's early presence in the eastern Mediterranean and Balkan regions—whether on the banks of the Danube, the Nile or the Euphrates—are much sparser than researchers have claimed. This is not to say it did not reach these areas: absence of evidence is not evidence of absence, and given the many imbalances in documentation, its appearance might easily have escaped notice. Explanations have focused on individual actors like Columbus or Rudolf II; or on momentous events, such as the Ottoman conquests. The conditions created by these emperors and explorers may have been instrumental in maize's spread, but

---

32 'It is held to have been first sown in our lands in the vicinity of Požega around 1611': Köröškeny, *Uputa*, 110; a legend repeated by Mayer, *Landwirtschaft*, 80; Stanojević, *Landwirtschaft*, 99; Humlum, *Zur Geographie*, 29; Hatt, 'Corn Mother', 904; Stoianovich, 'Le maïs', 1027, and many others.
33 Vrbanus, 'Ratarstvo', 227.

there is no evidence of anything like a dissemination strategy. However, we are still a long way from those Romanian cornfields.

Across the River and Beyond the Forest: Maize in Transylvania and Hungary

The lands that constitute the heart of Romania today—Transylvania, Moldavia and Wallachia—lay north of the Danube. But to a well-organized conqueror, a river is not a frontier, and in fact the Danube played an important part in the Ottoman military supply system in their European campaigns.[34] Moldavia and Wallachia, two principalities which had emerged in the fourteenth century, were already paying tribute to the Sultan by 1500. Transylvania was still part of the Kingdom of Hungary, but not for long. In 1526, the Ottomans advanced into central Europe and defeated the Hungarians at Mohács, on the right bank of the river. After Buda fell in 1541, central Hungary became an Ottoman province, and Belgrade and Temeşvar Ottoman fortresses. Transylvania constituted itself into a semi-independent principality, but also paid homage to the Sultan. All three principalities continued to be governed by Christian princes and were not generally subject to conversion or Muslim settlement. But they paid tribute either in money or produce to the Porte, hence their designation as 'tributary states'.[35] Their affairs were more and more bound up with the Ottomans, now at the height of their power.

These countries were of course prized for their rich natural resources, a lot of which made their way to Istanbul. But we should make two very important qualifications to the popular image of Ottoman rule as a period of unrestrained extraction. The first is that before the eighteenth century, relatively little of the tribute in kind was delivered in cereals, and there was little systematic or large-scale arable cultivation undertaken specifically for this purpose. The most prized products were sheep, salt, honey, wax, fish, and timber, grain less so. The second is that Ottoman dependency did not mean that these lands became cut off from European markets. On the contrary, trade with the cities and markets of central Europe not only continued but expanded, particularly in respect of cattle but also of other goods. Recent works by both Hungarian and Romanian historians give relatively positive evaluations of the economic situation of these provinces.[36] In general we can con-

---

34 Murphey, *Ottoman Warfare*, 87; Gradeva, 'Along the Danube'.
35 Kármán and Kunčević, eds, *European Tributary States*.
36 Kontler, *History of Hungary*, 159–62; Murgescu, *România şi Europa*, 30–50; Pálffy, *Hungary*, 73–81. For the tribute in kind I have followed Murgescu. There is some newer counter evidence: White,

1.3 Life in Ottoman Hungary. Ferenc Wathay, Songbook, 1604.

ceive of Danubian Europe in this period not as a fracture zone, as it is so often portrayed, but as one of contact and exchange.[37] There was no single direction of travel of plants or food products. Transylvania in particular was a fascinating crossroads of central European and Ottoman styles and influences.[38]

According to a later tradition, consigned to writing at the end of the eighteenth century by an anonymous author, maize entered Transylvania 'from the southern Turkish provinces', with 1611 being given as the nominal date of introduction.[39] Historians continue to favour a 'Turkish' explanation to this day.[40] Trade routes

Climate of Rebellion, 32 n. 59, 100–1 reports shipments of between 1,000 and 2,500 tons of Moldo-Wallachian grain or flour at several points in the 1580s. But he describes these as extraordinary measures.
37 Gradeva, 'Ottoman Balkans'; cf. Faroqhi, 'Trading Between East and West'; Jianu and Barbu, eds. *Earthly Delights*.
38 Benda, 'Obiceiuri alimentare'; Aslan, 'Turkish Flavours'; Fekete, 'Late Renaissance Garden Art'.
39 Anon, 'Ueber eine der ersten Ursachen', 123: 'nur aus dem Jahre 1611, aus den südlichen Türkischen Provinzen in Siebenbürgen bekannt'.
40 Lang, *Cuisine of Hungary*, 32; Fodor, 'Hungary Between East and West', 408; Bartha, 'Points of Connection', 51; Owen Jones, *Corn*, 48; Koch, *Distinctiveness*, 36.

into Transylvania across the Carpathians remained relatively active in the first half of the seventeenth century. But maize does not seem to figure in the surviving customs registers of Brașov, Sibiu or Cluj, or in Moldavian trade documents.[41] If maize came from Ottoman lands at all, it is tempting to imagine it arriving from a southwesterly direction, maybe from the region of Temeșvar. It is attested (as *kukurudz*) in a Romanian-Latin lexicon composed in the town of Caransebeș, southeast of Temeșvar, around 1650.[42] Caransebeș was an important link in the chain of commerce between Transylvania and the Balkans at this time.[43] Partly because of warfare and piracy in the eastern Mediterranean, overland routes from the Adriatic to the Danube began to flourish, conducted largely but not exclusively by Orthodox Christian merchants.[44] There are sightings of maize in Belgrade,[45] southern Hungary,[46] and Dalmatia, where merchants are known to have played a role in supplying it to the Venetian Republic during their war against the Ottomans in 1645–1669, even if 'the army is hard to convince to accede to maize bread'.[47]

But the first direct mention of maize in Transylvania is earlier and further north, at the fortress of Kővár (Cetatea Chiorului, today in Maramureș county). An inventory undertaken here in February 1639 recorded 6 *cubuli* of maize in storage, the equivalent of at least half a tonne.[48] In other words, it was probably more than a mere garden plant, but rather intended either for livestock fodder or for military provisions. The next mentions of maize are all in relatively northern or western localities: in Mád (today northeastern Hungary) in 1641; at Dej and Gherla in Transylvania, in 1652 and 1660; and at Hédervár in western Hungary, in 1658.[49] In all these mentions, the word used is *törökbúza*, which means 'Turkish wheat'. This term, sometimes taken to be a sign of an Ottoman origin, is almost certainly

---

41   On Brașov and Sibiu: Pakucs-Willcocks, 'Transit of Oriental goods'; on Cluj: Pap, 'Produse agricole'; on the Moldavian trade: Chelcu, 'Merchants from Iași'.
42   Anon, *Dictionarium valachico-latinum*, 96 (facsimile at 323). The dating to 1650 is somewhat tentative: see Chivu, 'Studiu filologic', 12–20; Chivu, '*Dictionarium*'.
43   Dan and Goldenberg, 'Le commerce balkano-levantin', 104–7.
44   Stoianovich, 'Conquering Balkan Orthodox Merchant'; Pedani, *Dalla frontiera al confine*, 61–62.
45   Zirojević, 'Biljni i stočni fond', 16; Garić Petrović, 'Maize Cultivation in Serbia', 263. On routes see also Riedler, 'Istanbul–Belgrade Route'.
46   Maize in Transdanubia: Balassa, 'Der Maisbau', 110; Sümegi *et al.*, 'Environmental History', 46–50.
47   Mrgić, 'Polyphony', 14–15. Adriatic merchants in Belgrade: Brown, *Brief Account*, 40; in Vienna: idem, *Account*, 74; at Temeșvar: Pippidi, *Hommes et idées*, 79–80; in Transylvania: Ciure, 'Contribuția'.
48   'Török buza cubuli cassovienses no. 6', in Makkai, ed., *Rákoczi iratai*, 437–38; cf. Balassa, *A magyar kukorica*, 41; Demény, 'Introducerea', 1245–46. The measure *cubulus cassoviensis*, named after the town of Košice, today in Slovakia, was larger than the average *cubulus*, amounting to between 84 and 125 litres.
49   Balassa, *A magyar kukorica*, 45.

a calque from the Latin *turcicum frumentum*, which, as I have argued above, constitutes no indication of the plant's origin.⁵⁰

Some historians of Transylvania have claimed that the earliest adopters of maize in the principality were the German-speaking Saxon population.⁵¹ Contemporary Saxon sources associate it rather with the Romanians. A chronicle from the town of Braşov reports that Transylvanians nicknamed the famous Romanian Prince Michael the Brave—who briefly ruled the provinces of Moldavia, Wallachia and Transylvania simultaneously at the turn of the seventeenth century—'Malai Vodă' (Prince Cornmeal), instead of the usual Mihai Vodă (Prince Michael).⁵² Although *mălai* here may refer to millet or millet flour rather than maize or cornmeal, the chronicle gives an indication of how Romanians were scorned for their different cereal habits, while also acknowledging that humble crops could be a source of power. Also at this time, the term *málé*, clearly a borrowing from Romanian *mălai*, begins to appear in Maygar sources from Transylvania.⁵³ More concrete evidence of the Transylvanian authorities' habitual association of the crop with the Romanian population comes in an article of the 'Constitutions' of Maros county, which states that Romanians commonly cultivated maize to avoid the tithe which officially fell only on wheat. They were also said to grow it outside the village bounds, another way of avoiding taxation.⁵⁴ In 1686 there was even an attempt to outlaw maize's cultivation by 'the poor inhabitants', as it threatened the production of wheat and other taxable cereals, which was considered 'very damaging to the landowners'.⁵⁵

Especially in northern Transylvania, some Hungarian nobles grew maize on their estates. But they generally used it for swine fodder rather than for human consumption, when acorns were not available. It is interesting to note that maize was grown here alongside pumpkins, a continuation of the American custom of 'companion planting'. There were even tomato seeds on the Rákoczi estates at

---

50 *Törökbúza* appears first as a gloss on *frumentum turcicum* in learned glossaries and reference works from the 1570s and 1580s: Sziksai, *Latin-magyar szójegyzéke*, 24; Clusius, *Rariorum aliquot stirpium historia*, 820. I am grateful to István Szalma for the second of these references.
51 E.g. Acsády, *A magyar jobbágyság története*, 319.
52 *Chronicon Fuchsio-Lupino-Oltardinum*, i:170, signalled by Hasdeu, 'Originile agriculturei', 53. I am very grateful to Andrei Sorescu for help procuring Hasdeu's article.
53 Balassa, *A magyar kukorica*, 92–94.
54 'Marosszék Constitutiói' (1610–1718), article 17, in *A magyar törvényhatóságok jogszabályainak gyüjteménye*, i:48.
55 Article XI of the Transylvanian Diet (19 October–6 November 1686), in *Monumenta Comitalia Regni Transylvaniae*, xviii:586–87; quoted in Teutsch, *Geschichte*, ii:372; Demény, 'Introducerea', 1247.

Nagysáros (today Vel'ký Šariš, Slovakia), although we do not know to what uses they were put.⁵⁶

In 1683, partly egged on by their Transylvanian allies, the Ottomans besieged Vienna and were defeated. In retaliation, the Habsburg army entered Transylvania and conquered the province. However, there was significant resistance from the local Hungarian elites, a faction of whom, led by the Prince Imre Thököly, continued to make common cause with the Ottomans, with the aid of a number of Balkan Christian troops.⁵⁷ During his campaign against the Habsburgs in the winter of 1691–1692, Prince Thököly exchanged letters with a number of Ottoman pashas and janissaries in Vidin, Edirne and other fortresses from whom he was receiving support.⁵⁸ In the first of these letters, sent from Požarevac to Omer, Pasha of Vidin in December 1691, he requested information about supplies and prices of biscuit, flour, barley or rice porridge because 'we ourselves have been forced to live only on cornbread (*kukoricza-kenyér*)'. It is here that the term *kukorica*, now the standard word for the plant in modern Magyar, appears for the first time, and there are numerous further mentions of it in these letters.⁵⁹

There may also have been maize at Smederevo, between Vidin and Belgrade, which was ransacked by the Ottoman army in their campaign of 1690.⁶⁰ A contemporary Ottoman 'Book of Victories' (*Nusretnâme*) from 1696, noted that maize

1.4: Prince Imre Thököly. Engraving by Jacob Peeters. Antwerp, 1686.

---

56 Benda, *Étkezési szokások*, 109–10.
57 Parvev, *Habsburgs and Ottomans*, 79–84.
58 On Vidin as a supply point at this time see Gradeva, 'War and Peace', 161; and Kovács, 'Legal Status', 15, who shows that Vidin was receiving supplies from Wallachia.
59 Thököly, *1691–1692-iki levelekönyve*, 105 (letter of 6 December 1691), also at 131, 193, 194, 195, 197, 202, 204, 211, 228, 294, 303, 307, 375, 398; and Thököly, *Késmárki naplója*, 393, 549, 560, 678.
60 Abdullah bin İbrahim el-Üsküdarî, campaign history (1690) cited by Katić, *Tursko osvajanje Srbije*, 88. The word used by el-Üsküdarî – *darı* – more usually means millet: maize is a possible but by no means certain meaning. I thank Tatjana Katić for this information.

(*mısır*) was grown at Temeşvar, alongside pumpkin, outside the fortress, when conditions permitted.[61] In 1697–1702, when their victory was finally assured, Habsburg administrators conducted a survey of the frontier territory of Slavonia revealing the presence of maize in over forty localities.[62] On the other side of the frontier, Ottoman officials recorded maize in as many as twenty-nine villages in Serbia, in a tax register from 1714.[63] Further north, around Oradea, Habsburg surveyors found maize being grown in at least thirteen localities from 1697–1713.[64] Also in the vicinity of Oradea, a tithe on maize, hemp and cabbage (*kukurucz, canabum et caulium*) was taken in the village of Gyalan (Delani) in 1721.[65]

The Maizing of Moldavia and Wallachia

If, then, maize is well attested in Transylvania and the middle Danube region well before 1700, might it have travelled eastwards from here, along the Danube or across the Carpathians? There is no direct evidence either to corroborate or reject such a thesis. Wallachian tradition attributes the plant's introduction to individual rulers: most commonly mentioned is Prince Şerban Cantacuzino, who ruled Wallachia from 1678 to 1688. This idea, promoted by Cantacuzino's descendants in the late eighteenth century, was dismissed by historian Nicolae Iorga in the early twentieth, although it is still current in popular treatments of the topic.[66] As an alternative explanation, Iorga did suggest tentatively that Şerban's brother Constantin Cantacuzino, a nobleman and scholar who studied in Padua in the 1660s, might have played a role. But this too is mere speculation.[67]

For Moldavia, a different theory has been proposed, namely that maize arrived from the Caucasus—having been brought through the Straits by Italian merchants—and was then exported back westwards through the intermediary of the

---

61 Silahdar Findıkhlı Mehmed Aga, *Nusretnâme*, trans. M. Guboglu in *Cronici turceşti*, ii:486.
62 Smičiklas, *Dvijestogodišnjica oslobodjenja Slavonije*, ii:65, 94–95, 98, 103–9, 113–14, 243, 247, 249, 250, 257, 259, 263–65, 271, 275–80, 282, 290. See also Vrbanus, 'Ratarstvo', 227; Vrbanus, 'Proizvodnja pšenice', 148.
63 Zirojević, *Istočno-zapadna sofra*, 79–80: in Kućanja and Majdanpek, mining areas east of Smederevo.
64 Ştefănescu, 'Începuturile': Telegd (today Telechiu, Romania) in 1697; Bálnaca (Bălnaca), Örvend (Urvind) in 1698; Kisősi (Auşeu), Kövesd (Cuieşd), Dombó (Delureni), Éleslok (Lunсşoara), Ürgeteg (Ortiteag), Tinód (Tinăud), Cécke (Ţeţchea), Vércsorog (Vârciorog) in 1712; Csarnoháza (Bulz) in 1713. Also in Kapocsány (Copăceni) near Oradea in 1720: Ştefănescu, 'Consideraţii', 174–75.
65 Ilea *et al.*, 'Documente', 423.
66 Iorga, 'Ancienneté', 186, 189. Popular treatments: e.g. Djuvara, *Le pays roumain*, 237; Toussaint-Samat, *History of Food*, 157; N. Constantinescu, ed. *Romania's Economic History*, 78; Roman, *Romanian Dishes*, 11.
67 Iorga, 'Ancienneté', 189–90.

Laz people (a Caucasian people active in the Black Sea trade).[68] As the active presence of Laz merchants in Moldavia and the Black Sea coast and their role in the transportation of grain is quite well documented, this hypothesis certainly merits consideration.[69] It is further supported by the existence of the word *lazut*, an early term for maize, in Ottoman sources;[70] and possibly by the intriguing early Magyar term *tengeri*, meaning 'maritime [corn]', attested from the late sixteenth century in northern Transylvania.[71] However, since maize is not clearly documented in the Caucasus any earlier than in Moldavia,[72] the acknowledged role of the Laz does not necessarily mean they brought maize.

Despite this, it is worth stressing that the Black Sea region remained an active site of international trade.[73] With the consolidation of Ottoman rule, it did not automatically become a closed 'Turkish lake', but continued to be frequented by numerous merchant communities, with links to the Mediterranean and beyond. As late as the eighteenth century, contemporary observers underlined that Moldavia's maritime relations extended well beyond the Black Sea shoreline, to Egypt and North Africa.[74] Like the Mediterranean, the Black Sea is significantly surrounded by mountains; of its various hinterlands, Moldavia was among the most easily accessible along river networks. There had also been a long tradition of overland trade through Poland, on what was the shortest route from the Black Sea to the Baltic. Merchants, then, did not necessarily only stop at the shore, but sometimes travelled upriver and settled inland. Tatar merchants also came from the Crimea and the steppe regions, sometimes settling in Moldavia.[75] But while there was no shortage of routes, there is still no solid evidence of maize.

Another potential source of evidence for the presence of maize in Moldavia and Wallachia comes in the form of place and personal names.[76] Given the largely pastoral-agrarian nature of the economy in these countries, their inhabitants frequently drew on the animal and botanical world when naming themselves or each

---

68 Haupt, 'B: Dans les Pays du Danube et la mer Noire', 90–91.
69 Iorga, *Istoria comerțului*, ii:32–33; Alexandrescu-Dersca Bulgaru, 'L'approvisionnement', 73–74.
70 İslamoğlu and Faroqhi, 'Crop Patterns and Agricultural Production Trends', 422; Bilgin, 'From Artichoke to Corn', 280 n. 93, considers the word *lazut* to be of Armenian origin, originally meaning millet.
71 Balassa, *A magyar kukorica*, 90–92; Kisbán, 'Maisnahrung', 269; Benda, *Étkezési szokások*, 109–10.
72 Dekaprelevich, 'Iz istorii kultury kukuruzy v SSSR', 367–68.
73 In English see King, *Black Sea*, 111–19; Malcolm, *Agents of Empire*, 321–24, both with ample references.
74 Cantemir, *Descriptio Moldaviae*, 74; Anonymous report of 1740, in *Călători străini*, ix:266.
75 Faroqhi, *Ottoman Empire*, 78.
76 For sources and a full discussion of all these terms, see Appendix.

other.⁷⁷ Intriguing names occur surprisingly early in documents: there was even a locality Mămăligă in Wallachia in the 1520s. But this is no proof of maize.⁷⁸ *Porumb*, which is the modern standard word for maize in Romanian, also appears in names of people and places in numerous early documents: but given that its original meaning was 'pigeon', these names are hard to interpret. *Cucuruz*, another common word for maize, is the name of a village a few miles south of Bucharest, attested as Cucurezi in 1575 and then as Cucuruzi from 1621.

A still more common term, *mălai*, features in personal and place names as far back as the fifteenth century. *Mălai* means cornmeal in modern standard Romanian, and maize or maize bread in some regional uses. But in early sources it is more likely to refer to millet, which was by far the most widely used cereal in southeastern Europe before the arrival of maize. So we should be careful about the meaning of *mălai* in a sale document from the village of Şoldeşti, Moldavia in 1646, which in the view of one enthusiastic mămăligologist constitutes evidence of the presence of maize.⁷⁹ Also in Moldavia, a Syrian traveller's passing observation from 1653 on the unusual character of the grain there, 'which in this country customarily exceeds the height of a man', might possibly constitute a reference to maize, given that few other cereals possess this quality, but again we are in uncertain territory.⁸⁰ Nor can we make any historiographically consistent mămăligă from the nevertheless soundly documented mention of a man called Mămălata in Onceni, a village on the Siret river, in 1661. In 1684, a large convoy of Tatar caravans arrived in Iaşi bringing a considerable quantity of *mălai*, which must have been quite a sight, but almost certainly not one of maize.⁸¹ It has also been claimed that Tatars raided maize from villages in the Rodna district, just over the border in Transylvania in 1717. By this date, maize was better established, but once again the terminology is questionable.⁸²

Speculation aside, more certain sightings of the crop appear in Moldavia in the 1690s. In the estate records of the Carp boyar family there is a declaration from 1692 by a certain Nacşu, perhaps a temporary resident, who requested 'to let us stay

---

77 Paşca, *Nume de persoane*; N. Constantinescu, *Dicţionar*, lii–liii; Giurescu, *History of the Romanian Forest*, 190–216; Milică, 'Nume de plante şi nume de locuri'.
78 Compare 'polenta', which not only in Italian but also in other languages long predates the presence of maize: even in English it is attested from the fourteenth century.
79 Şerban, *Vasile Lupu*, 50. The 'maize' mentioned by Mihordea, *Maîtres du sol*, 29, 33 is questionable on the same ground.
80 Paul of Aleppo (1653), trans. M.M. Alexandrescu-Dersca Bulgaru, in *Călători străini*, vi:93.
81 Neculce, *Letopiseţul*, 289. As we shall see below, this chronicler called maize *păpuşoi*.
82 Şotropa, 'Tătarii', 268. His source reads *frumentum saracenicum*, more usually buckwheat.

until autumn, as we have sown maize and other vegetables, and we will go in autumn, having no other business, we were just some people wandering about.' Without offering any further detail, this document nevertheless affords us a tantalizing glimpse of the type of semi-sedentarized cultivation that took place on the Moldavian plain. The classification of maize as a vegetable or garden plant is another revealing aspect of Nacşu's declaration.[83]

The following year—according to a slightly later chronicle—a Greek, Constantin Duca, was appointed Prince. On his arrival, Duca was in hock to creditors in Wallachia and Istanbul, and unfamiliar with the customs of the country. During his reign, a tax was imposed on maize, which the poor people had begun to cultivate in previously untilled land. Apparently

> A new custom was devised, [a tax] of two *orts* per *pogon*[84] on maize, for at this time people had fewer oxen and the poor folk of the country had started to make plots by hoeing, in forests and on disused land, below the forests they would sow maize, and that's what they fed themselves on; and no-one wanted to take up the plough any more. And that was the main reason it was decided to introduce the tax on maize.[85]

Another chronicler, Ion Neculce, writing half a century later and doubtless drawing on his predecessor, wrote that Duca

> devised a custom new to the country, of taking a tax of one *zlot* per *pogon* of maize and millet, which people had begun to grow by hoeing in cleared spaces, so as not to die of hunger, and he took four lei per *pogon* of tobacco. Useless measures, without rhyme or reason, and completely ineffective in alleviating want![86]

---

83 Declaration of Nacşu, 18 June 1692, Carp family papers, in *Studii şi documente*, vi, part ii:95: 'să ne lasă să sedem păn in toamnî, căci am fostu apucatu-ne de am sămănat păpuşoi şi de alte legumi, iară în toamnă să ieşim, că n'avăm nici o triab[ă], că am fostu înblându nişte oameni fără triab[ă]'. The source, obviously Moldavian, refers to 'Glodeani', today Glodenii-Gândului, Iaşi county (not Glodeanu, Buzău county, Wallachia, as per Giurescu, *Probleme controversate*, 125).
84 *ort*, a low-value coin; *pogon*, a unit of land measurement, roughly 0.5 hectares.
85 Anon, *Letopiseţul Ţării Moldovei* [c. 1712], in *Cronicele României*, ii:40.
86 Neculce, *Letopiseţul*, 357. This would also be the first mention of tobacco in Moldavia (in Transylvania and Wallachia it is attested slightly earlier): see Mihăescu, *Tutunul*, 84.

These narrative accounts, however imprecise,[87] nevertheless illustrate vividly how maize was perceived by elites in Moldavia as a poor person's crop which had insinuated its way into the country on the edges of villages and forests.

Other sources show that maize did indeed begin to be noticed by the authorities: a princely charter from 1713 permitted the abbots of Copou Monastery in Iaşi to take a tithe on any of the crop grown on their estates, including maize.[88] We also find maize in the village of Găgeşti in the Putna river valley,[89] in the southwestern part of the country, i.e. far from the capital. Here in 1717, a certain bandit Lupaşcu, a priest's son, was accused of having stolen a hundred *merţi*[90] each of millet and maize, and sixty of wheat, resulting in the prince Mihai Racoviţă ordering his lands to be confiscated and made over to the victim, Ştefan Pârvu.[91] Maize also features in an Italian-Romanian vocabulary list drawn up by the Roman Catholic missionary Silvestro Amelio in Iaşi in 1719.[92]

In Wallachia, early internal mentions are scarcer. A Gospel published in 1693 contains a (later) marginal annotation to the effect that 'In the days of Prince Constantin, maize came up in Wallachia, which it hadn't before'; but this cannot be taken to refer with certainty to the reign of Prince Constantin Brâncoveanu (1688–1714).[93] More promisingly, a letter by a certain Osman of Kule, who requested help in bringing maize (*mîsîr bugdayı*) and millet from the mountains to the water, has been dated to around 1700, and the locality Kule identified with Turnu, a fortress on the left bank of the Danube (today Turnu Măgurele, Teleorman county). But here again, the localization is tentative.[94] The first certain internal attestation of maize in Wallachia is at Hurez Monastery, Vâlcea county, in 1716–1717, where it was delivered to the occupying Austrian army: 'wheat and maize was given to the soldiers'; 'wheat and maize was brought into the village for the Germans'.[95] Never-

---

87   For example, Neculce misdated the beginning of Duca's reign to 1691 (1693 is correct).
88   Prince Nicolae Mavrocordat, charter to Copou monastery, 7 June 1713, in *Documente Iaşi*, iii:398.
89   Today in Boloteşti commune, Vrancea county.
90   *merţă*, [pl. *merţi*] a unit of capacity, estimated at 197 litres for Moldavia in this period. Stoicescu, *Cum măsurau strămoşii*, 204.
91   Prince Mihai Racoviţă, order of 7 October 1717, in Chelcu, 'Mărturii', 76.
92   Piccillo, *Il glossario italano-moldavo di Silvestro Amelio*, 70.
93   'În zilele lui Constantin Voievod au ieşit porumbul în Ţara Românească: că mai nainte vreme n'au fost': cited by Berciu-Drăghicescu and Ciobotea, 'Viaţa economică', 375n.20; but see the comments of Florea, 'Câteva consideraţii', 49–50.
94   Osman of Kule, letter [c. 1700], summary in Guboglu, *Catalogul documentelor turceşti*, ii:209.
95   Accounts of Hurez Monastery, in *Studii şi documente*, xiv:15 ('au fost dat mai nainte la catane la Urez grâu şi porumbu'), 16 ('au adus în sat Neamţilor grâu şi porumbu').

theless, by the second decade of the eighteenth century, foreign observers in both Moldavia and Wallachia described it as a regular crop.[96]

The End of the Beginning

By around 1700, then, around two centuries after it crossed the Atlantic, we finally find maize clearly established throughout the Carpathian and Danubian area. The plant's presence here was partly a product of these countries' situation at the intersection of trade routes, and partly a result of the dramatic encounters between Habsburg and Ottoman land armies in these provinces over the long seventeenth century.

Many other plants made their way across southeastern Europe during this period. One interesting example of this was the horse chestnut, which was native to the Balkans. Popularly rumoured to have been brought to Europe by the Ottomans as fodder for their horses—hence the name—it was in fact transmitted through elite circles, and was also the subject of botanical and nutritional scrutiny before becoming a familiar feature of west European streets and parks.[97] Other plants were transported to Europe for different reasons. Rhubarb, for instance, was highly prized for medicinal uses, and was often traded from or through the Balkans to Italy and further afield.[98] The tulip, which became the glory of Dutch and other west European gardens and paintings, travelled, sometimes overland, from Istanbul to Europe in the late sixteenth century.[99] The coffee bean was popular in Vienna by the mid-seventeenth century and was to conquer the city after the Ottomans failed to do so—in preparation for the siege of 1683, the Ottoman Grand Vizir, Kara Mustafa Pasha, had more than two tonnes of coffee beans stashed in the fortress of Belgrade.[100] It is likely that the Ottomans were also responsible for the introduction of rice from Asia and for encouraging its cultivation in the Danube region, where it is attested in the Banat from the sixteenth century.[101] Toward the end of the same century tobacco and paprika first appear in Hungary and Transylvania, initially prized for elite consumption and for medicinal purposes rather than as staples.[102]

---

96 For Moldavia in 1709: Bardili, *Reisebeschreibung*, 143; for Wallachia before 1716: Del Chiaro, *Istoria*, 18.
97 Lack, 'Lilac and Horse Chestnut'.
98 Rhubarb from Albania to Italy in 1518: *Monumenta historica Slavorum meridionalium*, 184; from Bulgaria to England in 1612: Foust, *Rhubarb*, 18.
99 Wijnands, 'Tulpen naar Amsterdam'; Salzmann, 'Age of Tulips'.
100 Reindl-Kiel, '*Simits* for the Sultan', 67. More broadly see Fotić, 'Coffee and tobacco'; Senciuc, 'Exotic Brew?'
101 Feneșan, *Vilayetul Timișoara*, 253–55; Amedoski, 'Introduction'.
102 On tobacco: Demény, 'Introducerea', 1248–53; on paprika: Halikowski Smith, 'In the Shadow'.

Such stories depend on the observations of contemporaries, which also depend on their idea of what is valuable. In this respect, maize attracted no such attention. It was not a factor in Ottoman or Habsburg military food supply, although the conditions created by warfare, with some regions experiencing extensive pressure while others languished, can be said to have contributed to its adoption. In such circumstances, it may have been natural for peasants to turn to it as a valuable resource in times of need. As elsewhere in the world, where traditional upland communities met encroaching imperial forces, it could be a classic 'escape crop', enabling people to live beyond the reach of authority.[103]

Regarding the precise routes by which maize arrived, we have questioned many existing hypotheses without being able to replace them with firmer answers. In some ways we should not be surprised or disappointed by this. Just as in China, where there is evidence that maize arrived both overland and on the southern and eastern seaboards, so in the Balkans there is no reason not to imagine that the crop followed different itineraries in a variety of circumstances.[104]

Exact information as to the people who transported maize is also frustratingly scarce. Attributions to different ethnic or social groups, such as Adriatic or Black Sea merchants, Romanian shepherds or even nomadic Roma are thought-provoking, but lack substantiation.[105] In general it should be borne in mind that there was considerable individual and group mobility across the Habsburg-Ottoman frontier at this time.[106] We are also tempted to repeat McCann's warning that 'those who advocate peasant agency and those who favor the idea of patrician innovation will find equally little to document their assertions'.[107] But by 1700 the researcher even of these peripheral countries is in a slightly better position. There are some indications of economic valorization of maize on the part of a few magnates, soldiers and entrepreneurs in these borderland regions. And we have a few fascinating glimpses of poor people using it on the margins of society. The authorities in these lands were not responsible for its introduction, but rather reacted to its presence when it came to their attention.[108] This would change slowly over the course of the eighteenth century, as we shall see in the next two chapters.

---

103 Richards, *Unending Frontier*, 81, 130–31; 'escape crop': Scott, *Art of Not Being Governed*, 201.
104 Ho, 'American Food Plants into China', 194–95.
105 Black Sea merchants, see above; Romanian shepherds: Bartha, 'Points of Connection', 51; Roma: von Lipmann, 'Geschichte', 336.
106 Recent works on this complex topic include Katsiardi-Hering and Stassinopoulou, eds. *Across the Danube;* Pešalj, *Monitoring Migrations;* and Landais, 'Enregistrer l'ethnicité'.
107 McCann, *Maize and Grace*, 62.
108 Cf., for the potato in western Europe, the arguments of Earle, *Feeding the People*, 24–55.

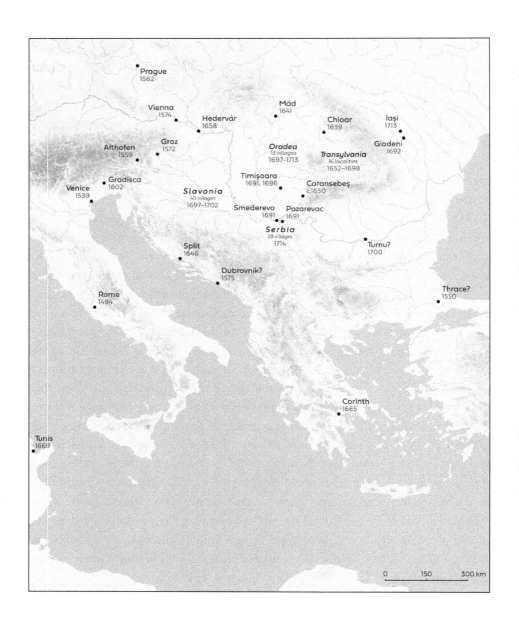

Map 1. Maize in Southeastern Europe, c. 1550–1700

32

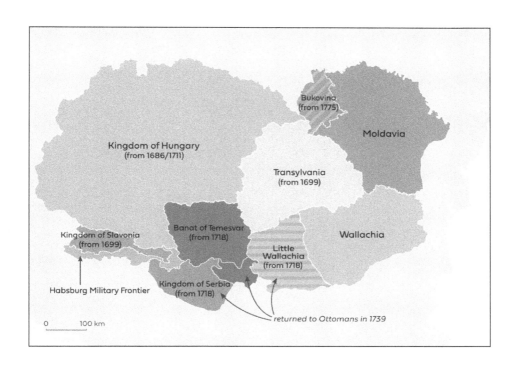

Map 2. Empires and Frontiers, c. 1700. Dates indicate periods of Habsburg rule

Chapter 2

Conquerors, Cultivators and Collaborators: Maize at Empire's Edge, 1700–1774

In January 1699, on the banks of the Danube at Sremski Karlovci, Habsburg and Ottoman envoys signed the Treaty of Karlowitz in the presence of English and Dutch diplomats who mediated the proceedings. The treaty confirmed the transfer of Croatia and Transylvania into the hands of the Habsburgs, who thereby became overlords of a substantial population of Croats, Serbs, Romanians and other subjects. Habsburg rule over Hungary was finally confirmed in 1711, and their gains continued when in 1718 they took over the Ottoman strongholds of Belgrade and Temeșvar. Belgrade became the temporary centre of a Habsburg Kingdom of Serbia, while the country around Temeșvar was reorganized as a 'Banate': it was ruled as the emperor's personal domain, and became a site of colonial experiment including intensive settlement by Germans and many other nations.[1] For a brief but important interval, the Habsburgs also held Little Wallachia, corresponding to Oltenia in today's Romania.[2]

Taken together, the gains of 1699–1718 constituted the largest single territorial expansion in Habsburg history, and one of the largest transfers of territory in early modern Europe.[3] The economic value of the lands of the middle Danube was known to contemporaries: according to a departing Ottoman chronicler, they were 'as fertile as Egypt'.[4] A merchant from Split described them as being 'situated in the heart of the most fertile Ottoman provinces', and hoped that the newly con-

---
1   Roider, 'Nationalism and Colonization'; Thomas, 'Anatomy'. The term 'Banat' meant the territory of a *Ban*, a historical term for a regional ruler.
2   Papacostea, *Oltenia*.
3   Kreuter, 'Attempts'.
4   Bartınlı İbrahim Hamdi, quoted in Feneșan, *Vilayetul Timișoara*, 247.

quered lands would bring products his way, in an expansion of the older Balkan trade.⁵ Serbia and Little Wallachia did not spend long under Habsburg dominion: in 1739, they were returned to the Ottomans. But the breach had been made, and there was maize to discover, even if the imperialists did not particularly like what they found, and still less what they ate.

The Habsburgs did what other empires did or would do: they undertook intensive mapping and investigation of their newly-acquired territories, or *Neoacquistica* as they were called in the bureaucratic Latin used in Vienna. At a time of urban growth and demand for supply in central Europe, it was to be expected that they should look to these lands in search of 'frontier foods'.⁶ One result of this was an extremely detailed report on Little Wallachia, compiled in 1723 by explorer and cartographer Friedrich Schwantz. Schwantz noted many aspects of economic and social life in the province, including the Wallachians' activities such as ploughing, tending vines and orchards, livestock raising and beekeeping. 'Their manner of eating is not delicate', he wrote; 'they can have wheat, meat, fish and plenty of game; but they lack the skill to prepare them'. In one of the earliest unambiguous mentions of mămăligă in any language (*Mameliga*), the Austrian cartographer described it as 'a kind of porridge cooked in a pot from maize meal and water'. But to Schwantz it was a 'defect' (*Defect*), one which could only be compensated for by the 'excellent and plentiful wine' (*gutte und viele Wein*) that the province offered.⁷

Schwantz was not alone in recording mămăligă in a mainly negative key. The boyars of Oltenia, responding to a request by the Habsburg Imperial commander to account for their income, mentioned tithes on wheat, barley, oats, millet, maize, buckwheat, hay and vegetables.⁸ But administrators wondered whether there was any point claiming maize, given the lack of an international market for the cereal.⁹ It was nevertheless taken for troops and sometimes fed to the horses in the absence of barley.¹⁰ In the 1720s the Habsburgs began taking measures for importing wheat and barley from Little Wallachia, for both local consumption and international export.

---

5   Alvise Mocenigo to the Doge of Venice, 20 September 1721, in Luca, 'Greek and Aromanian merchants', 328.
6   Hoffmann, 'Frontier Foods'.
7   Schwantz, 'Kurtze Erklährung', page 84 of pdf. Printed in Hurmuzaki, *Documente*, ix, pt. i:637; Rom. trans. M. Holban in *Călători străini*, ix:67. Stoianovich, 'Le maïs', 1027, cites similar disparaging Austrian remarks on maize in Serbia.
8   Boyars' response to General Stainville, 20 October 1719, in *Documente privind relațiile agrare*, i:285 ('triticum turcicum').
9   Papacostea, *Oltenia sub stăpânirea austriacă*, 71–72.
10 Niccolò da Porta, order of 1 January 1723, in *Acte fiscale*, 105; register for Mehedinți county, 1723, ibid., 117–24; register for upper Vâlcea, 1729–1730, in *Studii și documente*, v:148.

But boyars fought for the right to continue selling these crops, as well as maize and hay, across the Danube.[11] In the early 1730s, the Habsburg military governor of Transylvania, General Count Franz-Paul von Wallis, made an inspection of Little Wallachia. He reckoned the province deserted, finding nothing growing there—'except maize', he added disdainfully.[12] Likewise, the commander of the Banat of Temesvar, General Joseph Andreas von Hamilton, recorded the abundance of maize and other crops in the province, again in a disparaging manner, alleging that such plenty had a detrimental effect on the industriousness of the inhabitants.[13] This did not, of course, stop the Habsburg authorities from taxing it extensively.[14]

For these early soldiers, explorers and bureaucrats—just as for their French contemporaries in North America—maize was more than simply a plant. Rather, to them it was a marker of otherness, and to some extent of servility.[15] Such derogatory attitudes would prove hard to shake off: even in the 1770s, after the Habsburgs acquired further territory from the Ottomans in the form of the province of Bukovina, their soldiers and administrators made similar remarks. It was an obstacle to imperial tidiness, growing for example over field boundary stones which could not be properly identified.[16] A good administrator would boast to Vienna of getting rid of it: 'through our support and example, one sees now all kinds of crops flourishing throughout the country, and the plough is employed, where before one found only a few fields of maize'.[17] In many ways the Habsburgs thought of the border with the Ottomans as a classical 'barbarian frontier'.[18] In reality, as Jürgen Osterhammel has observed, they were up against a different and relatively well-organized imperial system.[19] And one aspect of this system happened to be the cultivation of maize. Maize, then, was a 'frontier cereal' not just in terms of its location on the edges of big empires or smaller fields, but in terms of its moral and social configuration.[20]

---

11 Papacostea, 'Contribuție', 243–44.
12 Von Wallis and von Rebentisch, report of 1731, in Hurmuzaki, *Documente*, vi:471; Rom. trans. M. Bulgaru, M. Holban, in *Călători străini*, ix:164.
13 Hamilton, *Chorographia Bannatus Temesiensis* (1734), in Veichtlbauer, *Zwischen Kolonie und Provinz*, 29.
14 Feneșan, *Administrație și fiscalitate*, 101.
15 Launay, 'Maize avoidance?' On Spanish colonial attitudes see Brandes, 'Maize', Earle, *Body of the Conquistador*, 143–53; on English ones: Chaplin, *Subject Matter*, 149, Gentilcore, *Food and Health*, 75.
16 Fiscal Adjunct J.F. Erggelet, report of 21 July 1787, in Vitcu, 'Hotarnica unor moșii', 422.
17 General Enzenberg, report on Bukovina, 1786, Hurmuzaki, *Documente*, vii:471.
18 On European-Ottoman gastro-frontiers: Dursteler, 'Bad Bread'; Petrică, *Topography of Taste*, 41–66.
19 Osterhammel, 'Kulturelle Grenzen', 109 n.33. See also Burke, 'Cultural Frontiers', 204–16.
20 Paz Sánchez, 'El trigo de los pobres'. While Hoffmann, 'Frontier Foods', referred to food brought from frontiers to urban centres, Paz Sánchez's concept of 'frontier cereal' (*un cereal fronterizero*) stresses how maize was used to mark moral and social boundaries.

CHAPTER 2

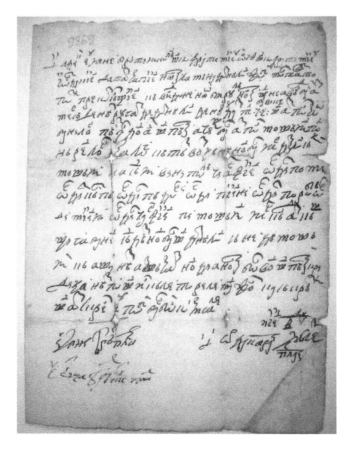

2.1 Friedrich Schwantz, Report on Little Wallachia (Oltenia), 1723

2.2 Brătianu brothers, letter of mortgage, Poenărei, Wallachia, 1728.

The Habsburg conquests meant that the Ottoman provinces of Moldavia and Wallachia acquired a much greater strategic importance as border territories in a reorganized Empire.[21] Henceforth, princes were appointed from a limited number of Orthodox Christian families resident in the Fanar district of Istanbul, where investiture took place. While the nature of the regime has been much debated,[22] the important point for the mămăligologist is that, after 1700, the princes actively sought to introduce reforms aimed at stabilizing population and particularly revenue. In these matters they were answerable to the Sultan but they also well understood that securing stable, well-managed territories was in their own interest: their personal fortunes depended on it. Although they were influenced to some extent by enlightened ideas, they also developed their own initiatives. The settlement and agrarianization of the provinces on each side of the Habsburg-Ottoman border can therefore be understood as taking place in parallel, albeit in asymmetric ways.[23]

Wallachian documents bear witness to the spread of maize. In June 1728, the brothers Iane, Oancea and Iordache Brătianu pawned their estate at Poenărei in Argeş county, to a merchant who was thereby entitled to all the produce thereof 'from the orchards or fields or forests or clearings or maize or honey or whatever is on the estate' for a period of three years.[24] By the 1730s, monastery registers recorded quite ample quantities of the plant.[25] For example, in 1738, the monastery of Hurez in Wallachia was attacked by irregular troops, who, as well as destroying many objects, apparently consumed substantial quantities of maize.[26] In 1739, 150 *kile* of maize was harvested at Vistireasa in Prahova county and 70 at Blejoiu de Sus in the same county, estates belonging to Târgşor Monastery. In 1740 the respective harvests were of 120 and 130 *kile*.[27] In 1746, the leading Orthodox hierarch of the province, Metropolitan Neofit of Ungrovlachia, undertaking a visitation of his office's landholdings, noted rich sowings of maize and other cereals on the church's estates at Fotoaia near Giurgiu on the Danube, at Obislavele on the banks of the Argeş river in Dâmboviţa county, and at Comana further downstream on the same river.[28] While in the early 1730s, Austrian observers had considered maize to be

---

21 Howard, *History of the Ottoman Empire*, 211–12.
22 Pippidi, *Hommes et idées*, 339–50; Philliou, 'Communities on the Verge'; Iordachi, 'Phanariot Regime'.
23 Constantiniu and Papacostea, 'Les réformes'.
24 Brătianu brothers, 'Zapis'.
25 Columbeanu, *Grandes exploitations domaniales*, 56–64.
26 'Foae de pagube şi jafurile ce au făcutŭ haiducii şi plăiaşii la sfânta mănăstire Hurezii' (1738), in *Studii şi documente*, xiv:57.
27 Şerban, 'Cîteva date', 258. A *kile* = 680 litres.
28 Neofit Cretanul, Journal (1746), trans. A. Camariano-Cioran in *Călători străini*, ix:338, 340, 345.

prevalent in the mountainous regions near the Transylvanian border,[29] by mid-century it was clearly cultivated all over the province.

In 1750, the Prince of Wallachia took a serious enough interest in the crop that he ordered a tithe to be determined on the basis of the surface area cultivated rather than according to the harvest. It has been argued that this was done to counteract the subterfuge of picking maize ears before the harvest, thereby avoiding taxation.[30] In a petition of April 1751, the villagers of Izvorul de Jos, Vlaşca county, complained that because of the greedy appropriations of the landlord, Mihalache Clucer, 'we haven't been able to sow either maize or garden plants; it is as if we were migrants'.[31] According to a note made in the coverleaf of a manuscript, the year 1756 was a particularly rich one in Wallachia for wheat, barley, maize, wine, millet and other crops. It is interesting to note the order in which the crops are listed, with maize and other cereals now placed ahead of the traditional vines and millet.[32] In 1770, a delegation of Wallachian boyars who presented a report to the Russian government detailing the country's resources singled out the upper part of Ilfov county around Bucharest, and Vlaşca, Dâmboviţa and Argeş counties, as areas of maize cultivation.[33]

In Moldavia, sources also indicate the private initiative of individuals. In 1735, four sisters, Ştefania, Ghinia, Ioana and Ileana, were forced to mortgage the estate they had inherited from their late father, Ioniţă Clijan, because the latter had died owing fifty bushels (*stamboale*) of maize to a Turk.[34] In 1738, a monk, Parfene Bărzul, settled a tenant on his estate at Sohod in Bacău county, who grew maize in his own private garden.[35] The following year, a chronicle reports, there was a general failure of the maize and millet crop owing to early autumn mists and frosts. The weather was so bad that part of the population had to flee to Ottoman and Polish territories, and the Prince reduced tithes.[36] In 1741, Ion Borundean of Bacău county issued a complaint against a certain Ştefan who had damaged his maize field of one and a half *pogons* (three-quarters of a hectare), allowing it to be tram-

---

29 Papacostea, *Oltenia*, 72–73; Hurmuzaki, *Documente*, vi:478.
30 Constantiniu, 'Situaţia clăcaşilor', 90; more generally, Olaru, *Writs and Measures*, 273–85. For tithes on maize in Moldavia, see e.g. *Uricariul*, xxi:206; *Documente privind relaţiile agrare*, ii:298, 475.
31 Petition of villagers of Izvorul de Jos to Prince Ghica, 14 April 1751, in *Documente privind relaţiile agrare*, i:505: 'toţi săracii şi-au pus porumbul şi grădini, iar noi şi ceilalţi oameni din sat, am rămas de nici porumbu n-am pus, nici grădini, tocma ca când am fi bejenari'.
32 *Însemnări de demult*, 119.
33 Wallachian deputies to Count Panin, St. Petersburg 1770, in *Genealogia Cantacuzinilor*, 468–73.
34 Testimony of 5 October 1735, in *Uricariul*, xxi:206.
35 Judgement of Prince Grigore Ghica, 26 March 1738, in *Uricariul*, x:204–5.
36 *Cronica Ghiculeştilor*, 498, 499.

pled by cattle.[37] That maize was already widely cultivated at this point is confirmed not just by the above miscellaneous data but by a country-wide audit of monastery income undertaken in 1742 on the orders of Prince Constantin Mavrocordat. The auditors recorded a substantial 350 *merți* of maize at Putna Monastery, while wages were being paid for the harvesting of 10 *pogons* (approximately 5 hectares) of maize at Bogdana Monastery.[38] In the region of Bacău, where there were Catholic communities, missionaries who visited found maize 'in abundance', sometimes in 'extraordinarily large vats'; it formed part of the priests' tithe.[39]

Elsewhere in Moldavia, maize could be a form of currency or wage payment: in 1746, a certain Gheorghița of Spinești in Putna county bought a clearing, paying partly in cash and partly in maize.[40] In 1752, boyar Teodor Palade was paying itinerant labourers in carp and cornmeal for scything undertaken on his estate at Mârzăști, outside Iași.[41] In 1754, maize was extremely scarce in the south of the country, and the population was reduced to foraging for acorns; they had to buy millet and maize at high prices from the northern parts, and from Poland.[42] The following year, the hegumen of Voroneț Monastery sued the people of Drăgoești who had allegedly taken fifty *merți* (up to a tonne) of maize from the monastery stores.[43] Also in 1755, the monks of Putna Monastery were obliged to disestablish a lake they had created on the course of the river Hucău on their estates in northern Moldavia, because the overflowing waters were causing damage to the maize crops of the neighbouring village of Boian.[44]

In the same year, maize was still considered a garden plant, but a taxable one: the residents on the estates of Dancu Monastery at Bucium, outside Iași, although not obliged to pay any tithe on their garden produce, were liable for their maize (and cabbage).[45] Another source for the generalization of maize comes in some documents concerning the organization of markets in Iași in the middle of the eighteenth century. In 1757, a tax was introduced on the weighing of flour in the city

---

37 Register of Constantin Mavrocordat, cited by Berceanu, 'Reformele', 218.
38 Bogdan, 'Sămile mănăstirilor', 225, 251.
39 'Abundance': Giovanni Maria Ausilia (1745), trans. M. Alexandrescu-Dersca Bulgaru in *Călători străini*, ix:313; tithes, ibid., 304, 322; 'extraordinarily large vats': Péter Zöld (1766), trans. I. Totoiu, ibid., 509.
40 Sale contract, 17 April 1746, in *Documente putnene*, i:78 (today Vrancea county).
41 Teodor Palade, estate accounts (1752), in Mîrza, 'Cheltuielile', 350.
42 *Cronica Ghiculeștilor*, 706, 707.
43 Prince Matei Ghica, order of 3 November 1755, in *Documente privind relațiile agrare*, ii:323.
44 Judgement of 23 June 1755, in *Documente bucovinene*, v:82 (today Boyany, Ukraine).
45 Villagers of Bucium, contract with Dancu Monastery, 4 June 1755, in *Documente Iași*, v:612–13; confirmed by Prince Ioan Theodor Callimachi, charter of 23 May 1760, in *Documente Iași*, vi:253.

market, to be granted to the newly-established monastery of St. Spiridon: maize was explicitly recorded as a taxable flour alongside wheat, barley, millet and oats.[46] If in previous decades, maize was associated mainly with poor folk eking out a life on the edges of the forest, by the middle of the eighteenth century it became a regular part of town and country life.

The reader may have noticed that a significant number of early mentions of maize in Moldavia and Wallachia occur on monastery lands, or records thereof. Monasteries occupied a specific place in the administration and economy of the principalities at this point. Historically, they had been endowed by medieval rulers and enjoyed a range of immunities from taxation.[47] A number of monasteries and their lands were 'dedicated' to Orthodox Patriarchal Sees in the Ottoman Near East (Alexandria, Antioch, Jerusalem), or to Mount Athos. Although they have traditionally been perceived as post-Byzantine institutions, in reality they bore some resemblance to the Islamic endowments in the Ottoman Empire known as *vakıf*: essentially ring-fenced trusts relatively independent of secular authority and responsible for a number of charitable and welfare functions for the benefit of the community, as well as, of course, religious devotion.[48] By the middle of the eighteenth century, as part of an attempt to increase state control, princes started to commission inventories of monastic incomes and landholdings in a way that they had not done before.[49]

There is no concrete evidence to suggest that maize was formally introduced to the principalities by any Orthodox religious authorities. What we are seeing here is perhaps an optical illusion, due to the fact that monasteries kept records where others did not. However, it is worth recalling that monasteries had extensive communication links through the Empire and also time to experiment with new crops. They were important locally as the sites of mills and fairs, and in these capacities are likely to have played a role in the crop's dissemination.[50] During times of war, their ample buildings and fortifications meant they were used by occupying armies as centres for quartering and supply.

---

46 Decrees of Princes Constantin Racoviță, Scarlat Ghica, Ioan Callimachi, Grigore Callimachi, from the period 1757–1763, in *Documente Iași*, vi:85, 149, 458; see also Tofan, 'Venitul cântarului', 234–35.
47 Chelcu, 'Legal and Tax Systems'.
48 Mutafchieva, *Osmanska sotsialno-ikonomicheska istoriya*, 118–33; Radushev *et al.*, 'Introduction'. The term *vakıf* is sometimes used in Romanian for monastery donations: examples in *DLR*, s.v. 'vacuf'.
49 Bogdan, 'Sămile mănăstirilor'; Columbeanu, *Grandes exploitations domaniales*. More broadly on the princes' attempts to assert fiscal control in this period, Olaru, *Writs and Measures*.
50 In 1779, Axente Pătrașcu of Târgu Neamț established a mill at Neamț Monastery, to whom he paid rent in maize: *Documente privind relațiile agrare*, ii:489.

Monasteries, like boyar families, were also owners of slaves, the vast majority of them Roma gypsies. Some of these practised trades like tinkering, butchering and gold-panning, or were musicians. Others served the household or performed agricultural labour.[51] A later source, from the 1780s, reports the Metropolitan of Moldavia as saying of some Roma slaves that 'they are happy, even though they have nothing to eat but mămăligă'.[52] There is some evidence that Roma gypsies acted as guards of maize stores.[53] At Hurez in Wallachia, maize was used to feed Roma slaves working in the monastery's forests.[54] Much later, we have a register of maize fed to the slaves at the Goldsmiths' Monastery in Bucharest.[55] There is no direct relation between monasteries' use of maize and their enslavement of Roma, which took place several centuries earlier than the plant's arrival. But among other things, maize must have been useful to monks as a cheap food supply for this purpose.

As already argued, we should not imagine the Ottoman frontier to have been strictly 'closed' to trade. The trade in cattle and horses to Germany, Austria, Hungary and Poland continued to flourish.[56] Many of the merchants of the principalities were, then, 'capitalists' in the literal sense of the word.[57] Cereals, however, were a different matter. In a memorandum of 1770, the Wallachian boyars presented the Ottoman claim to a monopoly on grain as a recent thing, replacing the traditional taxation of sheep, wax, hives and vineyards 'only in the last fourteen or fifteen years'.[58] A French diplomat reporting from Moldavia at the beginning of the nineteenth century stated, presumably on the basis of local informants, that Ottoman requisitioning of grain had only begun in 1761.[59] While this was hardly the case, Ottoman reliance on the Danube region as a source of grain became much more pressing when the Porte lost full control over the grain supply from Egypt after the revolts of 1755–1756, and also ceded Crimea to Russia in 1783.[60] The Porte itself, in a note sent to the Austrian internuncio in 1767, described the limitations on export

---

51 More detail on their legal and social conditions: Achim, *Roma*, 31–64; Iordachi, *Liberalism*, 127–64.
52 Obradović, *Ezopove basne*, 301.
53 Obradovici, *Carte de mână*, quoted below, p. 64; *Documente Callimachi*, i:549.
54 Letter of Hegumen Rafail, October 4 1790, *Studii și documente*, xiv:132.
55 Anon, 'Foaie' (reproduced in Illustration 7.1, below).
56 Cernovodeanu, 'Comerțul'; Murgescu, 'Der Anteil', 61–91.
57 Capital < *capita*, head of cattle. Cf. also 'stock'.
58 Wallachian boyars, response to questionnaire of Field Marshal Count Rumyantsev-Zadunaisky (1770), in *Genealogia Cantacuzinilor*, 461.
59 Charles Reinhard, report of 1807, in *Călători străini în sec. XIX*, i:274.
60 Alexandrescu-Dersca Bulgaru, 'L'approvisionnement'; Ağir, 'Evolution of Grain Policy'.

of grain and other foodstuffs from the principalities as a recent policy.⁶¹ At this time, the Sultan also began to crack down on the practices of Ottoman soldiers and merchants who, in contravention with traditional prohibitions, had taken to raising livestock or setting up farms north of the Danube, often in connivance with local Christian elites. This was done partly so that these lands be reserved for direct provisioning of the imperial capital.⁶² Before becoming 'the breadbasket of Europe', as Romania was sometimes called in the twentieth century, Moldavia and Wallachia were dubbed 'the storehouse of the Empire' (*devlet-i alienin kileri*).⁶³

These new measures meant that the Habsburgs could not officially purchase maize from the Principalities, although by this time they had begun to promote its transportation from the Banat to the free port of Trieste, from where it was exported across the Mediterranean. The Trieste merchants did not especially prize the Banat grain, which they adjudged to be impure, sometimes damp, and also involving higher transportation costs than that from Carinthia or Styria.⁶⁴ There were numerous discussions and proposals for extending trade in the Danubian area, but few concrete developments: in 1763 there were twenty-seven Habsburg consular agents in the Levant, but not one in the Balkans.⁶⁵

Other factors complicating the free circulation of goods were both military and sanitary. As part of their consolidation of control over Hungary and Transylvania, the Habsburgs set up both a military frontier zone against the Ottomans, and a *cordon sanitaire* against the plague, along the eastern and southern border of Transylvania. This involved intensive monitoring not only of people but also of foodstuffs.⁶⁶ In addition to this, there was the factor of war itself: the Principalities were a the-

---

61 '...was die Ausfuhr von Korn und anderen Fruchtgattungen aus der Wallachey ins Siebenbürgen anlanget ... dasz es den jüngsten Verfassungen oder Verordnung des Kays. Divans schnurstrakhs zuwider ist'. Contemporary translation of a *takrir* (clarificatory note) sent to Internuncio Brognard, August 1767, in Hurmuzaki, *Documente*, vii:39–40.
62 The earliest such orders are against merchants using the Danubian lands for winter grazing: Ahmed III, firman, July 1733, in *Documente turcești*, i:221–22. Later ones refer to *çiftliks* (farms, estates): Mustafa III, firman, August 1761, in *Documente turcești*, i:271–72; Moldavian petition, 1774, in *Uricariul*, vi:422; Sultan Selim III, firman, September 1791, in *Documente turcești*, ii:7. See further Perianu, 'Raiaua Brăilei', 296–98; Penelea, *Foires*, 31–33; Aksan, 'Whose Territory?'; Yıldız and Kokdaş, 'Peasantry in a Well-Protected Domain'.
63 Alexandrescu-Dersca Bulgaru, 'L'approvisionnement', 76; Aksan, 'Whose Territory', 70. The term is used consistently during the next decades, e.g. *Documente turcești*, i:285, 294, 319, 321; Raicevich, *Osservazioni*, 271; *Relațiile româno-otomane*, 640–42; *Documente 1821*, i:214; *Uricariul* vi:124, 125; *Mémoires et projets*, 149.
64 Andreozzi, 'L'aggravio dei dazi', 56, 57.
65 Heppner, *Österreich und die Donaufürstentümer*, 40.
66 Rothenberg, 'Austrian Sanitary Cordon'; Jesner, 'Adam Chenot'; Popovici, 'Establishment'.

Conquerors, Cultivators and Collaborators

3.1 J. J. Ehrler, *Peasant house and maize store*, Banat of Temesvar, 1774

atre of conflict between Ottoman, Habsburg and Russian armies on a regular basis in the eighteenth and early nineteenth centuries. Moldavia, Wallachia, or both provinces, were occupied by one imperial army or another for at least thirty years in the century between 1735 and 1836.

Military occupations both hindered and stimulated trade. Historically, the Ottomans had displayed little interest in requisitioning maize, although local officials may on occasion have sought to buy it.[67] During the 1768–1774 war, the young Emperor Joseph II, at that time co-regent with his mother Maria Theresa, made a tour of inspection in Transylvania, and noted that the peasantry, 'who could expect no help from their landlords', were dependent on the import of maize from Moldavia, which in turn depended on the goodwill of the Russian army which was occupying the latter province at that time.[68] During this time, European economists were beginning to reflect on the fact that maize could be a valuable reserve crop in

---

67 An Ottoman request to buy maize from the Habsburg governor of Semlin [today Zemun, Serbia] in 1769, mentioned by Mayer, 'The Price for Austria's Security, I', 270, seems to be an isolated instance. It is not mentioned in Aksan's careful studies of Ottoman provisioning: Aksan, 'Feeding the Ottoman Troops'; Aksan, 'Whatever Happened to the Janissaries?'.

68 'Schlussbericht des Kaisers Joseph II über seine Reise durch Siebenbürgen', 9 July 1773, in Joseph II, *Călătoria*, 739.

times of famine.⁶⁹ This might explain why Joseph took an interest in it, although beyond this remark, it seems not to have become part of Habsburg policy. He was right to observe that the Transylvanian elites were no fans of maize: agronomists of the time opposed its cultivation, arguing that it was labour-intensive and used up a lot of water, advocating its use not for food but for distilling spirits, mainly to prevent wheat being used to this end.⁷⁰ More generally in this period, Habsburg 'experts' began to promote the potato against maize, in the face of considerable resistance from the population.⁷¹ The Russian authorities, for their part, were apparently indifferent to maize, or their troops averse to it. According to a report by a field doctor in Russian service in Iași in 1770, the soldiers made their own bread from wheat or rye, but could not handle the 'Moldavian cakes' made of equal parts of wheat and maize flour, as these were not properly leavened, and therefore 'extremely bad for the stomach, as many of our men found out'.⁷² This would explain why they were happy for maize to be made available for export; a pattern which would continue up to at least 1830.⁷³

It has been argued that the quartering needs of the imperial armies in these lengthy and frequent periods of occupation created 'a sort of market', or at least stimulated the need for a better organization of sowing, harvesting and distribution of cereals in both provinces.⁷⁴ The same scholar even suggested that these inter-imperial conjunctures had the same effect on the local agrarian economy as the development of cities in western Europe, if admittedly on a smaller scale.⁷⁵ To a certain extent, the impulse for sedentarization, cultivation, commercialization and urbanization could be considered a by-product of this unusual situation.⁷⁶ Furthermore, the processes of procurement and negotiation over cereals gave local elites experience and more direct contact with the imperial metropoles, bringing them into broader patronage and communication networks across all three empires.⁷⁷

---

69 Carraretto, *Histoires de maïs*, 65–69; Finzi, '*Sazia assai*', 33–40.
70 Csetri, 'Débuts'; Frivaldszky, 'Reformjavaslat', 114. In 1757, there was a maize garden on the Jósika family estate at Branyicska (Brănișca, Hunedoara county), according to Fekete, 'Late Renaissance Garden Art', 19, but this appears to have been merely ornamental.
71 Müller, *Siebenbürgische Wirtschaftspolitik*, 29 (thanks to Oana Sorescu Iudean for this reference); Szabo, *Kaunitz*, 161.
72 Orraeus, *Descriptio pestis*, 123; Rom. trans. in *Călători străini*, x, part I, 78.
73 LeDonne, 'Geopolitics, Logistics, and Grain', 23; Taki, *Tsar and Sultan*, 117–18.
74 Ot̨etea, 'Le second asservissement', 300.
75 Ot̨etea, 'Constrângerea extraeconomică a clăcașilor', 1060.
76 LeDonne, 'Geopolitics'; Robarts, *Migration and Disease*, 86–88.
77 Philliou, *Biography of an Empire*, 35–36; Ağir, 'Evolution of Grain Procurement'.

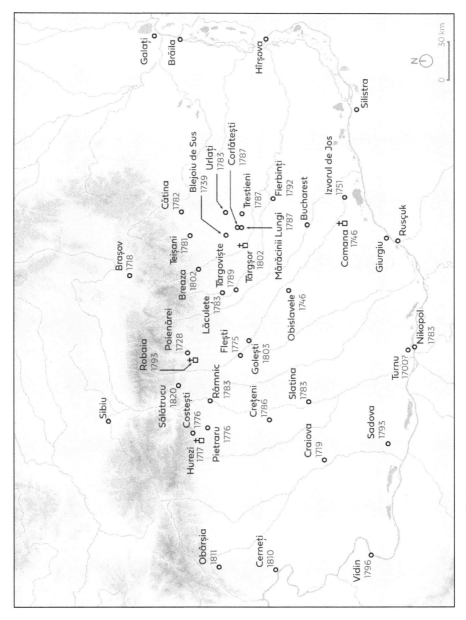

Map 3. Maize in Wallachia, c. 1720–1820

CHAPTER 2

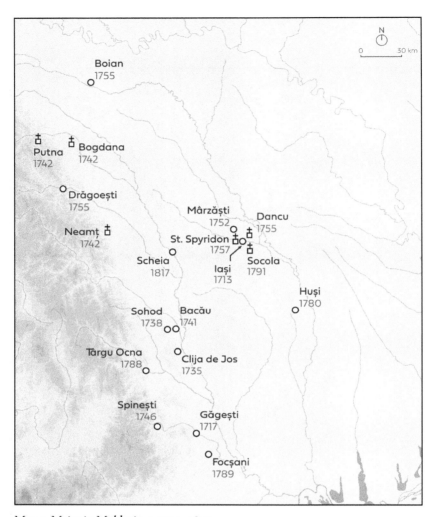

Map 4. Maize in Moldavia, c. 1720–1820

Chapter 3

Climate, Conflict, Contagion and Commerce: The Triumph of Maize, 1774–1812

The Treaty of Küçük Kaynarca, concluded between Russian and Ottoman representatives in a small village a few miles south of the Danube in July 1774, placed limitations on the traditional Ottoman right to exact tribute from Moldavia and Wallachia. Article 11 of the Treaty gave Russia freedom of navigation through the Straits, and the right to undertake exploratory trips overland or along the Danube. This jolted the Habsburgs—who had already enjoyed this privilege since 1718, but never made much use of it—into pursuing a more proactive commercial policy.[1] Finally, in 1782, they appointed an Agent in Bucharest, who described maize as being 'in great vogue', both for its ease of cultivation and for the reliability of the harvest.[2]

Domestic documents confirm the Agent's affirmations in abundance. In May 1776, for example, Chiril, a monk at Hurez Monastery in Vâlcea county, wrote to his superior promising to send twenty carts of maize and wheat from the villages of Petraru and Costești.[3] In July 1781, Iane, a priest from Vălenii in Prahova county, together with a certain Tănase Turcul ('Athanasius the Turk'), conducted a land survey in the nearby village of Teișani. Together, they found that Stan, the brother of Ilie and son of Mihai, was growing maize on land recently turned over to cultivation on the banks of the River Teleajen.[4] In June 1782, a group of four men in Catina, Buzău county—Manea, Neagu, Oprea and Isar—contracted to buy up the

---

1 Heppner, *Österreich und die Donaufürstentümer*, ch. 1, pt. 3.
2 Raicevich, *Osservazioni*, 56.
3 Chiril, letter to Hegumen of Hurez Monastery, May 11 1776, in *Studii și documente*, xiv:93; cf. letter of Ion Părăianu to same, 7 April 1783, ibid., 117–18.
4 Popa Iane, Tănase Turcul, survey of the estate of Ilie Pintea, 1781, in Sacerdoțeanu, 'Acte drăjnene', 192.

maize harvest in advance, clearly looking to speculate on the product.[5] In 1783, Reimer, a Saxon from southern Transylvania operating a glass factory in Wallachia, was purchasing cornmeal alongside wine and brandy.[6] In the same year, at Urlați in Saac country (today Prahova county), maize was being grown on estates belonging to the monks of Colțea Monastery.[7] At Obedeanu Monastery in Craiova, which housed one of the first schools in the city, maize formed part of the payment in kind that the teachers received.[8] In July 1786, the people of Crețeni in Vâlcea county were less fortunate: storms and hail destroyed several silos of wheat and maize.[9] Similarly, in Moldavia in September 1784, the maize could not be harvested because an early snowstorm caused much damage to the crops.[10] In October 1787, quite impressive quantities were harvested on the estates of the Metropolitan church at Trestieni, Corlătești and Mărăcinii Lungi in Prahova county.[11] The accounts of the church's estates at Gherghița, Borusul and Obedeanca in the same county show likewise that maize had become a dominant crop there, in some cases effectively practising a monoculture.[12]

In April 1790, the bakers of Bucharest were given permission to mix maize and millet with the usual wheat flour when making bread;[13] while in September the following year, the city's butchers were selling bacon from maize-fed pigs at a slightly higher price than bacon from pigs fed on acorns or beech nuts.[14] In Craiova in July 1790, Tudoran Mihail, the land agent of Oltenian boyar Ioniță Brăiloiu, reported a good crop of cereals but that the maize was suffering on account of the dry weather. 'If God shows mercy', he wrote, 'maybe there will be enough'.[15] In 1802, Aromanian merchant Vasile Țumbru, based in Brașov, bought 30 *kile* of maize from Breaza, across the border in Wallachia.[16] Not far away from Breaza, an inventory drawn up by Hegumen Dionisie at Târgușor Monastery, Prahova county, reveals 70 *kile* of maize, kept in two different storehouses, one at the mon-

---

5   *Studii și documente*, v:547.
6   Ispravniks of Râmnic, judgement of 14 May 1783, in Furnică, ed. *Documente*, 94.
7   Prince Nicolae Caragea, judgement of May 1783, in Iorga, 'Documente urlățene', 278.
8   Monastery accounts (1780s), in Bălan, 'Contribuții la istoria învățămîntului', 291.
9   Antonie Nicolantin, letter to Hagi Pop, 14 July 1786, in Furnică, ed. *Din istoria comerțului*, 131.
10 Enachi Kogălniceanu, marginal note from 1784, in *Însemnări de demult*, 122.
11 *Documente privind relațiile agrare*, i:758; cf. Șerban, 'Cîteva date', 259.
12 Columbeanu, *Grandes exploitations domaniales*, 66–68.
13 Wallachian Divan, order of 17 April 1790, in Urechia, *Istoria românilor*, iii:397.
14 'Slănină de râmator hrănit cu porumb' at 40 lei/oka, and 'slănină de râmator hrănit cu ghindă sau jir' at 36 lei/oka: price list of September 1791, in Urechia, *Istoria românilor*, iv:317.
15 *Studii și documente*, viii:109.
16 Limona and Limona, 'Aspecte ale comerțului brașovean', 546.

astery itself and one in the town of the same name.[17] In January 1803, boyar Radu Golescu had ground maize for sale on his estate in Goleşti, Argeş county.[18] In July the following year, an agent of the recently established British consulate at Bucharest, undertaking a reconnaissance mission in northern and western Wallachia, was offered maize for sale at Craiova by a local boyar, who was under the completely mistaken impression that the British had come to buy it up and take it for export through the Black Sea.[19]

In a patriarchal society such as Wallachia, growing and trading maize was mainly a man's game. Mainly, yet not exclusively: as recent research shows, even if they were subordinated from a legal point of view, a number of elite Wallachian women—particularly widows, but also nuns—could play a quite active role in commercial affairs.[20] In July 1776, Maria Berindeasa of Argeş county paid 5 *kile* of maize in damages due to Hera Bucşănescu, a minor official (*postelnicel*), after her cattle entered the latter's fields and damaged his crop.[21] In June 1779, Zmaranda Grecianu testified that she had been cultivating maize on the property of her recently deceased husband, Constandin Grecianu, which, she claimed, she did mainly for domestic use and not for commercial benefit.[22] In March 1783, Susana, the mother superior of the skete at Lăculeţe in Dâmboviţa county, petitioned the Prince of Wallachia because her peasants were evading tithes by growing maize rather than tending to the traditional vines.[23] In July 1802, Băluţă Teişanu wrote proudly to the Transylvanian merchant Hagi Pop that she had 400 *kile* of maize on her estate in Oltenia.[24] In Mehedinţi county in May 1814, Tiţa Armăşoaia, widow of the late Gligore Ciocăzanu, bought no less than 7878 *oka* of maize cobs from the boyar Nicolae Glogoveanu.[25] In Moldavia too, women were involved in maize transactions: a charter of 1776 shows the boyar's wife Vorniceasa Andronachi was collecting tithes of maize from the townsfolk of Bacău.[26] In March 1791, Marta, the abbess of Socola Monastery, together with her associates, Vinidicta, Iuliena and Anastasia, sold the income of the monastery's estates to the merchant Evanghelie

---

17   Hegumen Dionisie, inventory, August 1802, in *Documente privitoare la economia Ţării Romîneşti*, i:71.
18   *Studii şi documente*, viii:130.
19   Summerers, Bulletin, 1 August 1804, in *Rapoarte consulare şi diplomatice engleze*, 24.
20   N. Roman, 'Women in Merchant Families'.
21   Ispravniks of Argeş, judgement, 1776, in *Acte judiciare*, 160.
22   Department 2, judgement, 1779, in *Acte judiciare*, 782.
23   Prince Nicolae Caragea, charter of 7 March 1783, in Urechia, *Istoria românilor*, ii:395.
24   Băluţă Teişanu, Letter to Hagi Pop, 16 July 1802, in Furnică, ed. *Documente*, 225.
25   Receipt, 24 May 1814, in *Situaţia agrară*, 62. 7898 *oka* = c. 120 hectolitres.
26   *Documente bârlădene*, ii:186.

Boiangi for a period of a year, but retained the right to half of the estate's maize tithe.²⁷ While the number of women in a position to conduct trade was extremely limited in both principalities, the few who were played a clearly active part in the increasing commercialization of maize.

September Decrees and Swine Fodder: The state and its competitors

With the 'mainstreaming' of maize in this period, state intervention increased, and took a number of different forms. In Wallachia it was customary for the prince to announce in September that lawsuits would not be heard during a given interval, because the population needed to focus on the harvest. From the 1770s, maize begins to be mentioned in these 'September decrees', alongside the traditional wheat and grapes.²⁸ By the end of the century, this embargo on hearing lawsuits was extended to the maize-sowing period, and to that of hoeing: decrees to this effect were issued in April and June.²⁹

Another practice which attracted the attention of the authorities was the use of maize for animal fodder. According to a contemporary Armenian source, maize was only used to fatten pigs in Wallachia in the absence of acorns.³⁰ However, domestic documents show that the practice was more extensive than that. This should not surprise us, given the combination of the new fashion for maize and the longstanding tradition of livestock-raising in the principalities. Use of maize for this purpose worried the administration who claimed that it would result in food shortages for the general population. In January 1780, for instance, Oltenian boyar Vasile Pleşoianu mentions a princely order forbidding the feeding of maize to swine, and took action against a merchant who was doing this.³¹ But it seems that

---

27 Contract, 10 March 1791, in *Documente Iaşi*, ix:12.
28 Alexandru Ipsilanti, decree of September 1778, in *Acte judiciare*, 673; Nicolae Caragea, September 1783, in Urechia, *Istoria românilor*, i:257, 426; Nicolae Mavrogheni, September 1790, ibid., iii:428–29; Mihai Suţu, September 1791, ibid., iv:135; Alexandru Ipsilanti, September 1797, ibid., vii:95; Constantin Hangerli, September 1798, ibid., vii:497; interim governors of Wallachia, September 1806, ibid., ix:55–56; Ioan Caragea, September 1814, ibid., x, part A:620.
29 Sowing period: Ipsilanti, order of 14 April 1797, in Urechia, *Istoria Românilor*, vii:77; Grand Treasurer, order to the Ispravniks of Wallachia, 26 May 1813, in *Documente privitoare la economia Ţării Romîneşti*, i:156; Caragea, decree of March 29 1816, describes it as a 'custom': Urechia, *Istoria românilor*, x, part A:619–20. Hoeing period: Alexandru Ipsilanti, June 1797, ibid., vii:49–50; Constantin Hangerli, June 1798, ibid., vii:497.
30 Ingigian, 'Mărturii armeneşti', 273. Indeed, in 1794, Gheorghe Marinovici, a pig breeder from Sibiu, looked for maize in Wallachia only when he could not find acorns. *Studii şi documente*, xii:150.
31 B. Pleşoianu, letter to Hagi Constantin Pop, 25 January 1780, in Furnică, *Documente*, 69.

the elite of the province could disregard such interdictions: in 1775, at the estate of the Metropolitan of Wallachia at Fleşti in Argeş county, maize was being sold to merchants for swine fodder.[32] In August 1783, Barbu Ştirbei wrote from Craiova that he changed his swinefeed to maize, with good results: 'they are fat, and maybe some Serbian merchants will come from the Turkish Land'.[33]

The use of maize as fodder was regulated into the nineteenth century.[34] However, leading boyars would continue to request exemptions: boyar Ioniţa Brăiloiu made such a request to the ispravniks (sheriffs) of Romanaţi county in January 1792. In the following year, two monks, Paisie, Abbot of Sadova monastery in Dolj county, and Ioachim, treasurer of the Robaia skete, did likewise.[35] In 1807, on the occasion of a similar ban on feeding maize to swine, the aforementioned Barbu Ştirbei sought an exemption 'in order to sell maize to the peasants in need of food', which he was granted, provided that he did not sell on to merchants or to others who own swine.[36] In 1820, Ştirbei's nephew Dimitrachi Bibescu was continuing to feed his swine on maize, so he doubtless benefitted from an exemption too.[37]

The case of Ştirbei, one of the leading boyars of Oltenia, is interesting to note given that two of his great-nephews—Gheorghe Bibescu and Barbu Dumitru Ştirbei—became princes of Wallachia in the mid-nineteenth century, and founded political dynasties who played a significant role in local politics until 1945. Already at the end of the eighteenth century, Ştirbei was well connected. In January 1791, an exiled French royalist nobleman by the name of Charles-Marie, Count d'Irumberry de Salaberry, passed by his house in Craiova. At a ball in this city, de Salaberry was introduced to a Turk from Nikopol in Bulgaria, perhaps one of Ştirbei's maize-trading contacts. The Turk gave the French count his address, 'which would have been very useful to me if I were to have visited his town', de Salaberry remarked.[38]

In addition to his contacts in the Ottoman world, and with this exiled French count, Ştirbei later became acquainted with many members of the European elite,

---

32 Fleşti estate accounts, 1774–1776, in *Documente privind relaţiile agrare*, i:603.
33 *Studii şi documente*, viii:8.
34 See e.g. C. Canetzos, letter of 13 October 1821, in *Documente 1821*, ii:375; Glogoveanu, letter of 1822, in *Situaţia agrară*, 156. In 1823, the secretary of the Prince of Wallachia described the negative effect on the livestock trade of these interdictions, claiming they dated only from 1792: Arsaki to Fleischhackl, 20 April 1823, in Hurmuzaki, *Documente*, xx:821.
35 Urechia, *Istoria românilor*, iv:352–353.
36 Urechia, *Istoria românilor*, ix:620; xi:913, 914.
37 *Studii şi documente*, viii:56.
38 Salaberry, *Voyage à Constantinople*, 116–17.

in part through a visit he made to the Bohemian spa town of Karlsbad in 1796, where he met German, English, Spanish and Russian notables.[39] Picking up 'European' dining habits, his own tables were adorned not with mămăligă but with pineapples, wine and Transylvanian salami from Sibiu, as well as German-style sugar ornaments.[40] At the time of Salaberry's visit, the ladies of the house still ate while seated cross-legged on the ground, in Ottoman fashion, although Știrbei is known to have owned European tableware and napkins.[41] The Știrbei/Bibescu clan are just two of many Wallachian families, mostly from Oltenia, who transformed themselves into political dynasties in indepenedent Romania, partly based on their skill in cultivating and trading in maize in the late eighteenth century. Many others, including the Brătianu, Golescu, and Văcărescu clans, played a significant role in transforming maize into a commercially viable proposition. Behind the cosmopolitan airs and graces of the Romanian nobility of the late nineteenth and early twentieth centuries, there is an unmistakable trail of maize kernels.

Maize and the Trade in Spirits

The rise in cereal cultivation in the Principalities meant that grain, including maize, began to be used more extensively for the distillation of spirits. There was a tradition of distillation in Moldavia, usually from a base of fruit or wine pressings, but also sometimes involving cereals.[42] From around the middle of the eighteenth century, cereal-based spirits began to be imported into Moldavia from Poland, an activity initiated by Polish nobles and partially conducted by Jewish merchants.[43] In Wallachia in 1765, the Church spoke out against the sale of distilled alcohol by Jewish merchants, claiming that it was contaminated.[44] But elsewhere, ecclesiastical authorities collaborated with them, sometimes employing them on their estates.[45] Beginning in the 1770s, Moldavian boyars began to set up stills on their own estates, in some cases running inns: this was another reason for them to cul-

---

39 Știrbei, letters to his wife and to merchant Hagi Constantin Pop, published by Iorga, 'Un boier oltean'.
40 Iorga, 'Un boier oltean'; see also Lazăr, 'Food Trade', 322, 325.
41 Știrbei's order of tableware from 1781 in *Studii și documente*, viii:6; cf. Salaberry, *Voyage*, 116.
42 Székely, 'Food and Culinary Practices', 186–89; Felea, 'Cofeturi', 142–43.
43 Gonța, 'Începutul'. Jewish merchants: Iorga, *Istoria comerțului*, ii:71–72 (but see also Oișteanu, 'Jewish Tavern-Keepers', on the stereotypical dimensions of this ascription). Export of wine to Russia, on the other hand, was dominated by Cossack merchants (*cazaclii*): see Cereș, 'Exportul', 80–81.
44 Vintilă-Ghițulescu, *Patima și desfătare*, 103–4.
45 Prince Matei Ghica, order of 9 January 1756, in *Izvoare și mărturii*, 2–ii:18.

tivate cereals.⁴⁶ In 1777, Prince Grigore Ghica issued an order allowing only landlords to sell alcoholic drinks, while other inhabitants could not do so without his permission.⁴⁷ In December 1781, Sultan Abdul Hamid I, having been alerted to the issue by Polish representatives in Istanbul anxious to protect their countrymen's trade, issued a *firman* (decree) ordering Prince Constantin Moruzi of Moldavia not to impede the Polish trade in any way, in fact describing it as an established custom.⁴⁸ In the following month Abdul Hamid issued another *firman* outlawing 'the production and use of certain drinks' in Moldavia. He gave two reasons for his order. The first was that such drinks 'cause the dysfunction of the mental faculties and damage the spirit of wisdom'. The second was that 'as everybody knows, it is established that the necessary tribute for the daily nutrition of the inhabitants of my imperial seat should come from Wallachia and Moldavia, and from around the Danube'.⁴⁹ In 1783 the Metropolitan of Moldavia banned the use of wheat, maize and rye for distillation, drawing attention to the traditional ingredients used for this purpose (plums, damsons, grape pressings, old wine), and permitting only grains unfit for consumption to be used to this end. But this did not put a stop to the problem—peasants would allegedly dampen stores of grain with water in order to render them unfit for breadmaking, but good therefore for distilling.⁵⁰

While peasants acted surreptitiously, boyars could afford to be more open in requesting exemptions from regulations, just as they had done in relation to the use of maize for swine fodder. For example, in Wallachia in 1792, high-ranking boyar Great Ban Dumitrachi Ghica sought, and was granted, permission to make spirits from otherwise unusable maize and wheat grain on his estate at Fierbinți in Ilfov county.⁵¹ In general, the economic potential of distillation was a significant spur to the commercialization of agriculture and the rise of larger-scale cultivation of both wheat and maize, especially in Moldavia. The chaff remaining from the distillation process was further used as animal fodder.⁵²

---

46   Gonța, 'Producția de cereale'.
47   Grigore Ghica, order of 30 September 1777, in *Documente privind relațiile agrare*, ii:481; Mihail Suțu, order of 13 May 1793, ibid., 580.
48   Sultan Abdul Hamid I, Firman, 10 December 1781, in Duzinchevici, 'Contribuții', 231–32.
49   Sultan Abdul Hamid I, Firman, January 1782, in *Uricariul*, xx:308–11.
50   Urechia, *Istoria românilor*, i:211–12; order of Metropolitan Gavriil, 15 June 1783, ibid., ii:351–53; petition of the boyars, in *Uricariul*, iv:452–56.
51   Urechia, *Istoria românilor*, iv:350–51, 353, 390; vi:693, 694 (barley and wheat).
52   On subsequent developments see Gonța, 'Începutul'; Platon, *Domeniul feudal*, 26–38.

CHAPTER 3

Maize for the Shepherds: between Pastoralism and Capitalism

Every spring and autumn, the plains of Wallachia were traversed by Transylvanian shepherds, who migrated seasonally to the Danube to graze their flocks on the fertile plains on both sides of the lower reaches of the river, where, if an English traveller of the time is to be believed, the maize 'standing above six feet high, formed a rich and varied pasture'.[53] Although their main business was of course sheep, the shepherds also carried other goods with them on their return journeys to Transylvania. As a document from 1781 shows, local officials in Wallachia stopped a group of such shepherds and sought to limit the quantity of cornmeal they were transporting to 20 or 30 *oka* (around 30 to 45 kilograms). The shepherds objected to this, claiming that they needed a greater amount for their personal use.[54] What is more, as Transylvanians, they were Habsburg subjects. With the backing of the recently appointed Agent in Bucharest, they were able to petition for the maintenance of this right, which they claimed was traditional. 'In past times', they stated in 1784, 'it was permitted to take salt and cornmeal up the mountains; but the county officials have prohibited it, claiming that we are taking it into Transylvania'.[55] The matter was of sufficient importance to the Habsburgs that in 1786, the Austrian internuncio in Istanbul made representations about it to Sultan Abdul Hamid, who issued a *firman* ordering the Prince of Wallachia not to disturb such shepherds transporting cornmeal, as long as it did not affect the tribute (*zaherea*).[56] Abdul Hamid's successor, Sultan Selim III, repeated the order in 1791.[57]

Aside from officially sanctioned trade, both Habsburg agents and local princes were aware of contraband routes across the Carpathians and made use of them in their maize transactions. In 1786, the Austrian internuncio in Istanbul even wrote to his agent in Bucharest discreetly advising him to take advantage of the illicit enterprise of private traders to ensure the supply of maize into Habsburg lands.[58]

---

53 Craven, *Journey Through the Crimea*, 302. Cf., on the same route, Jackson, *Journey*, 257–58: 'very little corn was grown, except maize'; Lusignan, *Reise*, 44, 63: 'maize reached an extraordinary height'.
54 Complaint of 1781 against Mihalache, an administrator in Prahova county: *Acte judiciare*, 979. 20 to 30 *oka* – c. 30–45 kg.
55 Petition of May 1784, in Hurmuzaki, *Documente*, xix, pt. i:178; also later (1819) in Urechia, *Istoria românilor*, xii:417.
56 Sultan Abdul Hamid I, firman of 4 December 1786, in *Documente turcești*, ii:88; French version in Hurmuzaki, *Documente*, vii:518–21. Prince Nicolae Mavrogheni, orders of 1787 and 1788, in Urechia, *Istoria românilor*, iii:195–96, 634–35; Prince Mihai Suțu, order of 1792, in Hurmuzaki, *Documente*, xix, pt. i:621–23.
57 Sultan Selim III, firman of November 1791, *Documente turcești*, iii:19.
58 Von Rathkeal to Petrossi, 26 June 1786, cited in Oțetea, *Pătrunderea comerțului românesc*, 49.

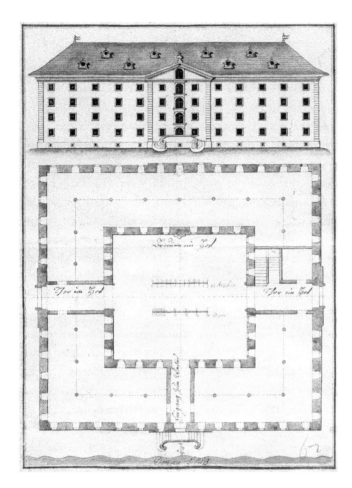

3.2 Plan for a cereal warehouse, Galați, 1793. Austrian State Archives

One of the reasons the Austrians countenanced the clandestine trade was that, by ensuring a regular food supply to southern Transylvania, it encouraged the Romanian population to remain there, and not to settle in Wallachia: in 1794 the Agent in Bucharest claimed to have managed to persuade over two hundred Romanian families to return to Transylvania, having arranged 'through good friends' for them to transport several hundred *kile* of maize across the mountains, thereby assuring their subsistence.[59] Clandestine transportation of maize from the Principalities into Transylvania and Bukovina continued through the early nineteenth century.[60]

---

59 Merkelius to Thugut, 6 October 1794, in Hurmurzaki, *Documente* xix, pt. i:715.
60 Bolkunov to Czartoryski, 14 June 1806, in Hurmuzaki, *Documente*, n.s., iv:547; Oțetea, *Pătrunderea comerțului*, 74–76.

CHAPTER 3

Maize beyond bounds

As already mentioned, maize did not form part of the traditional tribute goods which the Principalities were obliged to make over to the Porte. When, in 1782, a poor harvest resulted in a shortage of wheat, barley and millet in Wallachia, the Prince was unable to redeem the tribute through a payment in maize, and was forced instead to make grain purchases from Bulgaria in order to fulfil his obligations.[61] However, the following year, some of the tribute was delivered in maize, or at least Prince Mihai Suţu invited the Ottoman agent (*mutasarrıf*) at Nikopol to collect wheat, millet, barley and maize from the Slatina district of southern Wallachia.[62] At other times, princes would meet their obligations by purchasing grain from Russia, including a quantity of 3,000 *kile* of barley in 1798.[63] On several occasions, mindful of the need to supply the right kinds of cereals to Istanbul, princes issued orders for the people to sow not just maize but wheat, barley and millet, one even instructing his prefects to supply millet seed 'to those who have only been accustomed to growing maize'.[64]

In 1787, another inter-imperial conflict broke out, which was to last for nearly five years. During this war, both Habsburg and Ottoman armies started to show more interest in acquiring the crop. The Habsburgs, for example, were supplied with maize through river transportations up the Danube.[65] On the Ottoman side, rulers of Moldavia and Wallachia sometimes played a decisive role, both in raising militias and in furnishing supplies. In Wallachia in particular, Prince Nicolae Mavrogheni mobilized troops and resources for the Ottoman cause, sending officials 'from peasant hut to peasant hut', to extort maize from villagers in October 1787.[66] The following year, Wallachian boyars transported it westwards in large quantities to supply the Ottoman army as it advanced into the Banat.[67] In 1789, Ottoman *beşli-aga* Mustafa-Aga seized two thousand *oka* (around three tonnes) of maize from the Catholic monas-

---

61 Raicevich to Kaunitz, 27 August 1782, in Hurmuzaki, *Documente*, xix, pt. i:44. Ianache Văcărescu, who was Grand Treasurer of Wallachia in 1777, also reports having bought grain from Bulgaria to fulfil the tribute: Văcărescu, *Istoria othomanicească*, 139.
62 Prince Mihai Suţu, letter to mutasarrıf of Nikopol, c.1783, in Guboglu, *Catalogul documentelor turceşti*, ii:300.
63 Severin to Kochubey, 3 February 1798, in Hurmuzaki, *Documente*, n.s., iv:126.
64 Alexandru Ipsilanti, decree of 18 August 1779, in *Acte fiscale*, 264; quote from Nicolae Caragea, decree of 13 February 1783, in Urechia, *Istoria românilor*, i:256 n.3.
65 Anon, *Vollständige Geschichte*, i:322, 324.
66 Metzberg to Kaunitz, 26 October 1787, in Hurmuzaki, *Documente*, xix, pt. i:350–51. On Mavrogheni see more broadly Philliou, *Biography of an Empire*, 43–52.
67 Stoica de Haţeg, *Cronica Banatului*, 242, 245, 258; Anon, *Vollständige Geschichte*, i:322.

tery at Târgoviște in Wallachia, apparently with the connivance of two local inhabitants, Dobre a Vladi and Ion Rotopan, who were said to have informed Mustafa-Aga of the existence of the stores.[68] Requisitioning of maize was reported in Teleorman county during the same year;[69] Prince Mavrogheni in fact admitted to his masters at the Porte that plunder was the primary motivation of the ad-hoc troops he had managed to assemble.[70] After Mavrogheni's death in 1790, the boyar Ianache Văcărescu took over responsibility for provisioning the Ottoman troops.[71]

In Moldavia on the other hand, the ruling prince at this time, Prince Alexandru Ipsilanti, was more well disposed to the Austrians. In 1787 Ipsilanti gave express permission for maize to be exported into Habsburg Bukovina,[72] and Transylvanians were observed coming over the mountains to buy it.[73] Evidence that the Turks were beginning to learn about mămăligă comes also in the form of a Romanian-Turkish vocabulary list from Huși in Moldavia, probably dating from this war, where *mămăligă* is included in a list of necessary foodstuffs.[74]

Unlike either the Habsburgs or the Ottomans, the Russians apparently continued to show little interest in the plant during this conflict. A campaign account of the Russian-Ottoman confrontation mentions it only as an obstacle to the march of the Russian soliders across Moldavian fields, at Focșani in the summer of 1789: 'At sun-rise, the several lines advanced across the fields, covered with Turkey corn and other plants, which reached the soldiers' girdles'.[75]

Even after the end of the war of 1787–1792, maize continued to be exempted from the Ottoman tribute.[76] The local rulers, still answerable to Istanbul but now in better touch with their European neighbours, used this circumstance to profit from it. Indeed, one ruler of Moldavia from the 1790s, Mihai Suțu, was even nicknamed 'Prince Maize' (*Păpușoi Vodă*), on account of his serial cereal speculation.[77] In 1796, Suțu's successor in Moldavia, Alexandru Callimachi, arranged for the export of 9,000 *korets* (around 10,000 hectolitres) of maize to Habsburg Bukovina, through the agency

---

68 Ispravniks of Dâmbovița, report to the Wallachian Divan, 11 June 1790, in *Studii și documente*, i-ii:238–39.
69 Ispravniks of Teleorman, April 1790, in Urechia, *Istoria românilor*, iii:385.
70 Șakul, 'Evolution', 325.
71 Marquis de Lucchesini, Report to King of Prussia, 5 May 1791, in *Acte și fragmente* ii:326.
72 Metzberg to Kaunitz, Iași 25 April 1787, in Hurmuzaki, *Documente*, xix, pt. i:294.
73 Merkelius to Kaunitz, 23 December 1788, in Hurmuzaki, *Documente*, xix, pt. i:530 (Transylvanians buying maize in Târgu Ocna, Bacău county).
74 Ms. Rom. 2208, described by Brad Chisacof, 'Turkish Known or Unknown', 266.
75 Anthing, *History of the Campaigns*: ii:87.
76 Timoni to Thugut, 15 September 1795, in *Documente Callimachi*, i:52.
77 Wolf, *Beiträge*, ii:211.

of a Moldavian boyar in the latter province, Teodor Musteață.[78] In January the following year, the Russian consul in Iași reported that Callimachi made 'immense profits' by purchasing maize at a much lower price and furnishing it to the Ottomans.[79] In the autumn of 1800, Austrian agents in Bucharest and Iași asked the local rulers to keep them informed as to the available supplies of maize, and transmitted information to merchants in Transylvania concerning prices and quantities available.[80]

The so-called 'Phanariot' princes of Wallachia and Moldavia, appointed by the Sultan from the Ottomanized Greek-speaking Christian elite of the Fener district of Istanbul, have a persistently negative reputation in Romanian national historiography. According to a characteristic narrative history from the late nineteenth century, 'while the Greek indulged himself in silks and sables, in fats and pilaf dishes, the Romanian villager slept on the bare earth, having only a rock to rest his head, and the sky for a blanket; his only furniture a torn piece of treebark; and mămăligă his only food'.[81] This view was also cultivated by contemporaries. For example, a Wallachian chronicler wrote the following about the speculative activities of Prince Alexandru Moruzi in 1795:

> Moruzi was buying up wheat at 7 lei/*kile* and selling it in Bucharest at 40 lei/*kile*, preventing bakers from buying elsewhere except from the princely stores. And he did deals in maize too. He took money from all the big monasteries in the land, pretending it was a loan, to buy maize and give it to people without food; but he bought maize and sold it to the people at twice and three times the price and never gave the money back to the monasteries, rather he swallowed it himself.[82]

Complaints about Moruzi's handling of the harvest and the tribute clearly reached Istanbul.[83] In 1794 he wrote a lengthy report to Sultan Selim III, responding both

---

78 As reported by Timoni to Thugut, 2 February 1796, in *Documente Callimachi*, i:61; idem, 1 March 1796, ibid., i:63. Musteață, like several merchants, was of Aromanian Balkan origin. On him and other inter-imperial agents, see Costache, *At the End of Empire*, 30–72.
79 Anonymus report, 18 January 1797, in Hurmuzaki, *Documente*, n.s., iv:71.
80 Merkelius, letter to Hermannstadt merchant Hagi Constantin Pop, Bucharest, 8 October 1800, in Furnică, ed., *Din istoria comerțului*, 198; Hagi Pop, letter to the Prince, Sibiu, 15 September 1800, in Furnică, ed., *Documente*, 216–18; for Moldavia, Schilling, report of November 1800, in Hurmuzaki, *Documente*, xix, pt. ii:73.
81 Aricescu, *Istoria revoluțiunii*, 5.
82 Dionisie Eclesiarhul, *Hronograful Țării Românești*, 59. See also *Însemnări de demult*, 124, 173.
83 The rumours in Istanbul were reported to Moruzi by Ismail Gedikli of Brăila: letter of 12 June 1794, in *Documente turcești*, iii:77–78.

to complaints by Ottoman merchants that locals were withholding supplies of grain, and to petitions by boyars claiming they genuinely had none owing to the poor harvest. Moruzi informed the Sultan that he had sent men to seek out hidden supplies, including the use of bayonets to locate underground stores, and that the Metropolitan had sent orders threatening recalcitrant farmers with eternal damnation. Although, as usual, the great part of the Ottoman tribute was supplied in wheat, barley and millet, Moruzi underlined to the Sultan that even maize (*kukuruz*), which he defined as 'strictly necessary for the livelihood of the poor subjects (*reâyâ*)', had been supplied where it was available.[84] Moruzi also issued a decree in the Wallachian court assembly, charging the great boyars Brâncoveanu and Golescu with collecting grain in the different regions of Wallachia, while also asking for 'honest and experienced merchants' to be found to deal with the food supply.[85] In some parts, apparently, maize was unavailable because growers had responded to increased requisitioning by abandoning grain cultivation and replacing fields with plum orchards, which were not subject to tax.[86] As a result, Prince Moruzi was forced to purchase grain from Austrian suppliers, while the peasantry of Wallachia, even those in the west of the province, had to meet their own needs by importing large quantities from Moldavia, leading to price rises in the latter province too.[87]

The above account of Prince Moruzi's speculation in maize may seem to confirm the image of the Phanariot princes as rapacious spoliators, converting the natural produce of the Principalities into personal wealth. However, Moruzi—who spoke fluent French, adopted European habits and possessed 'a superior mind full of patriotic views', according to an English visitor—played a role, however imperfect, in promoting enlightened institutions in the two provinces, including schools and printing presses but also hospitals and other philanthropic institutions.[88] One of these was the hospital at St. Pantelimon Monastery outside Bucharest. In March 1795, the director of this hospital was attempting to apply more modern dietetic methods and sought to obtain lentils, garlic, onions and sour cabbage to feed the patients. When these were not found, Prince Moruzi ordered the hospital to purchase 5 *kile* of rice, maize and wheat such as could be found at market, to distribute

---

84 Alexandru Moruzi, Letter to the Porte, 13 September 9, in *Relațiile româno-otomane*, 623–29.
85 Moruzi, decree of 10 August 1794, in Urechia, *Istoria Românilor*, v:447; Merkelius to Herbert-Rathkeal, 29 August 1794, in Hurmuzaki, *Documente*, xix, pt. i, 710.
86 This happened in 1794 in Hărtiești, Argeș county, according to a report by the hegumen of Clocociov Monastery: Urechia, *Istoria Românilor*, vi:362; this and more in I. Constantinescu, *Arendășia*, 123.
87 Merkelius to Rathkeal, 27 September 1794, in Hurmuzaki, *Documente* xix, pt. i:713.
88 Livadă-Cadeschi, 'Financing Social Care'; quotation from John Sibthorp, diary, 4 May 1794, in Tappe, 'John Sibthorp', 469.

to the sick.⁸⁹ Moruzi also ordered the churches and monasteries throughout Wallachia to maintain reserves of grain including maize, as part of their social function in 'helping the community in times of need'.⁹⁰

In the following year, 1796, large quantities of Wallachian maize were sold across the Danube to the fortress town of Vidin, a practice which continued in the following two decades. For some years, this important Ottoman fortress had been ruled by a Pasha, Osman Pazvanoğlu. Pazvanoğlu was one of several Balkan strongmen in semi-open rebellion against the central authorities in Istanbul and seeking to carve out his own area of authority in the northwestern Balkans. It is significant that Pazvanoğlu's bid for autonomy, comparable in some ways to the autonomies being sought at the same time by Christian Serbs in the neigbouring Pashalik of Belgrade, were at least partly fuelled by regular supplies of Wallachian maize.⁹¹

Meanwhile, several boyars from Moldavia and Wallachia sought permission to trade cereals across Habsburg and Russian frontiers. Those with good connections would even lobby the Porte through European diplomats in Istanbul.⁹² In Moldavia, it was alleged that the Prince would clandestinely sell the right to export maize abroad, leading to the impoverishment of the inhabitants.⁹³ In the era of armies marching on their stomachs, maize never acquired the international fame of the potato or the sugar beet, both of which were introduced to the Romanian lands around this time, partly under Austrian pressure.⁹⁴ But it was nevertheless sought after and exported, and local actors concurred in this process.

Theorizing maize: Didactic literature, 1796–1813

Such assiduous interest in the last years of the eighteenth century led Romanians not just to grow maize, but to start writing about it, with both theoretical and practical aims. From the 1780s, under the influence of Enlightenment economic and pedagogical doctrine, a substantial body of—often translated—didactic literature

---

89 Order of Prince Alexandru Moruzi, 22 March 1795, in Urechia, *Istoria românilor*, vi:719.
90 Prince Alexandru Moruzi to Metropolitan of Wallachia, 10 October 1794, in Urechia, *Istoria românilor*, vi:766–68.
91 Aydın, 'On the Shores of Danube', 151–52. On conditions of production see Gandev, 'L'apparition'.
92 Request of boyars Balş and Depasta, reported by Timoni to Thugut, 19 April 1796, in *Documente Callimachi*, i:68–69; request of Nicolae Rosetti-Roznovanu to the Russian Ambassador in Istanbul (1820), in Costache, *At the End of Empire*, 129.
93 Moldavian Metropolitan and boyars, complaint to Tsar Alexander I against Prince Moruzi (June-July 1806), in Hurmuzaki, *Documente*, n.s., iv:631–32.
94 Bredt, 'Beiträge'; Jakubowski, 'Introduction of the Potato'. On sugar beet see Bodea, 'Préoccupations'.

was published in Romanian, especially in the Habsburg Monarchy.⁹⁵ However, it is perhaps not without significance that the first work of this kind to mention maize directly was published in Bucharest, at the height of the maize boom in that province, and possibly under the patronage of Prince Moruzi who had shown such an interest in the crop. In October 1796, a printer named Dimitrie issued a twenty-seven page brochure entitled *Certain Secrets of Working the Land and of the Art of Planting*, 'translated from a book by a teacher famed in the art of working the land'. In the preface, the translator castigated his Romanian-language readership by comparing their state of knowledge unfavourably with that of foreign peoples, and in the first instance their knowledge of maize:

> Other nations have better and more useful skills when it comes to working the land, and in short they make an effort to learn. ... But here in our country, we ourselves didn't even use to know what kind of plant maize was, nor what was the chickpea, nor aniseed, nor so many other crops and fruit, which our country bears forth today, and which flourish better here than in other parts. So if we were to learn different ways and means of growing our fruit and crops, wouldn't that be better? And bring praise to our nation?⁹⁶

Ten years later, Gheorghe Șincai's *Guidance on Field Economy* (*Povățuiri cătră Economia de Câmp*, 1806), published at the University Press in Buda, drew further attention to maize. Șincai—one of the leading figures in the Transylvanian Romanian Enlightenment—listed it in fifth place on a list of seven recommended cereals for cultivation, after wheat, rye, barley and oats, but before millet and buckwheat. However, he took care to record the different names given to it in Romanian in different regions: *cucuruz* or *mălai* in Transylvania; *porumb* in Wallachia; *păpușoi* in Moldavia; and *tenchi* in Oradea. He also offered advice on sowing, threshing, storage and other aspects of cultivation; and described it as 'the basis of the household among the great majority of Romanians'.⁹⁷

Șincai's guide was just one of a number of works printed at the time in Romanian and other languages, as part of a broader Habsburg project to enlighten and

---

95 Bodea, 'Préoccupations'; Edroiu, 'Economic Literature'.
96 *Oare care secreturi ale lucrării pământului și al meșteșugului sădirii* (Bucharest, 1796), preface, in *Bibliografia românească veche*, ii:388–89.
97 Șincai, *Povățuiri*, 35, 40, 55: 'Cucuruzul care e talpa casei în partea cea mai mare a rumânimei'. Cf. idem, *Elementa linguæ Dacoromanæ*, 33 (mention of *cucuruz* in a vocabulary list).

educate their subject peoples.⁹⁸ In 1807, also in Buda, a particularly interesting example of Romanian-language agricultural literature appeared, namely the *Handbook for a Well-Run Household* compiled by Grigorie Obradovici, director of schools in Caransebeș, a town in the Banat.⁹⁹ Obradovici was in fact of Serbian background, being the nephew of the well-known Serbian enlightener Dositej Obradović; and this handbook was translated from a similar work in Serbian.¹⁰⁰ But he prefaced his translation with an impassioned address to his Romanian readership which sheds valuable light on contemporary cultural attitudes to maize and national identity. According to Obradovici, the Romanians, unlike the Germans and Serbs,

> do not all grow wheat and all kinds of food; it is well known that the Romanians dwelling in the hills and mountains do not sow wheat, barley and oats, but only maize (*cucuruz*), they plant plum trees and raise livestock; and those who do sow wheat always produce poor quality ... even if they grow it, many buy and sell maize, saying maize meal is more nourishing than bread. The Romanian is more partial to sowing maize, and even if it bears fruit, he drives his horses, oxen or pigs into it; and even more plunderishly, the women steal maize out of the storehouse, distracting the gypsy [guard] with spindles, spoons, magic charms, riddles and other lies. So if the new crop doesn't bear forth, hunger is ready at the door, for they never keep any food supplies for two or three years ahead. ... as a result, he is always poor and needy.¹⁰¹

They therefore needed better guidance on how to plough and grow wheat, among other things (the book gives no information on how to cultivate maize). Obradovici went on to advise 'priests, teachers, gentlemen, administrators, merchants, craftsmen or even ploughmen' to read something of his book, and convey the knowledge it contained, so that ploughmen may learn how to work the land better; and in particular to follow the example of Germans and Serbs, who 'although ploughmen too, feed themselves, dress themselves and live better' than the maize-eating Romanians. This is a good example of how a nationalizing intellectual of the

---

98   For the broader context see Varga, 'Buda University Press'.
99   Obradovici, *Carte de mână*.
100 On Obradovici, and the socio-political situation of Serbs and Romanians in the Habsburg Monarchy, see Drace-Francis, 'Cultural Currents'.
101 Obradovici, *Carte de mână*, preface to the reader (unpaginated).

3.3 Romanian ploughman. Woodcut, Grigorie Obradovici, *Carte de mână*, Buda, 1807

Habsburg Monarchy in the early nineteenth century entertained negative stereotypes of the Romanian people. Obradovici's mămăligophobic approach to domestic economy illustrates how maize was treated not so much in terms of its nutritional or economic value, but rather as a signifier in a broader stigmatizing discourse about Romanian identity, perhaps internalized from the older Habsburg cultural and social attitudes mentioned earlier.

Against this general current, one somewhat short-lived Habsburg maize-processing project emerged in the 1810s. This involved the pressing of maize stalks, alongside maple, for the purposes of extracting sugar. Sugar had become a prized commodity in Habsburg lands from the late eighteenth century, but during the Napoleonic Wars their traditional supply routes were cut off.[102] In this circumstance, an enterprising doctor and agronomist, Johann Burger, published a treatise advocating the extraction of sugar from maize stalks, and also from maple.[103] Two short brochures expounding Burger's method were translated into Romanian by the noted Transylvanian patriotic writer Petru Maior, and published in 1812 and 1813.[104] Around the same time, a few enterprising Austrians also put

---

102 Good, *Economic Rise*, 55–56.
103 Burger, *Vollständige Abhandlung*, 389–93.
104 Bodea, 'Préoccupations'; Ursu, 'Cărți'; Tatay, 'Imagini'.

forward proposals to use maize stalks to obtain potash, or to make beer.[105] But none of these schemes seem to have been put into practice on any extensive scale. The making of sugar syrup with maize stalks apparently proved to be ineffective, as it required heavy processing and the use of young stalks, at the expense of the harvest.[106]

Famine, fecundity, freedom and control

Despite the educational, philanthropic and administrative efforts of rulers or writers, famine and drought remained real dangers into the nineteenth century. In 1811, according to a contemporary witness, there was 'a great hunger' in Wallachia, and the price of maize rose so high that the population were reduced to eating tree bark.[107] In April of that year, Constantin Golescu, ispravnik of Argeş county, resolved to go to Transylvania to buy maize to relieve the lack of food in the district for which he was responsible, and for which he obtained permission from the Wallachian Divan. Golescu proposed to buy 5,000 *cetverte* of cornmeal and maize with his own and borrowed money, and to sell it to the inhabitants at cost 'without any inflation of the price for profit'.[108] It seems, however, there was no dearth of maize in Wallachia in this year: at the end of May, the Wallachian Assembly reported to the Russian General Städter that they had expended 24,000 *kile* of maize on the feeding of construction workers who were building a bridge over the river Jiu at Sadova.[109] As in many societies, the state was privileging military imperatives over the needs of the population.

But the process was not, at least at this stage, one of colonial extraction—there could be benefits for the Romanian population either side of the Carpathians. We have seen how elites in Moldavia and Wallachia participated in this trade and indeed profited from it. Like other intermediaries in the Ottoman system of grain procurement, they used their prerogatives, and their relative remoteness from the imperial centre, to advance their own interests.[110] Further down the social scale,

---

105 Bright, *Travels*, 482–83.
106 Bright, *Travels*, 233.
107 *Însemnări de demult*, 130.
108 Wallachian Divan, Petition to General Städter, 21 March 1811, in *Documente privitoare la economia Ţării Romîneşti*, i:102–3. A *cetvert* ('quarter') was a Russian unit of measurement equivalent to 210 litres: see Stoicescu, *Cum măsurau strămoşii*, 247.
109 Wallachian Divan, report to General Städter, 29 May 1811, in *Documente privitoare la economia Ţării Romîneşti*, i:113.
110 Cf. Philliou, *Biography of an Empire*, 35–36; Ağir, 'Evolution', 119.

what sounds like a poor life may have had its advantages in terms of independence, and demographic historians have posited that maize may have played a role in boosting population growth.[111] The relationship between maize and longevity was already a contemporary meme: visiting Becicherec Mare in the Banat of Temesvar (today Zrenjanin, Serbia) in 1765, the Catholic abbot François-Xavier de Feller saw a painting of two Croats said to have lived to 172 and 164 respectively, off a diet of maize.[112] Two decades later, Transylvanian doctor István Mátyus reported Romanians living up to 120, 130 and 140 years of age, despite or because of their simple diet of mămăligă and cheese.[113] In the Bukovina, geologist Balthasar Hacquet met a Romanian man who was said to be 150 years old, which may have been an exaggeration attributable to 'the poor time-reckoning of this nation', and yet it seemed certain that over forty present-day families in the Dorna Candreni district were his descendants.[114] A visitor to Moldavia at the beginning of the nineteenth century was assured by the prince that 'he knew many vigorous men above 110 and 120 years of age' and stated that 'several were pointed out to myself at Fockshani who had passed a century'.[115] Historian William H. McNeill has ventured as far as to say that what potatoes and wheat did for Germany and Russia between 1700 and 1914, maize did for the Christian peoples of Ottoman Europe: by allowing them to live in the high mountain valleys, 'the political and economic balance of the Balkans began to shift'.[116]

McNeill's is a stick-your-neck-out proposition. While there can be said to be a correlation between the spread of maize, demographic growth and the desire for political independence, a direct causation is difficult to quantify with precision. His thesis is further weakened by his erroneous belief that maize was introduced into the principalities by Prince Constantin Mavrocordat only in the 1740s, thus positing a shorter and more dramatic change than the evidence supports. He was right, however, to stress that in remote regions, maize may have enabled populations to survive and even flourish outside state control. A document from Câmpulung in Bukovina (a province acquired by the Habsburgs from the Ottomans in

---

111 A recent study of China from 1770–1910 argues that maize contributed to a population growth of up to 19%, without, however, leading to economic or political development: Chen and Kung, 'Of Maize and Men'.
112 de Feller, *Itinéraire*, i:303; Rom. trans. I. Totoiu in *Călători străini*, ix:575.
113 István Mátyus, *Ó és Új Diætetica, apud* Florea, 'Considerații', 56.
114 Hacquet, *Neueste physikalisch-politische Reisen*, i:12.
115 Neale, *Travels*, 168.
116 McNeill, *Europe's Steppe Frontier*, 205–6, acknowledging that it remains 'largely hypothetical'; Quote from idem, 'American Food Crops in the Old World', discussed in McCann, *Maize and Grace*, 40–42. See also Langer, 'American Foods and Europe's Population Growth'; Komlos, 'New World's Contribution'.

1775), shows a group of village elders petitioning the provincial government about their inability to pay tithes:

> In our parts there are no beans, peas, lentils and so forth, nor fruit trees such as cherries, plums, damsons, pears, apples, which do not grow in the rocky mountain terrain, all we have in fasting periods is dried mămăligă (and many lack even that), while in times of yield, from one day to the next, mămăligă with cheese, and many lack even that... [117]

McNeill was also right more broadly to draw attention to the early rise in population in Wallachia and Moldavia, a real phenomenon which I believe to have been underestimated even by reputed historians of the Balkans.[118] It should be noted that the first reliable censuses conducted in the 1830s established a figure of two million for Wallachia and a million for Moldavia, in other words considerably higher than most estimates given for the preceding period.[119] Available data do not permit the establishment in detail of the kinds of direct causal relation that have been ventured by some non-specialists,[120] and a classic work warns us that 'perhaps the increase in population stemmed from a dozen or a hundred factors having nothing whatever to do with maize'.[121] But it is difficult to accept that there was no correlation between maize and population increase in Moldavia and Wallachia, and moreover between maize and the failure to register this increase—precisely because it enabled people to live unobserved.

Further—and again highly tentative—evidence of a relationship between maize and autonomy may be found in personal names. Several people called Mămăligă are mentioned in early sources: this in itself is an early indicator not just of the potential presence of the dish, but of its cultural meaning. Is there a relationship between what these people were called, and what they did? For example, in May 1661, a certain Mămălata from the village of Onceni, Moldavia, admitted to having harvested the grapes on a vineyard which he had already sold to a neigh-

---

117 Simion Păpușă et al., Petition addressed to the govt. of Bukovina [1793], in *Noth- und Hilferuf*, 292.
118 McGowan, 'Age of the *Ayans*', 652–53; Hitchins, *Romanians*, 58–59; Todorova, *Scaling the Balkans*, 237–61; Mazower, *Balkans*, 25–26.
119 S. Ștefănescu, 'Aspects de la révolution démographique'; L. Roman, 'Statistiques fiscales'. Compare, for Rumelia, McGowan, *Economic Life*, 85–87; for Hungary, Kosáry, *Culture and Society*, 15–17.
120 'In the Danube basin the population doubled in a very short space of time after the introduction of maize', claimed Nadal, 'Failure of the Industrial Revolution', 533.
121 Crosby, *Columbian Exchange*, 168; idem, 'Maize, Land, Demography'.

bour.[122] In June 1700, in the Șchei district of Brașov, a certain Vlad Mămăligă was one of a number of Romanian Orthodox elders who signed a declaration rejecting the terms of the Union with the Church of Rome that had been imposed by the Habsburg authorities.[123] On another list, this time of Romanian rebels involved in a famous patriotic revolt in Transylvania, a captain Ianeș Mămăligă is mentioned.[124] At the beginning of the nineteenth century, Ștefan Mămăligă, a free peasant in Covurlui county in Moldavia, appears as a particularly acquisitive and not always scrupulous buyer of land.[125] Without falling into nominative determinism, we may speculate, in a society where the transition to surnames from nicknames attributed on the basis of personal traits was still underway, a link between their 'mămăligonymy' and the types of freebooting or rebellious activity the documents report them to be engaged in. On the other hand, Chiril Mămăligă was clearly a pious person, as he paid for an icon in Alba county, Transylvania, around 1750.[126]

However, while maize could be a spur to freedom in some circumstances, it could be an accomplice to enserfment in others;[127] or, as Jevan Cherniwchan and Juan Moreno-Cruz have argued for pre-colonial western Africa, an accessory to sedentarization which can be a precursor to and facilitator of conditions leading to enslavement.[128] It is perhaps not by accident that among people named after maize in eighteenth-century Moldavia we find not only an Armenian merchant (Porumb, in 1701), but also a Roma slave (Păpușoi, in 1743).[129] A writer on the maize-growing Romanians of Transylvania wondered if they were really better in their lot than the black slaves of the plantations of America.[130] Moldavian documents from the beginning of the nineteenth century testify to the introduction of harsher labour dues, including hoeing, harvesting and transporting maize at the service of the boyars, tasks unheard of before 1800.[131] According to Moldavian agronomist Ion Ionescu de la Brad, these impositions could backfire: the peasants reacted by slashing the plants

---

122 Mămălata, declaration of May 20 1661, in *Ispisoace și zapise*, 3, pt. i:176–77.
123 Declaration, June 1700, in *Documente Șchei*, i:7.
124 Densușianu, *Revoluțiunea lui Horea*, 223.
125 Velichi, 'Acte covurluiene', 179. For further examples of mămăligonymy see Appendix.
126 Anon, 'Deisis'.
127 As argued e.g. by Levi, 'Diffusion of Maize in Italy'.
128 Warman, *Corn and Capitalism*, 60–65; Carney and Rosomoff, *In the Shadow of Slavery*, 56–59; Cherniwchan and Moreno-Cruz, 'Maize and precolonial Africa'.
129 *Documente bârlădene* iii:196, cf. Siruni, *Armenii*, 29; *Uricariul*, xxi:414, cf. Iorga, 'Ancienneté', 187.
130 Hacquet, *Neueste physikalisch-politische Reisen*, i:112.
131 Mitrany, *Land and the Peasant*, 29, 32, 39; Urechia, *Istoria românilor*, xi:28–30; Ciubotaru, 'Așezămintele agrare moldovenești'.

young, so that there would be less hoeing and carting work.[132] Some people began to offer their labour in order to obtain maize, also something rarely met with before: on 7 May 1800, Vintilă Crețu bought a *kile* of maize from Vasile Cocores in return for 10 lei and agreed to pay interest in the form of three days' corvée labour.[133]

---

132 Ion Ionescu, *Calendarul bunului cultivator* (1845), cited by Bărbulescu, 'O simbioză perfectă', 93.
133 *Documente privind relațiile agrare*, ii:722.

Chapter 4

Maize, *Raki* or Death: The Revolt of 1821 Reconsidered

In the years 1813–1817, as part of a Europe-wide subsistence crisis caused by repeated harvest failures, economic depression and other climatic factors, the population of Transylvania and eastern Hungary was in desperate need.[1] Surviving reports and notes show that the inhabitants were reduced to making mămăligă not from cornmeal but from ground-down cobs; they also had recourse to nettles, beech bark, acorns and other forest products.[2] There were attempts to bring emergency supplies from central Europe, and from the Banat.[3] As well as seeking relief from within their own territories, the Habsburg authorities appealed to their contacts in Moldavia and Wallachia for assistance. But conditions were not good here either, as the plague had broken out in 1813. Prince Ioan Caragea of Wallachia distributed maize at the urging of the Austrian consul, but it was bitter and hard to digest.[4] People fleeing the city hid among the maize fields. As this might lead to contamination, the Prince ordered such people (or their corpses, if they had died) to be brought to the quarantine stations.[5] Some villages, especially in the Carpathian mountains, refused to pay taxes, being unable to work and suffering much loss of life. They were supplied with maize by the boyars, following an 'enlightened edict' from Prince

---

1 Post, *Last Great Subsistence Crisis*; I. Constantinescu, 'Climă, agricultură și societate'; Stoianovich, *Balkan Worlds*, 35; Rus, 'Weather Anomalies'.
2 Ciorba, 'Alimentația de criză'; Hodgyai, 'Ínséges évek Biharban'.
3 Hodgyai, 'Ínséges évek Biharban'; *Însemnări de demult*, 131.
4 Fleischhackl to Metternich, 24 July 1813, in Hurmuzaki, *Documente*, xx:102.
5 Caragea, decree of 6 October 1813, in Urechia, *Istoria românilor*, x, pt. A:765; decree of 13 October 1813, in Urechia, 'Edilitatea sub Caragea', 546.

Caragea.⁶ The villagers of Blahnița de Sus in Gorj county were in dire straits, and could not pay their dues, as the maize had been caught by an early frost.⁷

Initially, in December 1813, Prince Caragea permitted the export of a mere 200 *kile* of maize across the Carpathians into the Hațeg region of southern Transylvania. However, the Habsburgs put pressure on the Porte to allow a larger quantity of 6,000 *kile* to be exported.⁸ The situation remained dire, and although Prince Caragea denied having personally obstructed the export of produce, it was not until the following summer that, after further lobbying by Habsburg representatives in Istanbul, a larger consignment of 50,000 *kile* could be exported from Wallachia.⁹

In Moldavia too, Raab, the Habsburg agent, was on the lookout for maize to help relieve the Transylvanian famine. In September 1814 he reported to Chancellor Metternich that the export ban on cereals still applied in all Ottoman territories, and could only be requested in special circumstances from the Porte; but that the export of maize was the prerogative of the Moldavian prince.¹⁰ Fearing that the Prince or other traders might manipulate the dire situation to raise prices, even though there was no shortage in Moldavia itself, Raab urged Metternich to intervene with the Porte and request an order from the Sultan permitting free trade in maize.¹¹ Sultan Mahmud II granted this permission as an exceptional circumstance on several occasions.¹² In Brașov, the Orthodox priest and teacher Radu Tempea—better known to posterity as the author of a Romanian grammar—procured a thousand bushels of maize from Moldavia and arranged for it to be distributed to the destitute inhabitants of the Burzenland (Țara Bârsei) region to the north of the city. He received a certificate of praise for his humanitarian efforts from Emperor Francis II in February 1815.¹³

However, in Moldavia itself, maize remained hard to obtain, or only available at extortionate prices, as several diary notes attest.¹⁴ A report of the French agent in Iași confirms this: the export of maize to Transylvania led to local shortages and a

---

6 Ștefan Clucer, Marin Butculescu, report to Prince Caragea, 7 May 1815, in *Acte fiscale*, 433–34.
7 Constandin Romniceanu, Răducan Fărcășan, letter of 4 November 1814, in *Acte fiscale*, 415–16.
8 Fleischhackl to Metternich, 5 December 1813, in Hurmuzaki, *Documente*, xx:126.
9 Prince Caragea to a Viennese counsellor, 25 June 1814, in Hurmuzaki, *Documente*, xx:197–98. 50,000 *kile*: Von Stürmer to Raab, 13 November 1814, in *Documente Callimachi* i:218.
10 Fleischhackl to Metternich, 13 July 1814, in Hurmuzaki, *Documente*, xx:169.
11 Raab to Metternich, 23 September 1814, in Hurmuzaki, *Documente*, xx:176–77; other reports in *Documente Callimachi*, i:221–25; ii:137, 212–13.
12 Grand Vizir Mehmed Emin Rauf Pasha, Request (*telhis*) addressed to Sultan Mahmud II, 1817, mentioning earlier approved requests by the Sultan, in *Relațiile româno-otomane*, 729–31.
13 Rescript of the Transylvanian Government, Feb 1815, in Lupaș, 'Date', 196–99.
14 Iordachi Sion, notes, in *Însemnări de demult*, 305; Petrache Gorovei, note of September 1819, ibid., 30.

doubling of prices, causing considerable hardship within the principality.[15] Some boyars complained about the speculative practices of the Prince, who requisitioned maize under pretext of needing it for the tribute, but then sold it over the Carpathians.[16] Others would also sell maize at high prices to villagers who had none, as did Grand Spathar Dracache Roset to the villagers of Șcheia, Roman county, in June 1817.[17] The following year, in the same village, a certain Giurgi Leorind was caught trying to steal maize.[18]

The conditions in the principalities in the 1810s were, therefore, typical in terms of the relationship between maize and social unrest. In a classic older study, for example, it was shown that rising cultivation and high prices of maize played a role in establishing the conditions for the Mexican Revolution of 1810–1821.[19] In the Balkans, on the frontiers between empires, between plagues and famines, and between legality and subterfuge, maize-trading could give wealth and experience to a socially aspiring person. After the famine of 1813–1817, the years preceding the revolt of 1821 in Wallachia saw exceptionally good harvests—a circumstance which, counterintuitively, can establish conditions for social change.[20]

One notable beneficiary of the local maize boom was the free peasant Tudor Vladimirescu, who would go on to become the leader of the 'national' party in the revolt of 1821. Born in around 1780 in Mehedinți county in Wallachia's wild west, Tudor was known to have risen in the social hierarchy from a relatively modest position. His ascendancy is usually ascribed to his role as a member of the *pandur* troops who acted in support of the Russians in the war of 1806–1812.[21] But Tudor's rise can also be attributed to his success in trading in maize from his native Oltenia, both south of the Danube and across the Carpathians. In his position as estate manager of the wealthy Oltenian boyar Nicolae Glogoveanu, he acquired some

---

15   Fornetty to Richelieu, 19 April 1816, in Hurmuzaki, *Documente*, xvi:1002; price lists from October 1816 to June 1817 compiled by Austrian Consul Raab, in *Documente Callimachi*, i:258. Cf. *Uricariul*, xiv:244.
16   Boyars Ghica and Balș, petition against Prince Callimachi, December 1816, cited in Taki, *Russia on the Danube*, 89.
17   Villagers of Șcheia, contract with Dracache Roset, 7 June 1817, in *Documente Callimachi*, i:542.
18   Iojă Ghercuț, witness statement, 26 March 1818, in *Documente Callimachi*, i:549.
19   Florescano, *Precios del maíz*; Van Young, *The Other Rebellion*, 71–5.
20   I. Constantinescu, 'Climă', 260. Compare White, *Climate of Rebellion*.
21   So-called *pandur* troops were deployed in Wallachia as light infantry or civil guards. Even before the 1806 war, they had taken an interest in maize: in December 1805 Prince Constantin Ipsilanti reprimanded the pandurs of Bucharest for stealing maize from peasant villages outside the city. Ipsilanti, order of 14 December 1805, in Urechia, *Istoria românilor*, xi:269. I thank Constanța Vintilă for drawing my attention to this source. See also Kutuzov, letter of May 1811, trans. M. Stroia in *Călători străini în sec. XIX*, i:419.

capital of his own, and in 1810 purchased a mill-race in the Cerneți river valley in Mehedinți county.²² In August the following year, he purchased some estates at Obârșia in the same county.²³ In a letter to Glogoveanu written in December 1816, Tudor claimed to have ten thousand *oka* (very approximately, fifteen tonnes) of maize ready to transport, 'for which I hope to get permission from Bucharest; and if I get permission for a hundred thousand, I would take on yours too, either buying it at an agreed price, or as a partner in profit'. This letter was sent from Orșova, north of the Danube on the Habsburg side of the frontier. Tudor was clearly in touch with traders on the Ottoman side, since he tells Glogoveanu that he has news from Istanbul.²⁴

The Time of the Consuls

In an influential book published on the eve of the 1821 revolt, William Wilkinson, the former British consul in Bucharest, adjudged the production of maize in both principalities to be of equal import to that of wheat, the latter being estimated at ten million *kile* or bushels.²⁵ Like many foreign observers, however, Wilkinson only considered it to have been for 'the nourishment of the peasantry', and seems to have been unaware of the by now extensive cross-border transactions in the cereal. Much of the maize-trading activity took place on the edges of the principalities, whether in Wallachian Oltenia or on the Habsburg-Moldavian border, and it seems Wilkinson did not get out much. He was reckoned, for example, a poor observer by his Austrian counterparts, who noticed that his circle of informants in Moldavia was extremely limited;²⁶ and his estimates of the tribute in grain made over to the Porte have been questioned by modern historians.²⁷ By 1816, the British government saw fit to withdraw its representation in Wallachia. In constrast, in the autumn of the same year, the French government appointed a new vice-consul in Bucharest, Formont. Profiting from the fine October weather, Formont made a reconnaisance tour of the mountains and forests of Oltenia. He related to his minister that Ottoman acquisition of maize in this province was

---

22 Hagi Gheorghe of Cerneți, letter of sale, 20 December 1810, in Vîrtosu, *Mărturii noi*, 22–23.
23 Constantin Dănciulescu, letter of sale, 24 August 1811, in Vîrtosu, *Mărturii noi*, 35.
24 Tudor Vladimirescu, letter to N. Glogoveanu, 12 December 1816, in Iorga, 'Scrisori inedite', 139; repr. in *Documente 1821*, i:106. Generally on Tudor's commercial activities: Oțetea, *Tudor Vladimirescu*, 80–83.
25 Wilkinson, *Account of the Principalities*, 75, 163–64.
26 'Der Wirkungskreise dieses General-Consuls dürfte hier in der Moldau nur sehr beschränkt seyn': Raab to Metternich, 25 November 1814, in *Documente Callimachi*, i:214.
27 Gonța, 'Producția de cereale', 240–41.

extensive, as they were anticipating a possible Russian declaration of war: 'the locals told me that they had not seen such a large number of Turks coming into Wallachia for over fifteen years.'[28]

Vice-consul Formont was onto something. While, as we have seen, the famine of 1813–1817 had opened up the export of maize to Transylvania under certain conditions, trade across the Danube into Ottoman lands continued, according to one local observer;[29] as did some Ottoman requisitioning. This trade was clearly not controlled from Istanbul, but conducted by frontiersmen just across the Danube, or even from an island in the middle of it. In 1814, for example, the best maize from the Glogova estates was taken by a certain Mehmet Tabak, in collaboration with other Turks from the island of Ada Kale, so only poor quality maize remained.[30] The islanders of Ada Kale came again in 1815 and took more maize.[31] In 1820 they did the same, on which occasion they also took *raki*.[32] According to traditional Ottoman doctrine, goods were not simply taken but paid for at a price fixed in Istanbul, a system known as *narh*.[33] Sources do not always permit us to follow what was paid for, what was taken in raids, or what was sold outside the official regime, although all these types of transaction doubtless occurred. Some of these 'Turks' had links with disgruntled *pandur*s whose regiments had been disbanded after the conclusion of the war of 1806–1812, and had chosen to cross the river.[34]

In April 1819, Sultan Mahmud II took an unprecedented decision. In a *firman* issued to the Prince of Wallachia, he gave permission for the usual tribute of millet, which had failed to be delivered to Giurgiu, to be substituted with maize (*kukuruz*).[35] In Moldavia in the same year, the tribute was also partly delivered in maize, something that the newly appointed Prince Mihai Suțu expressly agreed in Istanbul before leaving to take up office in the province. He spelled out the terms of its col-

---

28 Formont to Richelieu, 7 November 1816, in Hurmuzaki, *Documente*, xvi:1007–1008.
29 Philippides, *Geografikon tis Roumounias*, trans. N. Bănescu, 172. On the general conditions see Marinescu, 'Trade of Wallachia'.
30 Accounts of Glogova estate, 1814, in *Situația agrară*, 48–49; accounts of Toma Cherali, 2 October 1814, ibid., 66. See also Vîrtosu, *Mărturii noi*, 55–57; Perianu, 'Raiaua Brăilei', 324; and the testimony of Ion Trocan, 17 October 1812, in Iancovici, 'Unele documente', 127.
31 Accounts of Glogova estate, 1815, in *Situația agrară*, 70; Tudor Vladimirescu, letter of 28 January 1815, in Iorga, 'Scrisori inedite', 137–38.
32 Accounts of Glogova estate, n.d., in *Situația agrară*, 81.
33 For the classic model, White, *Climate of Rebellion*, 21–6; Murgescu, *Țările Române*, 179–182, summarizes the complex variations between 'free market' and 'fixed price' provisioning around 1800.
34 Oțetea, *Tudor Vladimirescu*, 99–103.
35 Firman of 12 April 1819, summary in Guboglu, *Catalogul documentelor turcești*, i:265. Sultan Mahmud may have been aware of a more general turn to maize cultivation elsewhere in the Empire at this time. For Anatolia, see İnalcık, 'Emergence of Big Farms'; for Egypt, Rivlin, *Agricultural Policy*, 113–14.

lection in some detail, advising the grain merchants of Istanbul to present themselves at Galați with money and numerous boats, where they would be able to obtain it at a fixed price. He asked, however, that Moldavian subjects (*raya*) be spared from selling it at below the fixed price, or they would in all likelihood no longer cultivate it.[36]

Not all Wallachian maize crossed the Danube or the Carpathians. It was alleged to have been used to bribe officials, as recorded in a criminal investigation conducted in Gorj county at this time.[37] Also in 1819, the inhabitants of the village of Raeț in Mehedinți county had enough maize to enable them to stockpile and to resist paying the customary taxes demanded of them by the authorities.[38] At the same time, it could be put to more civic purposes: in the following year, in the town of Slatina, Olt county, boyars raised funds from the sale of maize to endow a public school.[39] More modestly, in 1820 boyar Dimitrie Aman—the father of Theodor Aman, who would go on to become one of the most illustrious painters of Old Kingdom Romania—had a fence built at his property in Craiova out of maize stalks.[40] Official policy, however, ordered the population to concentrate on growing wheat and barley, as can be seen from a princely order issued to this effect in Wallachia in August 1820.[41]

In October 1820, the outgoing Prussian Minister to the Ottoman Porte, Count Friedrich Leopold von Schladen—later to be accredited to the Netherlands—left Istanbul at the end of his mission, together with his wife and a number of other Prussian barons, and passed through Wallachia on his way home. Having stepped down from his position, he was officially travelling incognito. But on his arrival in Bucharest in November he paid a visit to the reigning Prince, to the Russian consul, and to other local dignitaries. He also attended a ball, which was said to be brilliant by Wallachian standards, where the Prince organized 'all the national dances, Wallachian, Greek, Albanian &c.' for the benefit of his distinguished visitor, while

---

36   Prince Mihai Suțu, *takrir* (clarificatory note), Istanbul, c. June 1819, summary in Guboglu, *Catalogul documentelor turcești*, ii:436. Pisani, the Russian consul in Iași, gives figures for extensive furnishing of maize to Istanbul dating back to 1813: report, 2 Sep 1820, in Oțetea, *Pătrunderea comerțului*, 73. Gonța, 'Producția de cereale', 240 gives a figure of 220,701 *kile* for 1819. However, Moldavian boyar Conachi reported that only once since 1812 had a maize surplus been transported to Galați and that the port could not cope with the quantities delivered. Conachi, report to Divan of Moldavia, November 1830, in Istrati, 'Cu privire la exportul de grîne', 200.
37   *Studii și documente*, vi, pt. ii, 516.
38   Letter of Brâncoveanu, October 1819, in *Studii și documente*, v:206–7.
39   Poboran, *Istoria orașului Slatina*, 386.
40   Contract, December 1820, in *Corespondența lui Dimitrie Aman*, 56.
41   Prince Alexandru Suțu, order of August 1820, in Bulat, 'O poruncă domnească din 1820', 211.

von Schladen performed European dances with the wife of the Russian consul, attracting the admiring gaze of the local boyar ladies in attendance. Leaving the city, he was escorted on the rest of his journey through the province by his king's representative, Baron Ludwig Kreuchely von Schwerdtberg. Nearing the Habsburg border, the Prussian suite stopped for the night of 25 November 1820 at a staging post in the small village of Sălătrucu, in the foothills of the southern Carpathians. Here Consul Kreuchely expressly instructed their Wallachian hosts to prepare mămăligă for his minister, which he and other members of his entourage apparently enjoyed very much.[42] It is tempting to think that Kreuchely, who was an astute observer of Wallachian society, was not just eager to attend to his master's material comfort, but sought, through this small but significant gesture, to draw Count von Schladen's attention to the centrality of maize in the economy and politics of the principality. If so, he would certainly have had a point, as the events of the following year would show.

1821: The Cauldron Boils Over

Revolt broke out in both principalities in early 1821, following the death of the Prince of Wallachia, Alexandru Suțu. The son of a former prince, Alexandru Ipsilanti, marched into Moldavia from Russia in early March, while at the same time the Romanian leader Tudor Vladimirescu assembled a makeshift army of rebels in Wallachia. Although they were in fact both part of an attempted coordinated operation on the part of a Greek secret society to raise rebellion across southeastern Europe, the ambitions of Ipsilanti and Vladimirescu, and of their followers, soon came into conflict with each other. When they met in Bucharest in March, they determined to pursue separate courses of action. Ottoman troops crossed the Danube in May and quickly suppressed the rebellion. In June Tudor was assassinated by one of Ipsilanti's men, and his corpse thrown into a drain. But Ipsilanti's stand did not last long: his batallion was routed by the Ottomans a few days later, and he fled to Austria where although he was released from prison, he died in poverty in 1828.

The story of the revolt in the Principalities has often been dominated by a reading of it as a conflict between these two leaders: Ipsilanti, an elite Phanariot Greek, and the Romanian Vladimirescu, defender of the common people. Such narratives

---

42 Kreuchely von Schwerdtberg to von Miltitz, 14 December 1820, in Hurmuzaki, *Documente*, x:87–90; Rom. trans. G. Filitti in *Călători străini în sec. XIX*, i:916–20.

CHAPTER 4

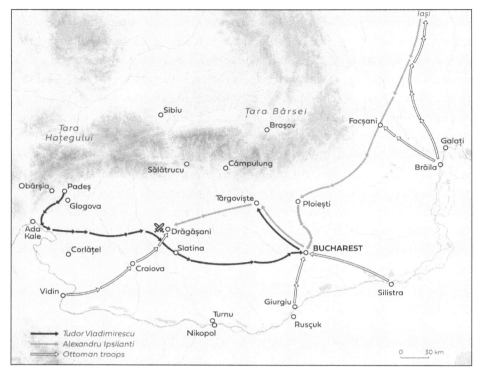

Map 5 Wallachia during the 1821 Revolt

extend back to the time of the revolt itself. However, historians have demonstrated conclusively that Vladimirescu was recruited into the Greek conspiracy, and that the interests of the parties were considerably more intertwined.[43] It has also long been known that many actors in the revolt were not just of Greek or Romanian origin, but of Serbian, Bulgarian, Albanian and even other backgrounds. Their national identity, although mentioned frequently in contemporary documents, was not necessarily a leading factor in motivating their actions or ideological positions. More recent research by Christine Philliou has made a strong case for showing that the convergence of interest between people of such different ethnic and social origins was at least partly a product of Ottoman structures of governance.[44] What has not been shown in detail is another thing that these different groups had in common: they were all extremely interested in maize.

---

[43] The older account by Oțetea, *Tudor Vladimirescu*, is still fundamental. In English, see Hitchins, *Romanians*, 141–52; Ardeleanu, 'Military Aspects'; and Pippidi, 'Balkan Hinterlands'.
[44] Philliou, *Biography of an Empire*. See also Yaycioglu, *Partners of the Empire*, 65–115.

During the revolt, stockpiling of the crop by all parties was widespread. Ipsilanti established his centre of operations in the vicinity of Târgoviște, Wallachia in May 1821, and took over several local churches and monasteries in order to store grain supplies, consisting principally of maize (the mill at Câmpulung, customarily used to process tobacco, was converted to make gunpowder).[45] Theft was also frequent during the revolt. According to one conservative satirical chronicler writing shortly afterwards, the entire purpose of Ipsilanti's venture was not national liberation but a pretext for plunder, including particularly obtaining maize under false pretences and selling it in Transylvania:

> He wasted and stole
> That tyrant Ipsilanti
> Together with the poor
> Thieves and scoundrels
> For they were so spiteful
> And hostile to the country
> That if they could
> They would have even taken the land
> They took oxen and cattle
> Broke the wine casks
> They didn't leave horses or weapons
> They swept up wheat and maize,
> Saying it was for the tribute
> They traded in them
> Took them all to Brașov
> Sold them for hard cash.
> Now stop and decide
> Why they rose up.[46]

Whether or not Naum's mămăligocentric explanation of the events was justified—in Brașov in July 1821, maize was 'very expensive', wrote the Serbian mer-

---

45 Fleischhackl to Metternich, Iași, May 12 1821, in Hurmuzaki, *Documente*, xx:623.
46 'Au risipit, au luat/ Acel tiran Ipsilant/ Dimpreuna cu calicii/ Tâlharii și măscăricii/ Că atât era pizmași/ Ș-asupra țării vrăjmași/ În cat de ar fi putut/ Să nu lase nici pământ/ Boi și vaci, ei au luat/ Buțile cu vin au spart/ Cai și arme n'au lăsat/ Grâu, porumb, l'au măturat./ Cu cuvânt de zahirele,/ Făcea negoț cu ele/ Toate'n Brașov le-au trecut/ Pe bani gată le-au vândut/ Stați acum și judecați/ Pentru ce au fost sculați'. Naum Râmniceanu, 'Pentru eteriștii crai greci', in *Cronicarii greci*, lxii.

chant Velija Pavlović[47]—those responsible were brought to justice and punished in the aftermath.[48] A contemporary chronicler, Ioan Dârzeanu, described the struggle for resources between the two main parties. According to Dârzeanu, Vladimirescu's men

> seized cattle by the herd, and especially sheep, cows and maize from the boyars, monasteries and merchants; wherever they found it they took the whole lot, pillaging like anything. They targeted especially the maize stores, breaking them open and letting them flow, causing even more destruction.'[49]

Some observers alleged that Tudor was in fact acting in league with the Ottomans against Ipsilanti's troops, supplying them with cereals and cattle.[50] Whatever the truth, when the Ottoman army occupied Wallachia after Tudor's death in June 1821, they looked for barley to feed their horses. Finding none, they requisitioned maize, just as the Habsburgs had done a century before.[51] A storehouse was built for this purpose in Craiova, with a capacity of 700,000 *oka* according to some sources.[52] Agents (*mumbașiri*) were appointed to collect maize in Saac, Prahova, Dâmbovița, Ilfov, Vlașca and Muscel counties.[53] If a later writer is to be believed, the Ottomans issued maize bread as regular rations to their Albanian auxiliary troops at this time.[54] As for feeding the people, an Ottoman official, Hagi Emin Aga, was appointed to oversee the distribution of maize.[55] In October 1821, the

---

47 Velija Pavlović, letter of 4 July 1821, *Studii și documente*, viii:146. Also in Orșova: Dumitrașco Popovici, letter of 11 May 1821, ibid., viii:142.
48 *Documente 1821*, ii:370; iii: 142, 259, 260, 265, 282, 350. See also Neacșu, 'Participarea locuitorilor', 97 n.2.
49 Ioan Dârzeanu, 'Revoluțiunea dela 1821' [1822], in *Documente 1821*, v:71. Ipsilanti's party did the same: ibid., 83.
50 Russian reports of July 1821, in *Documente 1821*, ii:257, 270. Their veracity is questioned by the editors in their introduction to *Documente 1821*, i:14. There are reasons why these agents might seek to pin blame on the recently dead Tudor; but the fact that they were aware of his role as a cereal supplier remains telling.
51 Kreuchely to von Miltitz, 6 January 1822, in Hurmuzaki, *Documente*, x:135.
52 Drexler, Austrian agent in Craiova, letter of 5 April 1822, in *Studii și documente*, viii:152, and Kreuchely, Prussian consul in Bucharest, letter of 13 April 1822, Hurmuzaki, *Documente*, x:143–44, both state 700,000 *oka*. The Austrian agent in Hermannstadt (Sibiu), reported a more realistic 70,000 *oka*: Lippa to Metternich, 13 April 1822, in Hurmuzaki, *Documente*, xx:714. The French agent in Bucharest reported 1500 *kile*: Bounin to Montmorency, 24 April 1822, in Hurmuzaki, *Documente*, xvi:1039.
53 Dârzeanu, 'Revoluțiunea', in *Documente 1821*, v:115.
54 Örenç, 'Albanian Soldiers', 508.
55 Dârzeanu, 'Revoluțiunea', in *Documente 1821*, v:120; Lippa to Metternich, 5 Dec 1821, in Hurmuzaki, *Documente*, xx:696.

Wallachian boyars complained about the Ottoman requisitioning, claiming 'it is being taken from the mouths of children, with sighs and tears', and that the inhabitants would soon be left without winter food.[56] In November, at Corlățel in Mehedinți county, everybody was safe, and there was some *raki* left after the depradations of the *pandurs*, but the maize news was contradictory: on the one hand, 'the Turks had taken all the maize', but on the other 'what was left was distributed to the people', to the tune of 3980 *oka*.[57] Individual merchants who had maize sought to take it to districts where there was none, to sell it to villagers for profit.[58] In Moldavia, some merchants continued to be permitted to export maize to Transylvania: merchant Costache Lipan received such an authorization in December 1821.[59]

In April 1822, the temporary governors of Wallachia issued an order to the local administrators to ensure that people sowed maize and millet, 'the customary food of the inhabitants', to ensure a sufficiency in the province.[60] In May, plenty of maize was sown on the estates of Nicolae Glogoveanu in Mehedinți county, and was 'looking fine'.[61] By June 1822, supplies were running short, and the interim governor of Bucharest, with the authorization of the Pasha, made half of the reserves available to the people.[62] In December, the authorities in Istanbul were aware that a number of troublemakers were travelling to the principalities, sometimes under the guise of grain merchants: they issued an order strictly controlling permission to travel to the area.[63] In January 1823 the inhabitants of Teleorman county had run out of maize: again the Prince ordered the boyars to open their reserves and sell it at a fair price, even giving credit to those temporarily unable to pay.[64] The people of Teleorman and other counties along the Danube were permitted to buy maize over

---

56 Wallachian boyars, draft petition, 6 October 1821, in *Documente 1821*, ii:368; boyars' memorandum of November 1821, ibid., ii:400.
57 Mihai Lăcusteanu, letter of 30 November 1821, in *Corespondența lui Dimitrie Aman*, 66; idem, letter of 1 February 1822, ibid., 68–70. 3980 *oka* = c. 5 tonnes.
58 C. Canetzos, letter to Hagi Ianuș, Craiova, 13 October 1821, in *Documente 1821*, ii:375.
59 I. Constantinescu, *Arendășia*, 169.
60 Order of *caimacams* Mihalache Manu and Constantin Negre, 10 April 1822, in Urechia, *Istoria Românilor*, xiii:282.
61 Logofăt Pătru, letter to N. Glogoveanu, 8 May 1822, in *Documente 1821*, iii:94.
62 Kreuchely to von Miltitz, 8 June 1822, in Hurmuzaki, *Documente*, x:163–164; Tancoigne to Montmorency, 25 June 1822, in Hurmuzaki, *Documente*, xvi:1052.
63 Order to Governor of Silistra and Mütesellim of Ruse, December 14, 1822, in 'Those Infidel Greeks', i:484.
64 Kreuchely to von Miltitz, 28 January 1823, in Hurmuzaki, *Documente*, x:207–8; Dârzeanu, 'Revoluțiunea', in *Documente 1821*, v:135.

the river without paying the customary import tax.⁶⁵ In Argeș county, meanwhile, people purchased cornmeal over the mountains from Transylvania.⁶⁶

The concern of the Wallachian elites to establish control over any transactions in maize comes across vividly in the numerous petitions which they despatched to the Ottoman Porte. In one such document, written in Greek, they 'heatedly requested' that they be permitted to trade any surplus maize freely, claiming that their neighbours in Moldavia already had this right.⁶⁷ However, it is not certain whether these maize requests ever reached the ears of Sultan Mahmud. Researches in the Istanbul archives have shown that the final version of this petition, translated into Turkish from Greek, omits the clauses which refer to the local boyars' maize demands.⁶⁸

In Moldavia too, the occupying Ottoman forces requisitioned substantial quantities of maize, even ordering it to be collected in advance of their arrival.⁶⁹ A report of December 1821 mentions a quantity of 75,000 *kile*.⁷⁰ In July 1822, the interim governors of the principality ordered that any reserves of maize that could be found in the provinces be sent to Iași.⁷¹ Just as in Wallachia, agents were sent out into the countryside to collect it.⁷² According to a local pamphleteer, they looted in large quantities, leaving none for the ordinary people.⁷³ The Moldavian boyars, like their Wallachian counterparts, resisted these measures by firing off petitions to Istanbul. In one such document, they complained that the Princes had put a stop to the local trade in maize, which they presented as a traditional right of the inhabitants, in order to establish a personal monopoly.⁷⁴ In another petition—there were many—

---

65 Prince Ghica to Constandin Câmpineanu, *caimacam* of Craiova, 25 January 1823, in *Documente privitoare la economia Țării Romînești*, i:270–81.
66 Corfus, *Agricultura Țării Romînești*, 256.
67 *Arzmahzar* of Wallachian boyars to the Porte, April 1822, in *Surete și izvoade*, x:290: 'παρακαλούν θερμώς'.
68 *Arzmahzar* of Wallachian boyars to the Porte, 1822, in Mehmet, 'Acțiuni diplomatice la Poarta', 72–76; see Mehmet's comments, 70–71.
69 Capitan Burtsov, report of July 1821, in *Documente 1821*, ii:269; Moldavian treasury, order of October 1821, ibid., ii:37.
70 Bucșănescu, letter to Metropolitan Veniamin, 13 December 1821, in Erbiceanu, *Istoria Mitropoliei Moldaviei*, 185–86. See also anonymous report, Feb 1822, in *Acte și fragmente*, ii:624; Kephala to Kreuchely, Focșani, 17 May 1822, in Hurmuzaki, *Documente*, x:156.
71 Ungureanu, 'Documente', 51.
72 Zahariuc, 'Începutul', 518, 534–36, 543.
73 'Nu mai era rânduială, era pradă și potop / Cu zapcii prin ortale, unde găsea lua tot; / Grâul, orzul, păpușoi ca râurile curgea, / Și peste cinci-șase zile, nu știa ce se făcea': Alexandru Beldiman, 'Tragodia Moldovei', in *Cronicele României*, iii:394.
74 *Arzmahzar* of Moldavian boyars to the Porte, 1822, in Hurmuzaki, *Documente*, Supliment I, pt. v:3; a similar document in *Uricariul*, vi:128.

the former Prince Mihai Suțu, grandson of Mihai Suțu, the notorious Prince Maize (*Păpușoi Vodă*) of an earlier generation, was even accused of having appropriated maize in order to make *raki* for illegal sale abroad.[75]

In any case, Ottoman traders continued to come to the principalities. The Sultan issued an order in 1826 which formally granted permission to the grain merchants of Istanbul to collect maize (*kukuruz*) and millet from Moldavia.[76] Ottoman authorities in the Danube forts also issued permits to merchants from Bulgaria to go to Wallachia and purchase maize at this time.[77]

---

75 *Arzmahzar* of Moldavian boyars to the Porte, 1822, in *Cronicele României*, iii:465.
76 Letter of twenty-two merchants and scribes of the Istanbul grain market (*kapan*) to Prince Ion Sandu Sturdza, 31 May 1826, in Guboglu, *Catalogul documentelor turcești*, ii:542. From the Moldavian side, see the recollections of Dimitru Radu Peicăneanu, reported by Meleghi, in *Uricariul*, xiv:246–48.
77 In December 1826, Ibrahim, Pasha of Vidin issued a travel permit to Dimitraki Hadzhitoshev, allowing him to travel to Giurgiu to purchase maize. Cited by Robarts, *Plague*, 232.

Chapter 5

Mămăligă 2.0:
Maize on the World Market, 1829–1856

The events of 1821 and 1822, however disastrous they were from the point of view of the revolutionaries' own short-term aims, precipitated major changes in the political organization of these borderlands. The 'Phanariot' system of appointing rulers from the Greek-speaking clans of Istanbul was ended: so-called native princes were appointed. In April 1828, Russian armies again marched into the principalities and across the Danube, crossing the Balkan mountains for the first time and defeating the Ottomans at Edirne. Peace was concluded there in September 1829, and Moldavia and Wallachia, while remaining autonomous and under their own princes, became formal protectorates of Russia. Tsar Nicholas I appointed one of his trusted generals, Count Pavel Kiselev, to oversee a comprehensive programme of domestic reorganization. Kiselev was responsible for introducing the so-called Organic Statutes which functioned as quasi-constitutions and placed their government on a rational footing. New frontiers were established: the Russians took control over the Danube Delta, and the territory up to two hours to the south of it was to be rendered uninhabited. The Ottoman fortresses at Giurgiu and Brăila on the north bank of the Danube were dismantled, and these towns and their extensive hinterlands incorporated into Wallachian territory. Muslims residing at these fortresses were obliged to sell up and leave within a term of eighteen months, and merchants could no longer enter either principality without express authorization. As part of this latter process, the Ottomans arranged to convey their people safely back to their territory, but also asked to be able to retrieve their stores of maize from Giurgiu: Ahmed Pasha of Rusçuk wrote to Kiselev explicitly requesting this in early 1831. We do not know if Kiselev replied.¹

What did this new order amount to? An important element was peace. When Russian troops withdrew in 1836, the principalities had been subject to military occupation for thirty of the previous hundred years. In the century up to 1939, they would experience this much more rarely, for a total of eight years.² A second outcome was health: a sanitary cordon was established along the length of the Danubian frontier, and a programme of vaccination against smallpox was undertaken. The securing of frontiers was accompanied by greater control over goods. The Sultan permanently gave up any right to requisition materials for the consumption of Istanbul. Special mention was made of grain, livestock and timber; and, for a period of two years, the taking of tribute in money. Perhaps most importantly, the entire Black Sea region was now almost entirely open to international trade, not just to Russia but to any nation. This would in due course transform the economy of both provinces.

Kiselev's reforms fixed not only the principalities' frontiers and the terms of international commerce, but also property relations, particularly the principles of land ownership and the structure of village communities. Up until this point, in so-called 'free villages', the peasants were considered masters of their land.³ In villages with a lord (*stăpân*), settlements were organized simply or not at all. Dwellings were dispersed across estates and people relatively free to move around on their master's land. From this point on, peasants were placed into categories based on how much livestock they owned, and given plots accordingly. Meanwhile the lord (now called *proprietar*, a new word in Romanian at this point) took control of the rest of the estate, which was designated as *rezervă*, also a newly introduced word. Overall, the peasants controlled less than half the land they had worked previously; and they were obliged more and more to work the lord's reserve.

In other words, at the moment when the principalities' external frontiers and international status were being established, there was a concomitant process of border-making on the local, estate level: demarcation of property, sedentarization of inhabitants, solicitation of their labour, even systematization of villages. Peasants did not concede this loss of land use lightly: in Wallachia they put up strong resis-

---

1   Ahmed, Pasha of Rusçuk, letters to Kiselev, 11 Feb 1831, 2 Mar 1831, summary in Guboglu, *Catalogul documentelor turcești*, i:525, 526.
2   In 1848–1851, 1853–1857 and 1916–1918.
3   Stahl, *Contribuții*, i:29–48.

tance in the whole period from 1832 to 1848.⁴ In Moldavia there was also considerable unrest: the introduction of the new property regime caused a number of villagers to attempt to emigrate into Bessarabia, where they perceived labour conditions to be lighter.⁵

Viewed in this way, Count Kiselev's reforms achieved two aims: on the one hand, they stabilized the territory of the principalities according to principles of international law; and on the other, they reformed their internal legal and social relations. Yet another new word, *capital*, occurs frequently in the Organic Statutes. But the authorities did not pursue a policy of completely unrestrained free trade. Kiselev was aware of the potential consequences of foreign commerce for the local food supply, and also perhaps of the competition it might pose for Russia's own grain trade. When, in 1830–1831, boyars lobbied the Russian administration for their right to export grain, just as they had done a decade earlier to the Ottoman Porte, Kiselev took a more cautious approach. He had been personally involved in ensuring that sowings were carried out in 1829, partly to ensure sufficient provisions for the Russian occupying army, and had, in times of shortage, ordered boyars and leaseholders to sell their stocks of maize to the peasants at a fixed price.⁶ In 1830, he permitted the export of a limited quantity of maize from Moldavia to Transylvania while reserving wheat and barley for his troops.⁷ He also waived any taxes on the import of maize from Moldavia to Wallachia: an example of how needs that arose in the course of a military occupation led to decisions tending towards the economic unification of the two principalities.⁸

Kiselev also provided for the establishment of grain storehouses in case of famine. This was not a totally new idea: it had already been mooted during the occupation of 1806–1812 by a Russian counsellor, A. I. Koronelli, who had proposed that Bulgarian settlers on monastery lands in Wallachia should not pay a tithe to the monasteries but rather set aside the grains for a reserve.⁹ Plans for reserve storehouses were first implemented at Focșani in June 1829,¹⁰ and would later be written

---

4   Hitchins, *Romanians*, 178–80; for Wallachia see esp. Corfus, *Agricultura Țării Românești*, 79–87 (resistance), 276–94 (systematization of villages). In Moldavia the exploitation of the reserve began slightly earlier: I. Constantinescu, 'Date noi'.
5   Platon, 'Cu privire la pribegirea locuitorilor'.
6   Corfus, *Agricultura Țării Românești*, 74–76.
7   Istrati, 'Cu privire la exportul de grîne', 203.
8   Onilov, *Generalul Pavel Kiseleff*, 163.
9   Kutuzov, letter of 16 July 1811, trans. M. Stroia, in *Călători străini în sec. XIX*, i:426; see also Ion Sandu Sturdza, letter of August 1827, in *Uricariul*, xiv:296–98.
10 Vasile Bonciu, letter of June 1829, in Grigoruța, 'Scrisori', 70

into the Organic Statutes drawn up in the following year.[11] Maize was especially prized for this purpose because it could endure longer in storage than other grains. Landowners were obliged to set aside at least a hectare of land for every ten families for the purposes of growing maize reserves. Separate regulations were drawn up for Bucharest, requiring each of the five districts of the city to keep supplies of 30 *kile* of barley or maize in special storehouses.[12] These laudable measures were hard to enforce in practice.[13] In Moldavia, a modification was introduced in 1833 which placed the obligation to set aside maize reserves directly on the peasants.[14] Still, there were over sixty thousand *kile* of maize reserves in the province in 1844,[15] and at the start of 1848, on the eve of the revolution, a new law was introduced there for the reorganization of the reserve system.[16]

While the Treaty of Edirne in 1829 is widely agreed to mark the opening of the Principalities to the world market, it should be noted that trade did not fall overnight into the hands of European powers. International ships did indeed begin trading in large quantities through the Danubian ports of Brăila and Galați. The number of vessels embarking and disembarking at these ports increased sixfold in the decade from 1831 to 1840; in 1843, a vessel bearing the United States flag entered the Danube, and one from Argentina in 1855.[17] However, at least before the mid-1840s, the role of the British and the French remained relatively reduced. The Ottomans continued to be the predominant importers of grain.[18] Moreover, even though maize was the main cereal cultivated, it was not the most exported. In 1834, for example, maize constituted over three-quarters of the cultivated surface area in Wallachia, and yet more than twice as much wheat as maize was exported through the Danube

---

11   Chapter V, Section iii of the respective Regulations in *Regulamentele Organice ale Valahiei și Moldovei*, 76–77 (for Wallachia), 275–76 (for Moldavia).
12   Potra, *Din Bucureștii de altădată*, 181.
13   Otetea, 'Le second servage', 341–42; Vintilă-Ghițulescu, *Evgheniți, ciocoi, mojici*, 317–19.
14   'Proiectul modificator al Secției VII a Capitolului III a Regulamentului Organic alcătuit de Sfatul Ocârmuitor la 20 Ianuarie 1833', Article 36, in Rosetti, *Pământul, sătenii și stăpânii*, 528.
15   'Vedomostie lămuritoare de sumele popușoilor aflați în magaziile de rezerv' (1844), in *Analele parlamentare ale României* 13–ii:330; Filitti, *Domniile române*, 587.
16   'Proiect pentru reorganisația magazalilor de rezervă chibzuit supt Prezidenţa Prea Înălţatul Domn Stăpânitor', January 27 1848, *Analele Parlamentare ale României*, 15–ii:830–36; confirmation, 15 April 1848, ibid., 1049.
17   Columbeanu, 'Contribuții la istoria marinei', 448–49.
18   Murgescu, 'Romanian Grain Exports', 60. However, it is likely that at least some was reexported. A report from 1839 mentioned 'great interest from Italy' in Moldo-Wallachian maize, including Genoa, Venice and Trieste. Anon, 'Commerce', 3. Colson, *De l'état présent*, 228, stated that maize went especially to Trieste, unlike wheat which went to several locations.

ports.[19] The great majority of maize continued to be grown on peasant lots rather than on the lords' reserve land: nearly three-quarters in Moldavia in 1833. Where it was cultivated more extensively on lords' land, as was the case in Vaslui county, this was probably for distillation rather than export.[20] There were also numerous technical obstacles to large-scale export, particularly the silting up of the entrance to the Danube Delta, which was the object of diplomatic contestation between Britain and Russia in the 1830s. These were only resolved definitively after 1856.[21] Even figures for British exports can be misleading due to the number of ships sailing under a British flag but in fact manned by Ionian Greek traders who served the internal Ottoman market. Romanian landowners continued to make use of their networks in Istanbul to sell maize there.[22] Some Bulgarians and Ottoman Turks also got involved in the maize trade at this time.[23] Still, production was rising fast and the pressure was on the peasants: in 1843, a German traveller would associate mămăligă not with anti-colonial independence but with submission: this dish was, he said 'as common as air' in the region between the Danube, the Black Sea, and the Dniester, and could explain how the Romanians had managed to live with the exactions of Austrian, Ottoman or Russian imperial rule with equal endurance.[24]

From the mid-1840s, western Europe was affected by multiple crop failures leading to a transnational subsistence crisis, felt most drastically in the Great Famine which decimated the population of Ireland.[25] Among the British government's actions to assuage the effects of the potato crop failure was the wholesale import of maize, principally from the United States, as a result of a deal made through the mediation of Baring Brothers in New York.[26] The British initially kept their maize imports secret, not wishing to disincentivize local relief efforts. But the worsening of the famine meant that the maize news spread—including to Transylvania, where they were reported in local newspapers from February 1846.[27] The officials who had

---

19 Corfus, *Agricultura Țării Românești*, 338 (cultivated area); Penelea, 'Considerații', 327 (Danubian exports).
20 I. Constantinescu, 'Date noi', 49–50.
21 Ardeleanu, 'Russian-British Rivalry'; Ardeleanu, *European Commission*, 29–77. On technical issues affecting trade upstream to Central Europe, see Gatejel, 'Overcoming the Iron Gates'.
22 Ion Ionescu de la Brad, letters of 1855–1856, in Ionescu and Ghica, *Corespondența*, 146, 153–55.
23 Davidova, *Balkan Transitions*, 74–75, mentions Mehmet Ağa Hacı Alişoğlu and Ahmed Hacı Ismailoğlu, in partnership with Bulgarian Tsviatko Radislavov, based in Shvishtov on the right bank of the Danube.
24 Kohl, *Hundert Tage auf Reisen*, 528.
25 Vanhaute *et al.*, 'European Subsistence Crisis'; Zadoks, 'Potato Murrain'.
26 O'Neill, 'Organisation'; Gray, 'Triumph of Dogma'; Salah Harzallah, 'Food Supply'.
27 *Gazeta de Transilvania*, 28 February 1846, cited in Ciorba, 'Drama celorlalți', 60.

initiated the scheme had not particularly thought through the practicalities: the maize arrived unmilled from America, but there were no mills in Ireland to grind it. Matters were made worse because the maize needed to be ground twice, and Whitehall baulked at the cost. Their ignorance of maize issues is perhaps somewhat surprising given that it had been put to extensive use for some time by British authorities in Australia, as cheap food for convicts,[28] not to mention its use by slaveholders in the United States for the same purpose.[29] When it was finally distributed, the cereal was, in a by now familiar pattern of maize aversion, rejected by many of the destitute—its yellow colour led to it being dubbed 'Peel's Brimstone' after the British Prime Minister Sir Robert Peel. 'Never was anything so calumniated as our cornmeal', wrote a British commissioner charged with maize distribution.[30] A rumour even spread around Ireland that those who consumed mămăligă would turn black.[31] Charles Trevelyan, the principal British Treasury official in charge of relief, tried to publicize maize by eating it himself both in mush and cake form, and issued several pamphlets with cooking instructions.[32]

Even when the many obstacles to the scheme were overcome, the supplies purchased from the United States proved insufficient. British commissioners began to look elsewhere for maize. In the House of Commons in May 1846, Benjamin Disraeli drew MPs' attention to the 'very interesting markets' of Hungary and the Danubian provinces, and bemoaned the fact that, of 1350 ships laden in the ports of Galați and Brăila, only six were British.[33] In October, the *Cork Examiner* learnt via an informant in Trieste that '700 vessels have left the Bosphorus with a favourable wind from the south, bound for the ports of the Black Sea and the Danube. The quantity of corn in store is so great that a sufficient number of transports cannot be found, although they have every where been sought for.'[34] The *Drogheda Argus and Leinster Journal* reported that 'the harvest on the banks of the Danube and the shores of the Red Sea has been excellent', and the *Illustrated London News* that 'very large purchases of maize, the produce of the Danube' had been made by the British Deputy Commissioner-General to the Forces stationed in Malta.[35] Prices rose in the

---

28 Cushing, 'Mysterious Disappearance'.
29 Kemmerer, 'Pre-Civil War South'; Hilliard, *Hog Meat and Hoecake*, 151–60; Covey and Eisnach, *What the Slaves Ate*, 80–83.
30 Sir Randolph Routh to Trevelyan, March 1846, in Woodham-Smith, *Great Hunger*, 73.
31 As reported by Anon, 'Irish Crisis', 249.
32 Woodham-Smith, *Great Hunger*, 73.
33 Disraeli, 'Speech to House of Commons'.
34 *Cork Examiner*, 19 October 1846, 4.
35 *Drogheda Argus and Leinster Journal*, 31 October 1846, 4; *Illustrated London News*, 9 January 1847, 19.

Danube ports of Brăila and Galați in 1847, and the year saw the single largest increase in the area of cultivation of arable land in the principality in the whole period. Many Moldavian landowners, and brokers in London and Liverpool, profited from the wholesale and speculative purchase of maize in western Europe.

Although the Moldavian and Wallachian maize had little effect in mitigating the effects of famine in Ireland, the venture had a transformative effect on British interest in the principalities. Figures show that 1846 was indeed the tipping point for British commerce: while no more than 110 British ships left the ports of Galați and Brăila from 1837 to 1845, there were over 700 sailings from 1846 to 1849.[36] During the revolutionary year of 1848, prices declined and 'the state of Europe paralysed the corn trade of the Danube', according to the British consul in Bucharest; but in the following year, one Moldavian observer reported over five hundred British ships heading for the Danube ports in search of maize.[37] The demand for maize and other cereals led to the establishment of the first British consular post on Bulgarian territory, at the Black Sea port of Varna, in 1847.[38] For a short period, consuls were even appointed to reside at Giurgiu, Tulcea and Ismail on the Danube.[39] There had in fact been a relative decline of maize production in Wallachia in the previous two decades—while in 1831 it had made up over 80 percent of the known harvest in the province, by the mid 1840s it was only at 50 or 60 percent. But in the years following 1846, maize production surged again: in 1850 it was at 78 percent, and 74 percent in the following year.[40] Britain was by far the largest customer, buying 67.4 percent of that exported through Galați, and 42.8 percent of what passed through Brăila.[41] The principalities had become, in the words of a German traveller, lands of 'wine, maize and folly'.[42]

The export of grain from Moldavia to Ireland in 1846–1847 was recorded in an idyll written by the man of letters and boyar Gheorghe Asachi, entitled 'The Highlander's Return from England', and performed on the stage of the National Theatre in Iași on 15 March 1851. In this work, Irina, a beekeeper's daughter, misses her betrothed Codrat, an uplander, who has been away for over two years, and is nearly tempted to forget him and marry Brădeanu, the village guard. But Codrat returns

---

36 Florescu, 'Rumanian Principalities', 63n.56; Cernovodeanu and Marinescu, 'British Trade', 713–14.
37 Colquhoun, 'Account'; Ionescu, *Escursiune agricolă*, 20.
38 Todorova, 'Establishment of British Consulates'.
39 Cernovodeanu and Marinescu, 'British Trade', 707.
40 Figures for 1831–1850 in Corfus, *Agricultura Țării Românești*, 338–79.
41 Ardeleanu, *International Trade and Diplomacy*, 112.
42 König, *Lebens- und Reisebilder*, 5.

and explains that he has been to 'England', which God has cursed with hunger, and was so far away that nobody except him dared to travel there. Upon arrival in Ireland, he says, he demonstrated the art of mămăligă-making to the local population. He overcame local suspicion by following the correct procedures, until the locals began cheering 'Bravo puding, bravo puding', ate the mămăligă and washed it down with rum-laced tea, before tipping Codrat generously with gold coins. These enable Codrat to pay off the family debts and marry his sweetheart Irina.[43] Despite the evidently fantastic nature of the idyll, there may possibly be some truth in the claim by Asachi, in a note on the published text of the play, that as well as 'speculators', some Romanians went to Ireland 'to demonstrate the best use of this product, which was not so well known to them'.[44] If so, there seems to be no report of them in Irish sources. However, Romanian diplomats at the time of the Union of the Principalities emphasized their philanthropic maize contribution when negotiating with British officials in the 1850s.[45]

The rise of the Danubian grain trade in some ways followed the pattern developed in imperial Russia through Odessa and other Black Sea outlets. But Russian exports were dominated by wheat, with an annual average of 1.2 million quartals of wheat as against only 49,000 of maize. The Danube ports, in contrast, exported on average 564,000 quartals of maize and 439,000 of wheat, in the interval from 1843–1852.[46] Contemporary observers explained this by declaring the maize of the Principalities to be 'of very good quality',[47] or even 'the finest in the world',[48] in contrast to the wheat, which was not as good as the Russian. The quality of Moldavian and Wallachian wheat was constrained by traditional techniques. The archaic practice of storing grain in large underground chambers, which often led to it rotting through damp, or taking on an undesirable earthy smell, was still attested in the middle of the nineteenth century, while threshing was still carried out through the method of trampling by horses, 'although some Proprietors have lately got Trashing Machines [sic] from England', according to the British Consul at Galați.[49] A French observer noted that

---

43 Asachi, 'Înturnarea plăieșului'.
44 Asachi, 'Înturnarea plăieșului', 80.
45 Alecsandri, 'My Mission to London', 542.
46 Figures in Ardeleanu, *International Trade and Diplomacy*, 271; Russian figures in Stoianovich, 'Russian Domination', 217–20; Maftei, 'Considerații'.
47 Colson, *De l'état présent*, 237.
48 Charles Cunningham (British Consul at Galați), report of October 1849, in Cernovodeanu, 'An Unpublished British Source', 39. The phrase is repeated in Skene, *Danubian Principalities*, i:420.
49 Cunningham, report of 1849, in Cernovodeanu, 'An Unpublished British Source', 39. Cf. Santoni, report of 1840, in Herlihy, 'Report', 126.

Wheat grain is susceptible to humidity, keeps badly and requires considerable and costly labour. Barley and particularly maize are of better quality. All the maize I saw in the Danube ports in 1853, was plump, clean, shiny and full.[50]

A British observer of the Russian political scene, Laurence Oliphant, travelling the shores of the Black Sea in 1852, understood the importance of maize in changing the international balance of power. Oliphant believed—not quite accurately, as we have seen—that the export of maize from Moldavia and Wallachia was 'an almost entirely new trade, Ireland having hitherto being the principal consumer'. He also pointed out 'the ruinous consequences of such a result to the southern shores of the Russian empire'. Oliphant went on to argue that the continuing Russian occupation of the principalities following the suppression of the revolutions of 1848 was motivated by a desire to put a brake on the Danubian grain trade in order to protect her own exports, and that steps should be taken to remedy this 'if England is ever to be independent of Russia for her annual supply of corn'.[51] Whether or not this was actually the case, it was certainly a widely-accepted view which significantly influenced the decision of the British and French to go to war with Russia in 1854.[52] If the latter was understood by contemporaries as a war of liberation, it was the liberation of maize just as much as of people.

---

50 Lefebvre, *Études diplomatiques et économiques*, 255–56.
51 Oliphant, *Russian Shores*, 345–49.
52 Ardeleanu, *International Trade and Diplomacy*.

Chapter 6

Independence, Capitalism, Disease and Revolt; Or, Why the Mămăligă exploded, 1856–1907

In 1856, after Russia's defeat in the Crimea, Moldavia and Wallachia were placed under the collective guarantee of the Great Powers by the terms of the Treaty of Paris. Commissions were established to grant them new autonomies. Debates began in assemblies in Bucharest and Iași. But their deliberations were soon overtaken by the Union of the Principalities, first under a local prince, Alexander Ioan Cuza, in 1859, then under a German, Karl of Hohenzollern-Sigmaringen, in 1866; leading finally to independence (1878) and the proclamation of Romania as a kingdom in 1881. This is broadly seen as a time of unification, institution-building and relative stability. Carol's forty-eight-year reign was, after that of Emperor Franz Joseph and Queen Victoria, the longest in European history of the period. Universities, academies, newspapers, hospitals and banks were founded; railways, roads and bridges were built; a more or less functional two-party parliamentary system remained in place. The Romanian Orthodox Church was established as a national institution; the Romanian Academy laid down the norms of the literary language.

From an economic and social perspective, the period has drawn much more sharply contrasting interpretations. The newly independent kingdom now became completely integrated into the global grain market, and cereals remained one of the country's major exports. Independence, citizenship and property rights were supposed to rescue the peasantry from the condition of being 'regarded only as machines, good for producing wheat and maize' and integrate them into a new national community.[1] They were indeed formally emancipated by the Rural Law of

---

1   In the words of Mihail Kogălniceanu, 1861, quoted by Iordachi, *Liberalism*, 207.

1864, but their lot did not necessarily improve. Farming techniques remained rudimentary. The population grew, but the infant mortality rate was by some margin the highest in Europe. Illiteracy remained high, especially in the countryside and even more especially among women. The maize reserves that had been set up in villages three decades earlier were disestablished, and the maize sold off.[2] Independent Romania, despite growing more maize, was not in a position to influence world markets, especially with the increasing domination of the United States—something which Romanian commentators were acutely aware of even in the 1870s.[3] The people of Romania and other southeast European countries were, in the words of one recent interpretation, 'Europe's guinea pigs'. In other words, far from being isolated from the currents of modernization and the global economy, they were more exposed than any other group to a sustained barrage of social experiments and political and economic change.[4]

Crudely put, on the one hand there is a narrative which interprets the period of independence as a modernizing era, anticipating the 'European integration' of the early twenty-first century; and on the other there is one which stresses Romania's increasing dependency on the forces of global capitalism, and its languishing in a state of underdevelopment as a consequence. These are not merely retrospective theories: the problem was posed in such terms at the time, including by figures such as Romania's national poet Mihai Eminescu, and the pioneering socialist theorist Constantin Dobrogeanu-Gherea, who developed the concept of 'neoserfdom' to describe the agrarian regime in Romania at the turn of the twentieth century.[5] Dobrogeanu-Gherea did not himself invent the notion: as early as 1874 a Conservative political thinker characterized the socio-political arrangements in Romania on the cusp of independence as 'serfdom of a new kind'.[6]

That cereal production increased in Romania during the second half of the nineteenth century has been well documented.[7] This was in synchrony with the development of global transportation and raw material supply systems, into which the new state was integrated. A lesser-known outcome of the Treaty of Paris was the estab-

---

2   *Legea pentru regularea proprietăţeĭ rurale*, Article 50.2. An attempt was made in Covurlui county to establish rural credit in place of reserves, by growing maize separately for sale: Ionescu, *Agricultura Mehedinţi*, 296.
3   For example, Cantacuzino, *America vis-à-vis cu România*.
4   Uekötter, 'Europe's Guinea Pigs'.
5   Dobrogeanu-Gherea, *Neoiobăgia*.
6   Rosetti, 'Despre direcţiunea progresului nostru', 134. For overviews on debates in this period, see, in English, Hitchins, *Rumania*, 55–89; Cotoi, *Inventing the Social*.
7   Tucker, *Rumanian Peasant Revolt*, 70; Axenciuc, *Evoluţia economică a României*, ii:51.

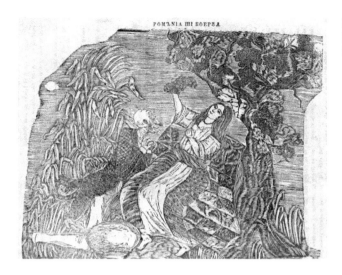

Image 6.1 Romania and the Boyar, 1861. *Bondarul* (The Drone) satirical magazine.

lishment of a "European Commission of the Danube", a neutral international body staffed by personnel from the signatory powers whose role was to ensure the navigability of this body of water through hydraulic and dredging works which made the river much more available to commerce. The Commission, a successful example of international cooperation which endured until 1948, was also important in facilitating export of maize from the Principalities.[8] Railways appeared too: the first lines—from Constanța on the Black Sea to Cernavoda on the lower Danube, and from Giurgiu to Bucharest—were built by British engineers who were granted concessions from Sultan Abdülmecid I at the end of the Crimean War, and then purchased by the Romanian government in 1878. A line was built traversing Moldavia and Wallachia, partly aimed at cementing the unification of the new state, but financed by Austrian, Prussian and British loans, and connecting Romanian raw materials to foreign markets. The building of railways was in fact a condition of Romanian independence as determined by the Powers at the Treaty of Berlin.[9]

In the same interval, the population of the new kingdom grew fast, from nearly four million in 1859 to nearly eight million in 1916; this despite the country having the highest infant mortality rate in Europe and experiencing significant emigration. What did not change a great deal, in contrast to international infrastructure and national demographics, were techniques for growing maize. By 1900, Romania had become in truth what early nineteenth-century social observers claimed it was:

---

8   Ardeleanu, *European Commission*.
9   Jensen and Rosegger, 'Transferring Technology'; Kellogg, *Road*, 68-91; Sugar, 'Railroad Construction'.

'a preeminently agrarian country'.[10] Of the 84 percent of the population who did not live in Bucharest, nearly everybody worked on the land. The population had increased by half, while the amount of land available had not.[11] While peasants now owned land by the terms of the Rural Property Law of 1864, their plots became smaller and smaller (from an average of 4.6 hectares in 1864 to 3.2 hectares in 1905), so they were virtually obliged to work on the large estates in order to survive. From a labour obligation of twelve days per year in 1830, to an estimated fifty-six days in 1860, the peasants were now reckoned to be spending up to two-thirds of their working time on the landowners' estates.[12]

The rural economy had moved definitively from a forest and animal base to an arable one; of the arable surface area, 94 percent of it was dedicated to cereals by the 1860s, and this remained fairly constant until after 1900.[13] Cereals remained at the heart of the country's export economy, representing 81 percent of exports in 1882 and 76 percent in 1912. Although maize exports declined slightly in proportional terms, production of maize roughly doubled. As an overall pattern, exports to Great Britain and Austria-Hungary dominated initially, but the principal destinations by 1912 were quite diverse, including to Italy (19 percent) and Belgium (24 percent), although this partially reflects the proportion of exports through port cities such as Genoa and Antwerp, rather than the point of consumption. Exports to Austria-Hungary collapsed after a customs war between 1885–1891.[14]

Despite the dominance of cereals in the Romanian export economy, the country's size compared to other maize-exporting countries (USA, Russia, Brazil, Argentina, Canada) meant that it was never in a position to determine prices on the world market, and there was no relation between the cost of production and the price of sale.[15] This meant that there was little incentive to invest in the quality of product. Scholars have pointed, entirely correctly, to the greed and irresponsibility of large sections of the landowning class, who often did not live regularly on their estates. However, even diligent landlords who took care over both the quality of their produce and the working conditions of those who laboured to produce it, would rarely profit from their investment. It is worth citing in detail the observa-

---

10 On the discursive development of this trope, see Drace-Francis, *Traditions of Invention*, 48-49.
11 31 inhabitants/km² in 1859, 46/km² in 1900: Axenciuc, *Evoluția economică a României*, ii:20–21.
12 Chirot, *Social Change*, 133–34.
13 Jormescu and Popa-Burcă, *Harta agronomică*, 147; Axenciuc, *Evoluția economică a României*, ii:51.
14 Chirot, *Social Change*, 122–24; Iosa, 'Comerțul cerealier', 248. The slight relative decline is due to the rise after 1900 of petroleum exports.
15 Axenciuc, *Evoluția economică a României*, ii:500; Murgescu, *România și Europa*, 123.

tion of a well-informed British journalist, T. Wemyss Reid, who visited Romania in 1878, the year of independence. Wemyss Reid visited first a wretched estate outside Bucharest, where

> I found thin and miserable crops raised on soil which, though with care and proper cultivation it might be made to bring forth almost any amount of produce, is now rapidly exhausted by the barbarous and slovenly fashion in which it is tilled. Everything produced on these estates - with the exception of the fruit and vegetables—was poor. [...] The maize was light in the head and ragged in the stalk, and the wheat was black and shrivelled.[16]

Following this, he then went to what was by all accounts a very well-run estate in Moldavia in 1878:

> Mr. S_____ has nevertheless accomplished marvels. It was a pleasant sight to look upon the immense fields, stretching towards the sombre background of forest, where already the autumn-sown wheat was springing, green and fresh, and where the well-drained, well-ploughed furrows told of the care exercised in cultivation. [...] When we went into the crowded granaries and inspected the vast stores of maize and wheat, the same contrast to the state of things existing elsewhere was presented to us. The grain would have compared favourably with that raised in any quarter of the world; and its appearance alone would have sufficed to show that the cereals of Roumania, under proper cultivation, need shrink from no competition. [...] But Mr. S. assured me that for this excellent wheat, quite equal to any ordinarily seen in the London markets, he could only obtain the price paid for the wretched crops of his neighbours.[17]

There were limited exceptions to the lack of investment in maize production and processing. For example, in Bragadiru near Bucharest, an industrial distillery was established in 1882 for manufacturing alcohol, which could process 340 hectolitres of maize per day. While the product was refined, the unused husks were used as livestock fodder. The maize alcohol produced at Bragadiru was exported to Bulgaria, Egypt, Turkey and Germany. On the estate of the Știrbei family at Buftea, to

---

16 Wemyss Reid, 'Rural Roumania', 89; also in Tappe, 'T. Wemyss Reid and Rumania'.
17 Wemyss Reid, 'Rural Roumania', 92.

CHAPTER 6

6.2 Emanoil Panaiteanu-Bardasare, *Road among gardens*, Iaşi, 1882

the north of Bucharest, efficient industrial equipment was brought in for processing maize and cotton. But these were exceptions, benefitting from proximity to transport networks and to capital, and from targeting new product markets.[18]

In the year 1888, the agricultural and pastoral peoples of the world were not happy, and a series of revolts broke out in different points across the globe. In the Dutch East Indies, the people of Banten province in Java rose up against their masters.[19] In the Scottish Hebrides, the crofters of Skye had been protesting increased rents and worsening labour conditions for a number of years, and pitched battles between peasants and landlords were ongoing; the British government even sent warships to Skye to establish control. In Trinidad there was similar unrest.[20] In Dufile, Equatoria (today's northern Uganda), local Islamic forces deposed the British-imposed governor Emin Pasha—a Silesian-born Jewish doctor who had worked as a quarantine officer in the port of Bar, in the Ottoman Adriatic (today part of

---

18 Further on structural obstacles: Wood, *Agrarian Problem*, 150–231 (details on Bragadiru and Buftea at 208).
19 Kartodirdjo, *Peasants' Revolt*.
20 Verteuil, *Years of Revolt*.

6.3 'Mama-Liga de Lux': cigarette paper packaging, Bucharest, c. 1900

Montenegro)—and were brutally surpressed by an expedition led by Henry Stanley. In northern Afghanistan, Turkic leaders rejected the authority of their British-backed Pashtun masters and were no less brutally put down.[21] Imperial Germany's establishment of the colony of German East Africa led to an extensive rebellion spreading along the coast.[22] In Brazil, Princess Imperial Isabel promulgated the abolition of slavery, but it was not enough to stabilize conditions: the following year, her father the Emperor was deposed and the country declared a Republic. The concatenation of events is remarkable given that these rebellious forces were not in direct communication with each other.[23] Many were products of what historian Michael Adas has called 'one of the most cruel contradictions of the era of colonization', namely a combination of population growth and political centralization which meant that peasants, pastoralists and other marginal peoples could no longer simply avoid central authority, but were brought into confrontation with it, at the moment when the state's technological and organizational capabilities vastly outstripped that of the population.[24]

---

21 Kakar, *Consolidation*, 180–204; Lee, *Afghanistan*, 390–95.
22 Fabian, 'Locating the Local'.
23 Kartodirdjo, *Peasants' Revolt*, 142, nevertheless posits that the Muslim (Ottoman) defeat in the Russo-Turkish War, or *perang Rus* as it was known, had a mobilizing impact on the peoples of Java.
24 Adas, 'From Avoidance to Confrontation', 218-19.

CHAPTER 6

Events in Romania in the spring of 1888 conformed to this pattern. The previous year's harvest had been poor due to a drought, and there was dissatisfaction with the ruling Liberal government who had been the dominant force in the new kingdom under Prime Minister Brătianu for most of the preceding decade. In December of that year, after a parliamentary debate to discuss the poor harvest, a law was passed permitting the purchase of 3 million lei worth of maize on the international market to sell to villagers on credit repayable within five years, especially in Wallachia which had been hardest hit. Some left-leaning politicians objected to the commercial nature of this solution, describing it as 'usury on mămăligă, which the peasant makes for his children with the maize sold him by the government'.[25] What really sparked the revolt, however, was allegedly a deceptive attempt by local Liberals to persuade villages to sign a message in support of Prime Minister Brătianu under the illusion that they were signing a petition requesting supplies of maize.[26]

The peasants produced no written programme of their grievances, but from the telegrams of village mayors and from government orders which are the principal sources of our information concerning the events of late March and early April of this year, it is clear that maize, or particularly the lack of it, was a central driver of dissatisfaction. Asked why they were in revolt, the inhabitants of Speteni, in Ialomița county, told army officer Captain Parapeanu that 'we are dying of hunger, we have no land, no pastures, no maize to eat and the mayor has stolen from us and deceived us with promises'.[27] In Eliza-Stoenești, also in Ialomița county, the peasants beat up the mayor and the notary. When the procurator showed up, they declared that 'we have no land to plough, the leaseholder put very harsh conditions, that we have no maize for food, that the mayor does not defend our rights but abuses them for the leaseholder, and that in the end we had no other recourse.' The procurator reassured them that the mayor would be put on trial and emergency steps had been taken to distribute maize, and then the peasants quietened down.[28] In Dascălul-Creața, Ilfov county, a certain Constantin Grigore took up a flag in front of a horde of his fellow villagers, shouting 'Let's kill the boyars, as we have no means to live, our children are dying of hunger and they don't want to give us maize'.[29] In Lipia-Bojdani, also in Ilfov, the peasants went to the mayor's office to

---

25 Deputy N. Voinov, in Adăniloaie, *Răscoala*, 115–16.
26 Procurator General C. Cociașu, 26 March/7 April 1888, in Bodea, 'Contribuții documentare', 162–65.
27 Colonel Iacob N. Lahovary, memorandum on the revolt in Ialomița county, in V. Kogălniceanu, *Chestiunea țărănească*, pt. ii: Anexe, 19-20; cf. Adăniloaie, *Răscoala*, 139.
28 Adăniloaie, *Răscoala*, 140.
29 Adăniloaie, *Răscoala*, 150.

request an order for the distribution of maize but the authorities had already fled. Instead they went to a wealthy innkeeper and destroyed his property, taking 7,000 lei from him and keeping him prisoner in the mayor's office.[30] In Fierbinți, Ialomița county, a rumour spread at the beginning of April that the mayor and some electoral delegates had gone to Bucharest and obtained money for the purchase of land and maize but used it for their own ends, 'hiding orders arriving at the mayor's office for the distribution of maize'. They beat up the delegates and smashed up the house of the mayor, who had fled to Bucharest.[31] In many villages the starving peasants ransacked the maize stores.[32] A delegation of peasants granted an audience by the Interior Ministry in mid-April summed up what they wanted in four points: land; reform of the law on agrarian labour contracts; re-establishment of the old units of measurement; and maize.[33]

In the words of leading Liberal statesman Mihail Kogălniceanu, the government, in mobilizing the army to quell the revolt, 'was crude and merciless. They shot down the peasants like dogs, without the latter having opened fire either in defence or attack.' Not only Chancellor Bismarck but even Sultan Abdul Hamid II expressed their concern at the state of the peasantry.[34] Order was restored, and maize distributed to peasants in need. But as a military officer involved in the suppression of the revolt acknowledged, its causes lay not in popular insubordination but in 'a bad and dishonest administration'.[35] Historians' reconstructions put the death toll at around 1,000. As the Romanian socialist author Constantin Dobrogeanu-Gherea noted, structural factors meant that the social antagonism between the people and the elites would result in a cycle of repression and revolt in the last years of the nineteenth century.[36]

In 1904, after a series of poor years, the harvest in Romania was a failure, even worse than that of 1887. Export was prohibited in August, and King Carol of Romania, reflecting on the fortunes of the past year, wrote in his diary of January 1905 that

---

30 Adăniloaie, *Răscoala*, 152.
31 Adăniloaie, *Răscoala*, 151.
32 Report in *România liberă*, 2/14 April 1888, in *Răscoala țăranilor din 1888*, 229. This report says maize is being ransacked 'everywhere'; specific cases were reported in Dudești, Dâmbovița county (ibid., 237); Orascu, Ilfov county (ibid., 242); Frumușeni, Ilfov county (ibid., 253).
33 Report in *Universul*, 4/16 April 1888, in *Răscoala țăranilor din 1888*, 231.
34 Mihail Kogălniceanu, Speech of 7 December 1890, in idem, *Opere*, v, part 5, 245–46.
35 Raport of Major Magheru, 1888, cited by Arion, *Pagini*, 6. Maize distributed: *Monitorul Oficial*, 8/20 April 1888, in *Răscoala țăranilor din 1888*, 251.
36 Dobrogeanu-Gherea, *Neoiobăgia*, 171–207.

For my country it has been the worst year of my long reign. We now suffer greatly the consequences of the bad harvest; two-thirds of the population must be fed by the state, otherwise people would be starving. Huge shippings of maize from South America are being distributed to the peasants.[37]

According to *Lloyd's List*, the leading London shipping publication of the time, 'the ill wind which the failure of the maize crop means to Roumania seems destined to blow some good to the British shipowner'.[38] The maize purchases were financed by loans from Berlin-based banks, and imported mainly from Argentina by British and Belgian entrepreneurs.[39] As we have seen, the practice of importing maize at times of poor harvest dated back at least to the early years of independence. The imported maize—dubbed *păpușoiu american*, using the Moldavian word for the plant—aroused suspicion, both among the peasantry and among local sanitary experts, who were eager to blame it for the widespread incidence of pellagra among the rural population.[40] Some maize available domestically was illegally exported to Russia and sold back to the government. The finance minister himself alleged in the Chamber of Deputies that some boyars, being unable to send their maize to England or Antwerp as they usually did, took it over the border to Bessarabia, disguised it as 'Russian maize' and then reimported it at a much higher price.[41] Shortages of maize caused quite serious agitation already in 1905 in some villages: it was cited, for example, as a cause of unrest in the village of Bălăceanu in Râmnicu Sărat county.[42] By 1906, things seemed to be looking up: the harvest had recovered, with over 600,000 tonnes being exported from Romania.[43]

---

37 King Carol I, letter of January, 1905, quoted in Marin, *Peasant Violence*, 85.
38 'Argentine Maize for Roumania', *Lloyd's List*, 10 August 1904, 8.
39 Hurezeanu and Iosa, 'Social, Economic and Political Condition', 34 refer to British entrepreneurs and to Disconto-Gesellschaft and S. Bleichröder banks. The Russian Ambassador in Bucharest, doubtless better informed, referred to a Belgian shareholding company in La Plata: Giers to Count Lamsdorff, 12 January 1905, in *Rapoarte diplomatice ruse*, 395. General information on the types of business organization engaged in this trade: Popescu, *Casting Bread Upon the Waters*, 74–83.
40 N. Gh. Cădere, *Însemnări de igienă rurală* (1910) cited by Giosanu, 'Diete tradiționale', 179; V. Babeș, *Studii asupra pelagrei* (1911), cited by Andreescu and Rogozea, 'Aetiology Theories', 94. US agents had already begun to distribute maize in Russia in the 1890s as part of a philanthropic but also business-led campaign: Zhuravleva, 'American Corn in Russia'. Import of US maize, partly under business pressure, had also become a regular practice in Mexico at times of harvest failure: Wolfe, 'Climate of Conflict', 475–76.
41 Emil Costinescu, speech in the Chamber of Deputies, 24 November 1905, in Hurezeanu and Iosa, 'Social, Economic and Political Condition', 35.
42 Hurezeanu, *Problema agrară*, 202.
43 Axenciuc, *Evoluția economică a României*, iii:372.

The revolt which broke out in February 1907 was probably the defining event in the social history of Old Kingdom Romania. It upset the image of a stable, gradually modernizing European constitutional monarchy and raised serious questions about the country's social and economic basis. The causes of the revolt were not immediate maize-hunger, but structural ones, involving population growth, shrinking of plots and wages, and an increasingly stark conflict between capital and labour, as well as the peasants' increased access to knowledge and social communication.[44] Some scholars have even used wheat cultivation and export (while neglecting maize) as an index for the preconditions of social unrest in Romania.[45] In reality, wheat and maize cultivation kept more or less equal pace throughout the second half of the nineteenth century. There was no drastic change in proportions; nor is there any strong correlation between zones of wheat and outbreaks of peasant unrest. In fact the correlation between maize production and peasant unrest in the year 1907 is much closer than that with wheat.[46] To the peasants, maize was a much more personal matter: while wheat was predominant on the large latifundiary estates, up to 85 percent of maize was cultivated on farms of less than 100 hectares.[47] In 1906, the rooves of around one in eight of all peasant dwellings in Romania were made of maize stalks.[48]

So it is not surprising that in 1907, just as in 1821 and 1888, there was a maize trigger to the unrest. This consisted not in the fact of shortage or crop failure, although the memory of 1904 must have been fresh in the minds of protagonists.[49] On the contrary, the crop of 1906 had been excellent. Foreign export continued throughout the year: 1.39 million tonnes of maize left the country, more than twice the volume of the previous year's exports.[50] Prices were particularly high in west European markets, partly due to poor harvests in rival exporting countries such as the USA and Argentina.[51] More immediately significant were the consequences arising from some measures adopted by the Conservative government to prevent a repitition of the disastrous shortages of previous years. In February 1905 a law was

---

44 Marin, *Peasant Violence*, 275–84.
45 Stahl, *Traditional Romanian Village Communities*, 96–97; Chirot and Ragin, 'Market, Tradition', 431, 436; Chirot, *Social Change*, 148-49.
46 Compare Jormescu and Burca-Popă, *Harta agronomică*, 154 (Map 148, average wheat production by county) and 174 (Map 161, average maize production). See also Graphs 1 and 2 below.
47 Mitrany, *Land and the Peasant*, 84n.1, 287 (figure from 1911).
48 Cazacu, 'Locuințele sătenilor', 550 (12.6 percent).
49 Cf. Mexico in this year, where unrest was ascribed directly to shortages: Wolfe, 'Climate of Conflict'.
50 Axenciuc, *Evoluția economică a României*, iii:372. King Carol noted in April 1907 that maize to the value of 35 million francs was imported in April 1907: Marin, *Peasant Violence*, 85–86.
51 Burtt-Davy, *Maize*, 525.

introduced providing for the reestablishment of maize reserves (which, as the reader will recall, had been abolished in 1864). But these reserves, just like the earlier ones, were to be funded by the peasants, in the form of a five-lei tax on those owning between 0.7 and 15 hectares of land. Although the tax was compensated by a four-lei reduction in general taxes—in real terms, then, being only a tax of one leu—it caused considerable unrest through the country throughout the winter of 1906–1907.[52]

Peasants in various parts of the country were still protesting this tax when the time for making agricultural contracts fell in February-March. On 19 February 1907, the inhabitants of Poiana Lungă in Botoșani petitioned the prefect requesting to be exempt from it, and assuming all responsibility for their personal welfare in case of shortage.[53] Three days later, on 22 February 1907, the inhabitants of Fântânele in the same county declared themselves 'utterly impoverished' and refused to pay the tax.[54] Another three days later, on 25 February, the inhabitants of Onești, Bacău county, stated the same.[55] In a report of 15 March, Gh. Constantinescu, the adminstrator of the Flămânzi estate which was the epicentre of the revolt in Moldavia, gave the maize tax as a primary reason for peasant dissatisfaction in the immediately preceding period.[56] In Gorj county, according to a *Siguranța* (Security Services) agent's report, protest against and resistance to the maize tax was general 'in all communes'.[57] The importance of the maize tax in unleashing the revolt was well understood by contemporaries, including the Liberal government which came into power in March: repealing the tax was the very first item on the programme they presented to the King.[58] News of the repeal was proclaimed in numerous localities as a means of trying to quell peasant unrest.[59] It is therefore correct for Donald Sassoon in his recent history of capitalism to classify what happened in Romania in 1907 as a tax revolt.[60]

The events themselves have been narrated many times, and need be summarized only briefly here.[61] At Flămânzi, peasants who, among other grievances, complained

---

52 Hurezeanu, *Problema agrară*, 88-89, 259-65; Eidelberg, *Rumanian Peasant Revolt*, 191–98, 224–26.
53 Petition of 19 February/4 March 1907, in *Documente 1907*, ii:75.
54 Hurezeanu, *Problema agrară*, 263.
55 Petition, 25 February 1907, in *Documente 1907*, i:363–64.
56 Constantinescu, report to Botoșani prefecture, 15 February 1907, in Bejenaru, 'Județul Botoșani', 225.
57 Captain's report, March 21/April 3, in *Documente 1907*, iv:303–4.
58 Liberal party manifesto, 12/25 March 1907, in Rosetti, *Pentru ce s'au răsculat țăranii*, 615–16.
59 Text of the law as proclaimed in Teleorman county, 12/25 March, in *Documente 1907*, iii:384–86; mayor's proclamation of the repeal in Dobriceni, Romanați county, in an effort to calm spirits: Iordache, 'Oltenia', 482.
60 Sassoon, *Anxious Triumph*, 124, 297.
61 See especially the recent analysis of Marin, *Peasant Violence*, with references.

of being fed with 'mămăligă from rotten maize',⁶² rose up against the leaseholders of the largest latifundiary estate in the country, and stormed the village hall. Their actions were imitated throughout northern Moldavia. By early March, news of their uprising reached Wallachia, and many peasants, especially in the southwestern counties, refused to take up the plough and marched *en masse* to the manors of their respective landlords. In response, the government mobilized over 120,000 troops and many peasants were shot, including in some localities by the use of heavy artillery. In many accounts of the repression, a figure of 11,000 peasant deaths is given, but given that the government destroyed much of the relevant documentation, the exact number cannot be established with certainty. However, even if a much lower figure of 2,000 deaths is accepted, the repression still resulted in the largest number of violent peacetime deaths in a single event in the country's modern history.⁶³

One particular feature of peasant activity that emerges strikingly from the documentation in Wallachia is that, in many instances, they did not seek to steal maize from their landlord. Rather, when storming their lords' manor houses, especially in Wallachia, they would set fire to their maize stores. A quite remarkable number of incidents of this kind are recorded in Mehedinți,⁶⁴ Dolj,⁶⁵ Romanați,⁶⁶

---

62 Petition of 2/15 March 1907, in *Documente 1907*, ii:101.
63 Marin, *Peasant Violence*, 5.
64 Mehedinți: maize ransacked, com. Braniștea, 10–12 March (*Documente 1907*, iv:228-29; cf. *Marea răscoală*, 493); manor houses destroyed at Gârla Mare, 13 March (*Marea răscoală*, 492), and at Gemeni, Vrata, Botoșești, Bălăcița, Izvoarele (com. Gruia), Tâmna, Corcova, Podu Grosului (com. Bâcleș), 15 March (*Documente 1907*, iv:201–2); Izimșa (com. Obârșia de Câmp), 1400 *kile* of maize and 50 *kile* of wheat stolen, 14–15 March (211); Gemeni (today Dârvari), stores of leaseholder Ioniță Marincu set ablaze, 14 March (220); Ostrovu Mare, com. Gogoșu, a store and ten carts of maize destroyed, March (224–25); Rogova, 15 March, maize stores 'completely burnt' (*Marea răscoală*, 495); Stigniţa, Padina Mare, maize stores burnt (*Marea răscoală*, 496).
65 Dolj: Galicea Mare, a maize store set alight, 9 March (*Documente 1907*, iv:44); Livezi (today com. Podari), manor house and maize stores burnt, 11 March (47, 48-49); Horezu Poenari, maize store of Virgiliu Tîrnoveanu set alight, 11 March (47-48); Valea Stanciului, 11 March (*Marea răscoală*, 458); Drănic, property of C. N. Mihail completely burnt down, inc 360 *kile* of maize, 11–12 March (49); Băilești, Prince Știrbei's maize stores set alight, 12 March (*Marea răscoală*, 451); Verbița, likewise (ibid., 453); Urzicuța, 13 March (ibid., 455) Țimburești, com. Murta, March, 3 barns (*Documente 1907*, iv:88); Mârsan, maize and wheat stolen, hay set on fire (88); Negoiești, 14 March, maize stores destroyed (98); Bistrețu, 14 March, maize stores destroyed (100–101); Teasc, maize stores burnt (*Marea răscoală*, 466).
66 Romanați: comuna Golfin (today Robănești), 300–350 *kile* burnt, 13 March (*Documente 1907*, iv:122); Comuna Zvorsca, a cattle shed and 2 maize stores set alight, 14 March (129); Colibași, 13–14 March, manor house, carriages, maize stores (131, see also 174); Gubandru (today com. Baldovinești), maize stores, 13 March (*Marea răscoala*, 478); comuna Băleasa, wheat and maize stores, 13–14 March (138), com. Brastavăţu, 14 March (*Documente 1907*, iv:109), Buzducu estate, com. Popînzălești, before 19 March (113–114), comuna Dobrun, 14 March, Nicolae Luță set fire to the store of Ionică Brătășanu (140–142; see also 160); Scărișoara (today com. Băbiciu), 1,000 *kile* of the leaseholder's maize destroyed

Olt,[67] Vâlcea,[68] Teleorman[69] and Argeș[70] counties between 9 and 15 March 1907. This manner of protest suggests firstly that the peasants were not immediately dying of hunger, or they would have taken the maize rather than burnt it. The burning of the maize was rather a symbolic act of vengeance, partly against the above-mentioned tax and partly against the profiteering of landlords and leaseholders. It seems that maize in Wallachia, as in other peasant regions of Europe, 'had greater ontological weight than other foods, other aspects of the world, and most other entities in general.'[71] Secondly, the actions of villagers here were not particularly determined by the rise in wheat cultivation and export in Wallachia, as has been argued by some scholars.[72] Rather it was more likely part of a historic tradition of rebellion, especially in the provinces of Oltenia or Little Wallachia, where there were still memories of the uprisings of 1821 and 1848. Memories of the revolt in the Oltenian region were kept alive in popular song, which explicitly invoked the region's *haiduc* or bandit tradition, and the burning of maize:

---

during the revolt, undated (145–46); comuna Racovița (today com. Voineasa, jud. Olt), some stores set ablaze, others opened and the maize left to pour out (153); Jieni (today com. Rusănești, jud. Olt), four large maize stores set on fire (156–57); Rusănești de Sus, Voineasa County, 14 March, maize stores smashed up and set on fire (160); in Știrbei and Dobriceni communes, the peasants believed the government had issued an order to pillage (165); Strejeștii de Jos, maize stores destroyed, 14–15 March (*Marea răscoală*, 484–85); Câmpeni, 150 peasants led by priest and schoolteacher demanded money or half the maize. Despite the landlord replying that they could take it all, they attacked him and then destroyed the maize, setting fire to it but also carrying it off, 500 *kile* was burnt, 14–15 March (*Documente 1907*, iv:121); comuna Balș, before 19 March (115),

67 Olt: at Drăgoești (today in Vâlcea county), all the property of leaseholder Popescu was burnt. What maize remained was carried off by the inhabitants, 16 March (*Documente 1907*, iv:320); at Vulturești, Mr. Moșoiu's property was laid waste, but a maize store remained at Batia (329)

68 Vâlcea: Bălcești, Obogeanu's maize stores overturned, March 13 (*Documente 1907*, iv:241); Rămești, manor, maize cobs and all property burnt, 14 March (254–55); Laloșu, 33 inhabitants accused of stealing the maize of Haralambie Davidescu. Not all were guilty, some returned the stolen maize (292–93).

69 Teleorman: at Zimnicea, peasants sack the maize store of D. Arsenie, 10 March (*Documente 1907*, iii:383); Maize, potatoes, barley, rape etc. distributed on estate of H. Chazeski in Rădoiești, 10 March (Badea *et al*., 'Wallachia', 127); at Călinești, north of Alexandria, 10 March (128); at Meri Goala, 11 March (129); at Siliștea-Gumești maize was set on fire 'in a drift of blind hatred', March 11 (130); at Băltați, 12 March, 'they ravaged the grain stock' (130–31); wheat store house burnt at Slobozia-Mândra, 12–13 March (131).

70 Argeș: at Băseni-Stârci (today Stârci, com. Costești), the manor of Dumitru Miciu was ransacked, cobs gathered and set alight in the courtyard, 13 March (*Documente 1907*, iv:389); Lăunele de Jos (today in Vâlcea county), two maize stores of Traian V. V. Ropcea were set alight, 15 March (391).

71 Pina-Cabral, 'Minhoto Counterpoints', 197.

72 Chirot, *Social Change*, 148-54.

> Green leaf of nettle
> The men of Jiu are coming
> Give us guns and pitchforks
> And we'll join the haiducs
> And will set off all together
> And rid the land of thieves
>
> At Horezu Poienari,
> At Gângiova and Orăşani,
> The maize stores are ablaze
> With food taken from the poor.[73]

Despite the extensive and shocking nature of the revolt, acknowledged by nearly all parties, it did not immediately lead to significant land reform. This came only later, in the period 1917–1921, and was motivated not by a desire to build up a prosperous peasantry but by fear of revolution and by the severe reduction in profits to be made from cereal exports in the post-war dispensation.[74]

In the words of Queen Marie of Romania, written as a patriotic evocation for an English audience in 1916, Romania was idyllically portrayed as

> a fruitful country, a country of vast plains, of waving corn, of deep forests, of rocky mountains [...] A country where peasants toil 'neath scorching suns, a country untouched by the squalor of manufactories.[75]

But for the Romanian peasants who survived the bloodbath of their country's engagement in the First World War—over half a million of them were killed during the conflict—the land was still waiting.

---

73   Trifu, '1907 în poezia populară', 74, 75.
74   Eidelberg, 'Vasile Kogălniceanu', 81–82.
75   Marie, *My Country*, 5-6

CHAPTER 6

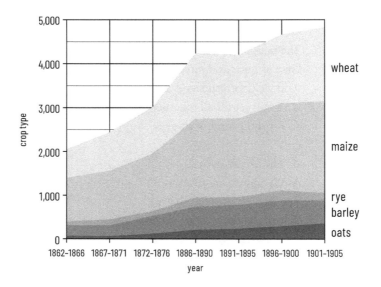

Graph 1: Cereals cultivated in Romania, 1862–1905 (hectares)
Source: *Anuarul statistic al României, 1908*, data reproduced in *Documente 1907*, i:34–35.

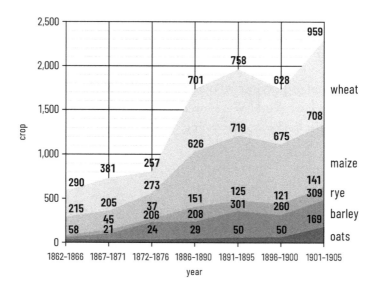

Graph 2: Cereal export from Romania, 1862–1905 (thousands of tonnes)
Source: Axenciuc, *Evoluția economică*, ii:369–372.

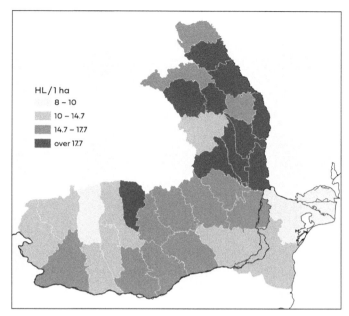

Map 6: Average wheat production by county in 1907
Source: Jormescu and Popa-Burcă, *Harta agronomică*, 154 (map. 148)

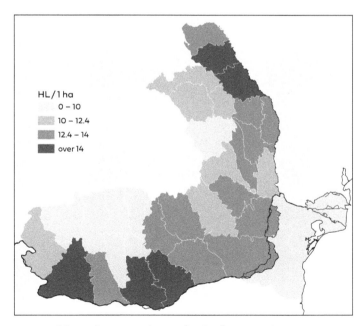

Map 7: Average maize production by county in 1907
Source: Jormescu and Popa-Burcă, *Harta agronomică*, 174 (Map 161)

Chapter 7

Manna valachorum – Recipes at the Interface

Sources record the existence of some kinds of cereal cake or mush in seventeenth- and early eighteenth-century Moldavia; but these almost certainly refer to millet.[1] In Transylvania there is an even earlier reference to Romanians enjoying millet cakes baked on hot coals, in the Latin poem *Ruinæ Pannonicæ* published in 1571 by the Saxon pastor of Mediasch, Christian Schäser.[2] But the first credible mention of a maize-based dish occurs in the first years of the eighteenth century, in the memoirs of the Transylvanian aristocrat, rebel and gourmand Miklós Bethlen, which he wrote while incarcerated in a Viennese jail on account of his resistance to the Habsburg takeover of Transylvania. Wistfully recalling the food that he had enjoyed in his youth, Bethlen noted the dish *balmos*, which he apparently liked very much.[3] Today, *balmos* (*balmoș* in modern Romanian) refers to a dish of mămăligă baked with cheese and sheep's milk. As Bethlen did not go into details, it is impossible to determine with certainty whether the *balmos* enjoyed was specifically prepared with cornmeal. He was, however, involved in a proposal to cultivate maize in Transylvania in 1703, so he would have been familiar with the plant.[4]

---

1 Iorga, 'Ancienneté', 186 (Bandini); *Călători străini*, v: 275 (Pal Beke); vii:107 (Vito Piluzzi); viii:315 (Erasmus von Weismantel); Cantemir, *Descriptio Moldaviæ*, 108. For previous attempts to trace *mămăligă* recipes, see inter alia Kreuter, 'Zuckerwerk'; Vintilă-Ghițulescu, *Patima și desfătare*, 25–26; Petrică, *Identitate culinară românească*; eadem, *Topography of Taste*, 105–9; Epure, 'Alimentația locuitorilor'; Jianu, '"Taste of Others"'; eadem, 'Polenta or Mămăligă?'; Dragomir, *Curatorul de zacuscă*, 223–30.
2 'The Wallachian lives off cheese and milk, and cakes made with millet flour cooked on hot coals': Christianus Schesaeus, *Ruinæ Pannonicæ* (1571), signalled by Bodale, 'Informații documentare', 57.
3 Bethlen, *Önéletírása*, i:130; idem, *Autobiography*, 130. Bethlen began composing his memoirs around 1708.
4 Lukinich, 'Egy erdélyi kereskedelmi társaság', 475; Moga, 'Politica economică austriacă', 102.

CHAPTER 7

Count Bethlen was not the only Transylvanian aristocrat forced into exile by the consolidation of Habsburg rule in the principality at the beginning of the eighteenth century. His younger contemporary Kelemen Mikes was one of a number of Hungarian Protestant rebels who sought refuge in Ottoman lands after 1711. Mikes's *Letters from Turkey*, a series of epistles addressed to a fictional aunt, were published posthumously and constitute a rich evocation of life between empires at the beginning of the modern age. In several of these letters he bemoans his fate as an exile. For example, writing from Edirne in December 1717, he complained that 'I would rather have been a cabbage pot in Transylvania than any coffee cup of the Sultan'. But he went on to praise the Ottoman white bread in the following terms:

> Our store of bread is placed here, therefore let us eat of it without complaint as long as it remains, and let us not say that it would be better to eat *málé* in Transylvania than wheat-bread here.[5]

As with Bethlen's *balmos*, we cannot be certain what Mikes's *málé* refers to, although the word was used in Magyar to mean maize, and therefore by extension maize bread.[6] Whatever cereal was involved, his remark suggests that *málé* was by now a characteristic Transylvanian food.

Mikes was born and raised in the Háromszék (Trei Scaune) region of Transylvania to the northeast of Braşov. If he had been at home when he wrote his letter, he might not have found much to eat at all, or so we learn from a tantalizing reference in a Romanian-language document from 1718. In this year there was a great drought in the region to the north of the city, so bad that the wells dried up. The price of wheat and millet had risen out of the reach of ordinary people, who resorted to grinding hawthorns, orache, and bulrush roots. At this point, tragically for the modern mămăligologist, the manuscript annotation recording the above account of the famine is torn. But what remains of the document tells us that in these dire circumstances, maize was ground and '*mămă...*' (presumably mămăligă) was made.[7] This, then, was clearly famine food. According to another eye witness, the population also had recourse to linseed cake, made from the dregs of an oil press.[8]

When the Habsburgs conquered Oltenia among other territories in the early eighteenth century, mămăligă found its way into the imperial archives. As noted

---

5   Mikes, *Török országi levelek*, 16–17; Mikes, *Letters from Turkey*, 9.
6   On Magyar meanings of *málé* at this time, including maize: Balassa, *A magyar kukorica*, 92–94.
7   Anonymous notes, Braşov 1718, in *Însemnări de demult*, 116.
8   Radu Tempea, *Istoria sfintei beserici a Şcheilor Braşovului*, cited in Andron, 'Calamități naturale', 18.

already, the explorer Friedrich Schwantz was the first of these to mention mămăligă, in a report on Oltenia composed in 1723; but his description of it as cornmeal boiled in water, that can be cut with a knife, can hardly be counted as a recipe.[9]

During the same decade, Viennese officials began to be troubled by reports of vampirism among the Orthodox population inhabiting these borderland territories. These were widely discussed across learned Europe and were proving an international embarrassment.[10] The problem clearly did not go away: reports compiled thirty years later by two of several medical specialists hired by Empress Maria Theresa to bring order to these frontier provinces give a little more detail on the dish. In 1753, Johann Georg Tallar, a German physician who had studied in Strasbourg and Mainz and served as a military surgeon to the Imperial army, including many years of experience in Wallachia and Serbia, was charged with investigating, and establishing rational explanations for, incidences of vampirism in the Banat, specifically in the villages of Klein Dikman and Rakasdia.[11] While mainly concerned with the problem at stake, Tallar's report, drafted and submitted in 1753 but not published until 1784, contains ethnographic information on the life habits of the local Orthodox (Serbian and Romanian) inhabitants, including a description of mămăligă as follows:

> Their bread is a dough of Turkish corn meal mixed with boiling hot water, which they season almost daily with uncooked beans; this turns spontaneously into a self-toughening slime (*glutinosum spontaneum*).[12]

As Peter Mario Kreuter has noted, Tallar's mămăligological interests were a by-product of his official brief, which was to find a material explanation for the vampire apparitions that were so disturbing the peace of Her Majesty's realm. The easiest thing for the doctor to do was to blame the mămăligă.[13]

Tallar was not the only European 'expert' to be deployed on the Habsburg border by the Viennese authorities in this decade. In 1755, another physician in the Empress's service, a Luxemburger by the name of Adam Chenot, was appointed director of the newly-established quarantine at Rothenthurm on Tran-

---

9   Schwantz, 'Kurtze Erklährung und Bericht'.
10 Mézes, *Doubt and Diagnosis*.
11 Today Ticvaniu Mic and Răcășdia, Caraș-Severin county, Romania. On Tallar and the correct dating of his account, see Mézes, 'Georg Tallar'.
12 Tallar, *Visum repertum*, 30.
13 Kreuter, 'Zuckerwerk', 190.

sylvania's southern frontier (today's Turnu Roşu, Romania). Here he wrote a treatise on the plague which appeared in Vienna in 1766. Chenot's thesis—like Tallar's—went beyond its specialist remit and touched upon the living conditions of the Romanians, in a region some hundred and fifty miles further east. According to Chenot,

> The Romanians' diet is for the most part cereal-based. Millet, doused in water and honey, and baked in ashes, serves as their bread; this is sometimes supplemented by a mash, which they prepare by adding cornmeal to boiling salted water, stirring it with a stick, until it becomes more solid and even in consistency, and then mixing it with cheese.[14]

From the 1770s, the lands of southeastern Europe became once again the theatre of war and the object of potential partition between empires; and, partly because of this, the object of increased interest on the part of many other international researchers and officials. This coincided with the expansion of the literary public sphere and a rise in European publications about the region and its peoples. Mămăligă-related information ceased to be the preserve of medical specialists, and appeared in a diverse range of topographical and ethnological reports in various European languages. The dish drew the attention of the Bohemian mineralogist Ignaz von Born, writing from the Banat in June 1770, who called the dish *mălai*;[15] Venetian naturalist Francesco Griselini, writing from the same province a few years later;[16] Florentine antiquary Domenico Sestini, who travelled through Wallachia in 1779–80;[17] Franz Joseph Sulzer, an officer and lawyer of Swiss origin who settled there for a number of years;[18] Austrian agent Ignaz Stefan Raicevich, who reported mămăligă being served with salt, milk, fresh cheese, or even with salted fish, accompanied by wine or grain-based spirits;[19] and French count Alexandre d'Hauterive, an emissary of the French embassy in Istanbul, according to whom

---

14 Chenot, *Tractatus de peste*, 55; Jesner, 'The Physician Adam Chenot'.
15 Born, *Briefe*, 11–12. In the English translation of this work (by Rudolph Raspe, later famous as the author of the *Adventures of Baron Munchausen*), *mălai* is described as a 'bisquet': Born, *Travels*, 15.
16 Griselini, *Lettere odeporiche*, 206; cf. Ehrler, *Banatul*, 53 ('Mamelika'); Steube, *Von Amsterdam nach Temiswar*, 125 ('Sprinza Malai und Raki').
17 Sestini, *Viaggio*, 15–16.
18 Sulzer, *Geschichte*, i:365.
19 Raicevich, *Osservazioni*, 249.

a pot is placed on the fire, and when the water boils, flour is poured in until it dissolves. The paste takes the shape of the vessel, it is eaten hot, and despite not having the appetite of a Romanian, I can testify that it is pretty good.[20]

Galician Johan Budinszky, on the other hand, inspecting the province of Bukovina for the Habsburg government in 1783, reported that mămăligă was usuallly boiled for fifteen minutes and stirred vigorously.[21] From Bucharest in this period there is even a report of 'corn Coffee houses', by no less a personage than British political economist Jeremy Bentham, who passed through the city in 1786 on his way to Russia. Although it is tempting to imagine a type of coffee made from maize being served in these establishments, his reference is more likely to be to a millet-based drink, known locally as *bragă*.[22]

The number of testimonies is itself evidence of the increasing European interest in, or even surveillance of, the human and physical resources of southeastern Europe. Sestini's account is important not only for the details of its preparation, but also for his comments on how the dish was prepared differently by the peasants and by the boyars:

> *Mammaliga* is made in the following manner: water is boiled in a big cauldron or kettle, and then cornmeal is thrown in in proportion to the amount of water, or to the quantity one wants to make, and then it is stirred with a big stick until it becomes consistent, like polenta made with chestnut flour, and this can be kept in the house, and portions cut for one person to eat, and this is called *Mammaliga Kruda*, eaten by the peasants in place of bread. There is also the custom of pressing it, making it hard, and then the people eat it with a little meat or fish; but it is more commonly prepared either with milk, or cheese, with raw onions or garlic, or even with lentils, or beans, and that is all that can be used to prepare it. And it is better when cooked in milk, than in water. But when it is fried in a pan with butter, it is called *Mammaliga Boja-*

---

20 d'Hauterive, *Mémoire sur la Moldavie*, 319.
21 Budinszky, *Die Bukowina*, 30. I am grateful to Philippe Blasen for this reference.
22 Jeremy Bentham, Letter to William Eaton, 9 January 1786, in *Correspondence*, iii:439. *Bragă* is similar to Russian *kvass* and Turkish *boza*; its ubiquity is attested to by the proverbial saying *ieftin ca bragă* ['cheap as *bragă*']. In Bucharest there was a guild of *bragă*-purveyors, known as *bragagii*, with twenty members in 1792 – see their charter in Urechia, *Istoria Românilor*, iv:287–88; viii:669. A decree of 1814 specified that *bragă* was a poor person's drink and that it was made with millet: *Documente București*, 690. In Moldavia it was made with barley or rye: Dudnicenco, 'Băuturile alcoolice', 179.

raska, and is genuinely good, almost like the polenta of the Lombards, prepared in the same way with wheat flour.[23]

The dish seems to have been enjoyed by Transylvanian elites too: in 1787, Johann von Heydendorff, a young nobleman from Hermannstadt visiting Vienna, wrote home to his father that he dined on a meal of mămăligă with milk, to assuage his homesickness.[24]

Von Heydendorff was not the only Transylvanian Saxon mămăligophile to pass through Vienna in the 1780s.[25] In the same decade, Andreas Wolf, a young man from the village of Grossau near Sibiu, travelled to the imperial capital to study medicine. It is typical of the social and geographical mobility of the era that upon graduating, Wolf moved to Moldavia where he served as physician to several princes during the 1780s and 1790s. Some years after returning to Sibiu, he published a two-volume set of 'Contributions towards a Statistical-Historical Description of Moldavia', which is one of the best contemporary accounts of the province. While complaining about the excessively fatty Moldavian diet—which, apparently, 'a German stomach could not easily accommodate'—Wolf spoke warmly of mămăligă, stating that it was rare for a meal to be served without it. He characterized it as 'a very simple peasant dish thousands live off, which any ten- or twelve-year-old could prepare'. But he also testified personally to having enjoyed it at the Prince's table on many occasions, garnished with freshly pressed nut oil and icing sugar. At the Metropolitan bishop's table, however, it was more likely to be served mixed with '*Brense* (a sort of cheese)', and the dish was called '*Mamaliga embrinsite* (Eingekäsete Mamaliga)'.

Wolf's recipes have a cultural meaning beyond the simply picturesque—they almost provide a gastronomic allegory of the balance of power that prevailed in Moldavia, between the Istanbul-appointed prince, with his sugary cosmopolitan tastes, and the cheesier, more down-to-earth bishop, in touch with the habits of his flock.[26] He also gave a detailed description of the peasants' mode of preparation:

> The peasants fill a cauldron or pan quite full with maize meal, pour water over it and add salt. They leave it on the fire to cook well, until it reaches a stronger

---

23 Sestini, *Viaggio*, 15–16.
24 Heydendorff, letter to his father, 7 December 1787, cited by Ittu *et al.*, *Din istoria bucătăriei fine*, 93.
25 Generally on mobility in this period, see Vintilă, *Changing Subjects*.
26 The garnishing of *mămăligă* with sugar was also recorded in 1840s Wallachia by the French doctor Caillat, *Voyage médical*, 23. More on sugar and status: Kreuter, 'Zuckerwerk'; Jianu, '"Taste of Others"', 439–41.

consistency, like bread. They then wrap the vessel in towels, and, holding it between their feet, they stir the mixture with an ell-long stick. When this is done, they put the dish on glowing coals for a few minutes, then take it to the table, where they turn out the mămăligă, which thus bears the form of the vessel. This meal is taken often, hot or cold, in place of bread. Some consume it with freshly milked milk, or with cheese, or pork fat; others cold with plum sauce, or pickled cabbage soup, etc.[27]

Wolf also praised the practicality of mămăligă from the peasants' point of view—it kept them healthy, provided good nutrition without excessive effort, could be used to feed their livestock as well as themselves, and more particularly afforded them some freedom of movement:

> Should they go into the forests and mountains, they need only take a certain quantity of cornmeal, a small cauldron and some salt, and they need not worry about bread or indeed any other foods.[28]

Mentions of mămăligă in Romanian-language sources remain rare. One is to be found in an 1822 petition addressed by a party of Moldavian boyars to the Ottoman Porte, which refers to 'mămăligă from maize which is the common bread of the inhabitants'.[29] There were, on the other hand, many more travellers who passed through the principalities in the early nineteenth century and recorded their impressions of mămăligă in favourable or less favourable terms. Their writings were central to the intertextual coagulation of a coherent mămăligological discourse, so frequently was it described by western observers as 'the principal food of the peasantry'; 'the basis of the people's food in both principalities'; 'the food of the peasantry'; 'the usual food of the people'; 'the usual food of ordinary Wallachians'; 'their ordinary food ... sometimes mixed with milk'; 'the principal food of the inhabitants of the villages of Wallachia', whose victuals 'always consist of maize polenta (called *mămăligă*)'.[30] This was the key period in which mămăligă 'came to the boil' and coalesced in the European imagination. By the middle of the nineteenth cen-

---

27 Wolf, *Beiträge*, i:263–64; also in Kreuter, 'Zuckerwerk', 196–99.
28 Wolf, *Beiträge*, i:38.
29 *Arzmahzar* of the Moldavian boyars, in *Uricariul*, vi, 125; also reproduced by the chronicler Dârzeanu, 'Revoluțiunea', in *Documente 1821*, v:129–34.
30 *Călători străini în sec. XIX*, i: 180, 273, 377, 573, 650 706, 755, 850; also Dalby, "'It is in Truth an Island'", 416.

tury, the association between mămăligă and the Romanian lands was strong enough that when, in Berlin in 1856, the world-famous German explorer and geographer Alexander von Humboldt, by then in his late eighties, met a traveller recently returned from Wallachia, his first question was about mămăligă.[31]

Writing back

The fact that European scholars, doctors, geographers and military men were assiduously canonizing the national cuisine did not go unnoticed in Bucharest. In the words of Wallachian boyar Constantin 'Dinicu' Golescu, writing in 1826,

> Europe is full, as of other things, so of such books. There is no corner of the Earth so overlooked, no country, no city, no village unknown to a single European, so long as he knows how to read. But we, in order to know our country well, have to obtain this knowledge by reading some book written by a European.[32]

There is an awareness of European cultural hegemony here, a mămăligălogical knowledge-colonialism which might correspond to that of the valorization of the material. But Golescu did not see it that way. He recommended—using, significantly, an agrarian metaphor—that Romanians 'should share such knowledge with our compatriots and plant it in our land, in the hope of a hundredfold yield'.[33]

Before setting off on a tour of Europe in 1824, Golescu had himself cultivated and traded in maize across the Habsburg-Ottoman border,[34] as indeed had his father before him.[35] So it is hardly surprising that he took a great interest in the crop during his account of his journey, noticing its presence in numerous localities.[36] Beyond this, Golescu did not write about mămăligă himself. But his call for Wallachians to embrace European forms of knowledge was taken up by contempo-

---

31 Rudolf Neumeister, *Erinnerungen*, cited in Iorga, 'Un martur german', 145.
32 Golescu, *Însemnare*, 4–5; in English as Golescu, 'Learning from Enlightened Europe', 101.
33 Golescu, *Însemnare*, 6; Golescu, 'Learning from Enlightened Europe', 102.
34 *Documente privitoare la economia Țării Romînești*, i:102–3.
35 Radu Golescu selling maize in 1803: *Studii și documente*, viii:130.
36 Golescu notes maize in Transylvania (*Însemnare*, 12, 13, 17), Hungary (27) and Lombardy (132); around Vienna (78) and Munich (176) it is slightly less cultivated; but in Graz it is the most frequent crop (103), as it is around Padua (119) and in the Banat (137). He attributed its introduction in Wallachia to Constantin Mavrocordat (6), an opinon he may have adopted from the Greek historian Dimitris Philippides, given his self-confessed reliance on 'books written by some European'. Cf. Philippides, *Geografikon*, 173.

raries. The Romanian lexicon published at Buda in 1825 glosses mămăligă as '*puls, vel polenta e zea mayis* (Latin), *pulyitzka* (Magyar) or *der Kukuruz-Mehl-Brey, die Mamaliga* (German)'.[37] A topography of Wallachia compiled in Greek by the doctor Constantin Caracaș and published in Bucharest in 1830, offered a description of mămăligă from a medical point of view. While 'quantitatively good', Caracaș wrote, 'it is not sufficiently nutritious to meet the needs of their heavy and forceful labour.'[38] Six years later, Moldavian nobleman Constantin Vârnav did the same in a medical dissertation defended at the University of Buda, in which he described mămăligă as 'the manna of the Romanians' (*manna valachorum*). In some ways, these texts were tributary to the discourse of European writers—Vârnav listed many of them in his quite thorough bibliography, although at the same time he did not hestitate to point out which foreign mămăligologists could be relied on, and which were out of date.[39]

The above account may give the impression that the diet of the inhabitants of Moldavia and Wallachia was 'conquered' by maize by the middle of the nineteenth century. It should, however, be noted that millet and even buckwheat continued to be used to make mămăligă until quite late. Numerous narrative sources attest to this. One traveller in Moldavia at the end of the eighteenth century, Baron von Campenhausen, mentioned mămăligă but also stated that it was improved with the addition of millet, in which case it was called *malay*.[40] In Wallachia, the petty boyar and memoirist Tache Merișescu recalled being served millet-based mămăligă in an out-of-the-way village inhabited by Bulgarians, in around 1810.[41] At a slightly later date, 1835, the Transylvanian traveller Ion Codru-Drăgușanu passed through Wallachia and visited the locality of Călărași, where he briefly took on work as a cook and prepared millet-based mămăligă (*maliga de méiu*).[42] While Baron Campenhausen had asserted that the addition of millet improved the dish, these

---

37 *Lesicon*, 371. This dictionary also offers entries for *malai* and *malata* (370). For modern theories of the origin of the word *mămăligă*, see Appendix.
38 Caracaș, *Topografia Țării Românești* [1828], 112 (πολυντα in the original Greek, 310).
39 Vernav, *Rudimentum physiographiæ Moldaviæ*, 19–20.
40 Campenhausen, *Bemerkungen*, 54. Buckwheat *mămăligă* was also a thing in Moldavia, 'which they also call *mămăligă*, even though it looks nearly black', see Wolf, *Beiträge*, i:36. Orraeus, *Descripio pestis*, 123 says *mămăligă* was made in Iași '*ex aequali proportione farinae tritici & frumenti turcici (Mays dicti)*'. In *Călători străini*, x, part ii, 78, I. Totoiu translates *farina tritici* as millet flour (which might well have been used, but winter wheat flour would be a more literal rendering).
41 Merișescu, *Tinerețile unui ciocoiaș*, 82.
42 Codru Drăgușanu, *Peregrinulu transelvanu*, 6. Codru-Drăgușanu also quotes the following verses: 'Mancare, n'ai cere rara;/ Pane, fia de secara,/ Dar' vai, totu la mamaliga,/ Cá si ieri, de méiu, te striga' (9–10).

Romanian writers classified the millet-based version of the dish as an inferior one, with a 'smell of poverty'.⁴³ But from here we can infer that it was still in relatively widespread use. In a few parts of Wallachia and Dobrogea, principally along the Danube, millet was still cultivated, and mămăligă made from it, around the turn of the twentieth century.⁴⁴

Early Romanian cookbooks

The middle of the nineteenth century was a key period in the Romanian literary nation-building process. This meant, alongside the production of other literary genres, the appearance of the first printed cookbooks in Romanian.⁴⁵ The first and perhaps best-known of these is the book *200 de rețete cercate* (200 Tested Recipes) published by Mihail Kogălniceanu and Constantin Negruzzi in Iași, Moldavia in 1841. Kogălniceanu and Negruzzi reckoned this a 'revolutionary' act: an attempt both to extend the literary language, and to transform local tastes in a European direction, moving away from the traditional 'Oriental' cuisine that had set the tone in the principality.⁴⁶ For this reason, and perhaps because it was considered so easy to prepare that it did not require instructions, there is no mention of mămăligă in this fascinating work, from which readers could otherwise learn how to make *bœuf à la mode* (bou di modă) or innumerable gelatine dishes. In another work, written in French for an international audience, Kogălniceanu affirmed that mămăligă was 'the customary food of the Gypsies', associating it thereby with a different, and—in the eyes of the Romanian elite—inferior ethnic group.⁴⁷

In 1849 a book appeared in Bucharest under the simple title *Carte de bucate* (Cookbook).⁴⁸ Virtually nothing is known about the author, Maria Maurer, except what she tells us in the preface, namely that she had compiled the recipes two years previously, 'for the benefit of my beloved pupils', most probably in a private boarding house. Recent research and a new edition has revealed little more. Maurer's useful

---

43 Vintilă-Ghițulescu, Introduction to Merișescu, *Tinerețile*, 29–30.
44 Giuglea, 'Crâmpeie de limbă', 600; Stratilesco, *From Carpathian to Pindus*, 230 ('Millet is almost out of use now'); Jormescu and Popa-Burcă, *Harta agronomică*, 174–77.
45 General overviews in Cazacu, *Story*; Nagy, 'O scurtă istorie/ A short history'; Nacu, 'Survey'. A bibliography of cookbooks by Burzo, 'Culinaria'.
46 Kogălniceanu and Negruzzi, *200 de rețete cercate*; Notaker, 'Romania'.
47 Kogalnitchan, *Esquisse*, 23: 'la nourriture ordinaire des Cigains consiste dans la mamaliga, qui est une espèce de polenta faite avec du maïs ou blé de Turquie'. Campenhausen, *Bemerkungen über Russland*, 164. From here it made its way into reference works: van Wijk Roelandszoon, *Algemeen aardrijkskundig woordenboek*, vii:1887; Heister, *Ethnographische und geschichtliche Notizen*, 22.
48 Maurer, *Carte de bucate*.

7.1 List of maize given as rations to Roma slaves, Zlătari Monastery, Bucharest 1834

book does however contain a recipe for *mămăliguță cu cașacval*, in fact a kind of oven bake with successive layers of mămăligă, cheese and butter.[49] As the editor remarks, this is highly likely to be a translation of a polenta recipe, although an exact source is hard to identify.[50] Despite this work going through a number of editions, Maurer's *mămăliguță* did not become part of any 'national' repertoire until much later.

One aspect of contemporaneous social analysis which focused particularly on maize came from circles within the country's developing medical profession. In particular, doctors' attention was drawn to the rising incidence of pellagra, a disease now known to be caused by niacin deficiency but then blamed particularly on the monotonous maize-based diet of the peasants. Pellagra had already been signalled by medics in Moldavia from the 1830s to the 1860s; but it was only later that a social discourse on the connection between mămăligă-consumption and pellagra developed strongly.[51] Sociologists and medical experts frequently denounced mămăligă, either as an unhealthy diet, or as a consequence of the highly unequal agrarian-social relations obtaining in independent Romania. Historical justifications for abandoning maize were advanced, including a claim to the effect that Romanian soldiers of medieval times had carried white bread attached to their saddles.[52] Historian Constantin Bărbulescu, in an ample analytical survey of these discourses, has shown clearly how this fitted in with a broader 'social imagology' concerning the peasantry: a negative take on mămăligă was aligned with contemporary ideas such as social Darwinism and anxieties about national degeneration. As Bărbulescu writes, 'mămăligă ceased to be simply a core food item to become a social symbol'.[53]

Curiously, not many anti-mămăligă crusaders actually denied any nutritional value to the mush. Rather, their critique was shaped by their reception of specific international debates, and in some cases by a vision of mămăligă as a malignant product of 'improved agriculture' and modern 'labour organization', in contrast with an imagined past.[54] Noted historian and economist A. D. Xenopol put forward a gradualist approach to the replacement of mămăligă, involving the establishment of communal ovens in villages. These, Xenopol believed, could serve two

---

49 Maurer, *Carte de bucate.*, 53.
50 Lazăr, introduction to Maurer, *Carte de bucate*, 20, adjudges this recipe to be from Piedmont.
51 Andreescu and Rogozea, 'Aetiology Theories'.
52 Based on a remark by Polish chronicler Marcin Bielski, published in Romanian translation in 1865 (Bielski, *Sprawa rycerska*, 164, 168) and widely popularized, for instance by Crăiniceanu, *Igiena țĕranuluĭ român*, 186; Xenopol, *Istoria Românilor*, iv:144.
53 Bărbulescu, *Physicians*, 90–122 (quote at 95). See also idem, '"The Peasant's Food"'.
54 Doctors Istrati and Lupu, cited in Bărbulescu, *Physicians*, 113.

concurrent aims: firstly, they could be used to dry maize, which he believed would mitigate the incidence of pellagra; secondly, they could be used to bake bread and accustom the peasants with a wheat-based diet.[55] As well as campaigns to introduce wheat bread, there was even a minor campaign to replace maize with soya beans in Romania in the years after 1900.[56] Mămăligă nevertheless remained the universal staple food for the vast majority of the population of Romania in the first half of the twentieth century.[57]

The campaign against mămăligă in Old Kingdom Romania bears remarkable similarity to that waged contemporaneously in other dependent countries, such as Mexico, where some social critics derided maize as the food of 'inferior races', while others sought to integrate it into national repertoires. As Rachel Laudan has argued, 'in one modernizing nation after another, factions arose that argued that to compete globally its citizens had to shift to eating wheat bread', and Romania was no exception.[58] Late-nineteenth century officials' disdain for mămăligă and the advocacy for wheat was, then, in synchrony with debates occuring in other parts of the world. But their discourse also echoed earlier ones from the inter-imperial history of the region, if we recall the observations, made already in the eighteenth century, of Habsburg imperial administrators on the diet of the Romanians.[59]

A brief look at some of the representations of mămăligă in periodical literature and popular books towards the end of the nineteenth century reveals its almost exclusively negative connotations: 'You would be hard pressed to deny that the Polynesian or the Hottentot eats better than our peasantry: they may eat raw meat, but it's still better for them than mămăligă with boiled unripe damsons', argued socialist and feminist writer Sofia Nădejde in the review *Contemporanul* in 1884.[60] A sketch from 1888 represents a beleaguered father, unable to earn enough to feed his children on anything better than mămăligă: 'everybody except poverty has forgotten about us', he wails as he hands out portions to his starving offspring.[61] In a satire on 'Peasant Logic' published in the humorous review *Calicul* (The Poor Man) in 1889, a peas-

---

55   Xenopol, *Mijloacele de îndreptare*, 29. The idea of kiln-drying maize had developed in the US in the 1840s, at the time of the Great Famine in Ireland. Communal ovens had been introduced by law in Italy in 1902, and Austria in 1904: for details see Ginnaio, 'Pellagra', 13; Flamm, 'Die Pellagra'.
56   Popovici-Lupa, 'Mijloacele'. On soya: Mihail, *Soia*; Urbeanu, *Importanța soei*; Urbeanu, *Evoluția chestiei soiei*; Urbeanu, *Neoiobăgia și capitalismul*. I am grateful to Andrei Sorescu for telling me about Urbeanu.
57   Scrob, *From Mămăligă to Bread*, 62–70.
58   Laudan, *Cuisine and Empire*, 269, 302; see also Otter, *Diet for a Large Planet*, 48–71.
59   See Chapter 2 above.
60   Nădejde, 'Hrana', 603.
61   Boteanu, 'Din mizeriile vieții', 371.

ant is ridiculed for ordering his wife to make mămăligă with sausage and pickled cabbage, instead of obeying the doctor's dietary instructions—'it doesn't matter if I'm ill for four days rather than three'.[62] An anecdote published in Transylvania in the same year portrays a Romanian and a Saxon sharing a meal, to which the former brings mămăligă and the latter cheese; the Romanian manages to appropriate all the latter's cheese while leaving his own mămăligă uneaten.[63] Elsewhere, mămăligă with dried plums is considered poor food, a way of 'lying to your hunger'.[64] In this period, neighbouring populations referred to Romanians pejoratively with reference to mămăligă, calling them *mămăligari* (mămăligă-eaters) or *mamalyzhniki*.[65]

The above may in part explain why, despite being universally recognized as the main food of the population, mămăligă was not usually codified in the field of cuisine. One exception was a very detailed account of various mămăligopoeic practices in the Moldavian region of Romania, made at the turn of the twentieth century by the teacher and folklorist Mihai Lupescu, and partially published in the review *Șezătoarea* in 1898 under the rubric 'Cuisine of the Romanian peasant'. But a book-length edition of Lupescu's culinary ethnography did not appear untill 2000.[66] Lupescu reports that the term is used fairly loosely, including the possibility of making *mămăligă cu cartofi*, i.e. mashed new potatoes, during the fast before the Feast of the Virgin Mary (31 July-15 August).[67]

Mămăligă is only briefly referenced in early twentieth-century Romanian cookbooks. One very comprehensive work first published in 1902, which went through at least eleven editions, Ecaterina Comșa's *Buna menajeră* (The Good Housekeeper), contains over 1250 recipes, including over a dozen for different types of white bread, but only one containing maize, and not for mămăligă but for a cornmeal cake.[68] Even more encyclopedic was Sanda Marin's *Carte de bucate*, first published in 1936. Marin included nine maize- or mămăligă-related recipes, but this is out of a total of over 1500, and there is no special section or indication distinguishing it as a national food or speciality.[69] The other important work from the inter-

---

62 Anon, 'Logica țăranului' 24.
63 Sima al lui Jón, *Ardeleanul glumeț*, 20.
64 Anon, 'Bucate bune', 602.
65 *Săvremmenik* (1889), cited by Detchev, 'Dress, Food, and Boundaries', 32.
66 Lupescu, 'Bucătăria țăranului: mămăliga'; idem, *Bucătăria țăranului român*, 126–31.
67 Lupescu, *Bucătăria*, 131; cf. Dimitrie Dan, quoted in Giosanu, 'Diete tradiționale', 178.
68 Comșa, *Buna menajeră sau carte de bucate*, 395.
69 Marin, *Carte de bucate*, 254: the nine recipes are for *mămăligă fiartă, mămăligă pripită; urs de mămăligă; mămăligă prăjită, mămăligă cu brânză la cuptor; mămăligă la cuptor; balmuș; mămăligă cu ochiuri*, and *friganele de mămăligă*.

war period, Constantin Bacalbașa's *Dictatura gastronomică* (1935) includes only a few maize recipes in the second edition, as communicated by a correspondent: *alivenci* and *mălaiul*, oven-baked maize cakes with sour milk; and *gir de mălai cu lapte*, all marked as regional Moldavian specialities.[70] Of these interwar classics, Marin's cookbook was in fact adapted in new editions during the Communist period and the repertoire made to fit in with the socialist conceptions of the role of nutrition and gastronomy in a socialist society.[71] The 1971 popularizing book *In the Footsteps of the Renowned Romanian Cuisine* mentions three mămăligă dishes, but in none of them is the reader told how to prepare mămăligă, only how to combine it with other ingredients, such as eggs, cheese, or butter.[72] The same is true of a *Literary-Gastronomic Album* published in 1985.[73] Meanwhile, in works on Romanian gastronomic history, *mămăligă* is almost completely absent.[74]

In striking contrast to the above, a short work in French, published under the title *Les bons plats roumains*, on the occasion of the 1937 Paris World Fair, gave a prominent place to mămăligă. *Les bons plats roumains* came with handsome illustrations by graphic artist Lena Constante, and a preface by Léon Thévénin, a journalist and French-language tutor to the young Prince Michael (later King Michael). Thévénin eulogized the country's 'elegant rusticity, its at once primitive and refined charm' (on the eve, it should be noted, of the country's descent into dictatorship). Unlike in any cookbook aimed at a domestic audience, mămăligă is defined here as 'the national dish, the bread of the Romanian peasant'—and given an ample separate chapter with no fewer than thirty-two recipes. While the majority of these envision mămăligă as an accompaniment to a French-style main course—*mamaliga à l'agneau, mamaliga au ragoût de porc*, and so forth—the prominent place given to mămăligă is in striking contrast to similar Romanian-language publications.[75]

The most detailed cookbook published in recent years, Radu Anton Roman's *Romanian Dishes, Wines and Customs* from 1998, gives slightly more attention to mămăligă than earlier Romanian-language works, offering thirteen recipes and a

---

70 Bacalbașa, *Dictatura gastronomică*, 64–65; recipes credited to D-na Laurenția Bacalbașa, school inspector.
71 Ghita, 'Altering Cooking and Eating Habits'.
72 Ciobanu and Brote, *Pe urmele renumitei bucătării românești*.
73 *Album literar gastronomic*, 102 has a recipe for *mămăligă* with walnuts.
74 Passing mentions in Cazacu, *Story*; none at all in Ulieriu and Popescu, *Trei secole*.
75 Anon, *Les bons plats roumains* (*mămăligă* recipes at 40–44). An English-language version of this book was published in 1939 with the title *Savoury Rumanian Dishes and Choice Wines*, probably on the occasion of the New York World's Fair in 1939 (thanks to Dan Burzo for this reference). It was reissued in 1999 as Anon, *Savory Romanian Dishes*.

greater degreee of ethnographic commentary. However, Roman gives pride of place to bread in his selection of more prominent and culturally important Romanian recipes with which he begins his book. 'Wheat is sacred', writes Roman in the preface, affirming that the majority of Romanian ritual foods, Christian or otherwise, are connected to it. Roman insists also on the sacredness in Romanian rural popular culture of other 'profane' plants such as nettles, wormwood, buds and flowers of willow and apple, vines and lovage; but maize is not among them.[76] However, in a by-now familiar move, the hierarchies are reversed in an abridged English-language edition of this work which appeared in 2008. Here, the mămăligă recipes are placed at the very front of the book, and related proudly to the ancient tradition of the Dacians.[77] This conforms to the general pattern, namely that while mămăligă was neglected in domestic publications, it was codified more frequently and more prominently in works destined for foreign consumption.

The Making of Mămăligă

Cookbooks, although wonderful sources both for attestation of food stuffs and dishes, and for cultural attitudes to them, do not ultimately answer one key question: who actually made the mămăligă? It is often an unwritten assumption that women do the cooking in traditional societies. This is well documented, for example, in the case of the tortilla in central America, where research has shown how much back-breaking women's labour went into the careful preparation of this maize bread.[78] The evidence in Romania is somewhat more equivocal. While many ethnographers follow a convention of ascribing agricultural work to men, and spinning, cooking and household work to women, it is clear that women also worked in the fields, including planting maize, and also that men made mămăligă often.[79] Sometimes this is the result of an implicit use of the traveller's use of 'men' to refer to people, and it is also affected by the fact that they did not have the occasion to observe women at work in the home. Similarly, cookery books were often explicitly

---

76 Roman, *Bucate, vinuri și obiceiuri*, 18, 21. Roman mentions *mălai copt*, *mălai ca la Moldova*, *mălai dospit*, *mălai dulce*, *mălăuți*, *mămăligă cu lapte*, *mămăligă cu magiun*, *mămăligă de cartofi*, *mămăligă pe fructe*, *mămăligă pe pături*, *mămăligă pripită*, *mămăligă umplută*, and *mămăliguță cu brânză și smântână*.
77 Roman, *Romanian dishes*, 7–14: layered *mămăligă*, *mămăligă* with cheese and cream, balmosh, and *mămăligă* dumplings à la Bukowina.
78 Earle, *Body of the Conquistador*, 145.
79 To cite only foreign travel accounts, e.g. Wolf, *Beiträge*, i:36; Caracaș, *Topografia*, 112. Women working the fields: e.g. Lehmann (1782), in *Călători străini*, x, pt. i:559.

addressed to women, as part of a social programme.[80] But this does not mean that they reflect actual real-life practices, particularly of rural society. In sources such as literary memoirs, the making of mămăligă is often ascribed to mothers and aunts, also perhaps as a matter of convention. For example, in a collection of essays on food subjects by leading Romanian intellectuals published in 2012, novelist Mircea Cărtărescu recalls his aunts making mămăligă in his grandfather's home, remembering how it was turned out of the cauldron and cut with string after being left to cool.[81] Similarly, philosopher Gabriel Liiceanu remembers his mother preparing mămăligă mixed with cubes of bread, and also offers a recipe for *alivenci*, a Moldavian sweet cake made with maize, white cheese and eggs, which likewise reminds him of his mother.[82] In Aglaja Veteranyi's novel *Why the Child is Cooking in the Polenta*, the protagonist describes the making of mămăligă as the work of her grandmother.[83] There are counter-examples, however. For instance, cookery writer Irina Georgescu ascribes many food preparation practices to her female relatives, but tells us that the mămăligă-making was her grandfather's task.[84] The question is one of many arising in this book that deserves further research, and we hope a further milling of sources, particularly from ethnography, travel, and social history, will enable us to give a clearer picture.

---

80 E.g. Maurer, *Carte de bucate*; Comșa, *Buna menajeră*.
81 Cărtărescu, 'Mierte fierte', 60–61.
82 Liiceanu, 'De la mămăligă cu pâine', 155, 163–4.
83 Veteranyi, *Why the Child*, 70.
84 I. Georgescu, *Carpathia*, 54.

Chapter 8

'The sparrow dreams of cornmeal, and the idle man of a feast day': Mămăligă as Metaphor

In foreign-language fictional works about Transylvania or Romania, mămăligă features primarily as a marker of local colour. Examples include British popular novelist Anne Manning's *The Interrupted Wedding* (1864);[1] Austrian Leopold von Sacher-Masoch's novella *Basil Hymen* (c. 1875);[2] German Karl Bleibtreu's *Ein Freiheitskampf in Siebenbürgen* (c. 1900);[3] Frenchman Jules Verne's *Le Château des Carpathes* (1892);[4] Queen Elizabeth of Romania's short story 'Vengeance: a narrative of Romanian mores' (published under the pseudonym Carmen Sylva, 1892),[5] and perhaps most famously, Bram Stoker's *Dracula* (1897), where, in the opening pages, narrator Jonathan Harker eats mămăligă for breakfast in Bistriţa, along with paprika and stuffed eggplant, and makes a note to himself to try to obtain a recipe.[6] Whether he succeeded is never revealed, and for a reason. In *Dracula*, as in all these works, mămăligă is a scene-setting note, rather than a protagonist or cliffhanging element central to the narrative.

In neighbouring Hungary, maize serves as the name of an 'everyman' character in a classic work of national literature, Kukorica Jancsi ('Johnny Corn'), protagonist of the epic poem *János Vitéz* (John the Valiant) by the famous poet Sándor Petőfi.

---

1   Manning, *Interrupted Wedding*, 101, 187.
2   von Sacher-Masoch, *Basil Hymen*, 7. For Sacher-Masoch, mămăligă is a Ruthenian speciality ('die Polenta der Kleinrussen').
3   Bleibtreu, *Ein Freiheitskampf in Siebenbürgen*, 20, 37, 175, 245–46.
4   Verne, *Le château des Carpathes*, Chapter 4.
5   Carmen Sylva, 'Vengeance', 864.
6   Stoker, *Dracula*, Chapter 1.

CHAPTER 8

János is nicknamed Johnny Corn because he was found abandoned in a maize field as an infant. From here he goes on to have a whole series of gallant adventures, which served as a symbol of Hungarian national bravery in schoolbooks and popular representations in the nineteenth and twentieth centuries.[7] Other maize-growing countries around the world have codified the plant in literary representations: a prominent example is Nobel Prize-winning Guatemalan novelist Miguel Ángel Asturias's modernist masterpiece *Hombres del maíz* (Men of Maize, 1949). But in Romania, there is no such equivalent figure. The story of maize and mămăligă in the country's literature, culture and art is more one of absence than of presence.

One splendid early exception is to be found in the work of Transylvanian writer Ion Budai-Deleanu. Around 1800, Budai-Deleanu, who worked as a Habsburg functionary in Lemberg (today L'viv, Ukraine), composed a mock-epic historical poem *Țiganiada* (The Gypsiad), a fictional rendition of the fortunes of a band of Roma Gypsies in the armies of medieval Wallachian ruler Vlad the Impaler. In this poem, mămăligă is noted several times as a characteristic food of the Roma: Vlad is portrayed as supplying his troops with 'many hundreds of baskets of flour, for mămăligă at lunch and dinner'.[8] When in their camp, the Roma enjoy larded mămăligă (*mămăligă cu untură*).[9] One character dreams of entering the gates of heaven, where he finds

> Rivers of sweet milk down dale,
> And streams of butter flowing by,
> Their banks are of soft mămăligă,
> Baked loaves, flatbreads and *mălai*.[10]

While Budai-Deleanu was surely aware that the carbohydrate-rich riverbanks of his fifteenth-century Wallachian dreamworld could not have been banks of maize, his repeated invocation of the dish was probably also influenced by the time in which he wrote. As Andrei Oișteanu has noted, in this work mămăligă represents a poor person's plenty or even their vision of paradise—a veritable mămăligotopia.[11]

---

7 Petőfi, *János Vitéz*. Many thanks to Zsuzsanna Varga for telling me about Kukorica Jancsi.
8 Budai-Deleanu, *Țiganiada* [A], in idem, *Opere* ii:33.
9 Budai-Deleanu, *Țiganiada* [A], in idem, *Opere* ii:242.
10 'Rîuri dă lapte dulce pă vale / Curg acolo și dă unt păraie, / Țărmuri-s dă mămăligă moale, / Dă pogăci, dă pite și mălaie': Budai-Deleanu, *Țiganiada* [B], in idem, *Opere* i:252.
11 Oișteanu, *Moravuri și năravuri*, 39; see also Cornea, 'Le paradis des affamés'. On mămăligă in Romanian folktales, see Cioancă, 'Pentru o poetică a imaginarului'

Budai-Deleanu also drafted a shorter mock epic, *Trei viteji* (Three Cavaliers), which features a Kir Kalos Cucureaza ('Good Sir Cucureaza'), a Greek parvenu, originally a seller of pastries and salt fish in Istanbul, who has risen to boyar rank in Wallachia.[12] Another character in *Trei viteji*, Mişca, who manages despite his low birth to join the ranks of the nobility, displays his pride and sense of rank by affirming that 'I have no inborn inclination for *mălai* or mămăligă; my taste is rather for cakes'.[13] Budai-Deleanu's mock-epics remained unpublished until the late nineteenth century, and had no influence on the emerging Romanian national literary tradition.

Throughout the nineteenth century, references in formal literary works in Romanian national literature are generally incidental. Mămăligă makes walk-on appearances in texts set in the countryside such as Ioan Slavici's 'Gura Satului' (Village Talk, 1878), Ion Creangă's *Amintiri din copilărie* (Memories of Childhood, 1881), or Sofia Nădejde's 'Vieaţa la ţară' (Life in the Country, 1886) but it is in no way central to the representation of rural life in these literary classics.[14] In Duiliu Zamfirescu's *Viaţa la ţară* (Life in the Country, 1894), a serialized panorama of rural life in this period, mămăligă is mentioned only as a dish that the children of the noble protagonists are taught by their Scottish governess to avoid.[15] Similarly, independent Romania's most renowned landscape painter, Nicolae Grigorescu (1838–1907) painted peasants, oxen, geese, shepherds, haystacks and many other aspects of rural life; but neither maize nor mămăligă is represented in his œuvre. The portraitist Theodor Aman (1831–1891), whose father was a noted maize-trader from the region of Oltenia, produced a small oil painting of 'Gypsy women preparing mămăligă', thus associating the dish with another ethnic group than the Romanians. The work, unsigned and undated, is not generally considered part of the Romanian visual canon and appears never to have been subject to critical discussion.[16] The same is true of an engraving portraying a 'mămăligă gathering' (Fig 8.1). In general, the absence of staples or export crops from the visual artistic repertoire is perhaps a feature of regimes of representation in colonial or semi-colonial lands.[17]

---

12 Budai-Deleanu, *Trei viteji*, in idem, *Opere*, ii:271. 'Kir Kalos' means 'Sir Good' in Greek, but is a pun on Romanian *cârcălos*, 'messy, dirty'.
13 Budai-Deleanu, *Trei viteji*, in idem, *Opere*, ii:272: 'în mine nu sîmţ, nice spre mălaiu,/ Nici spre mămăligă, eu nice-o plăcere/ Însă gura mea tot plăcintă cere'.
14 Slavici, 'Gura satului', 120–3; Creangă, *Amintiri din copilărie*, 29, 31, 55, 58, 68; Nădejde, 'Schiţe din vieaţa la ţară', 299, 301.
15 Nacu, 'Survey', 88.
16 Aman, 'Ţigăncuşi la mămăligă'.
17 Cf. Ireland, where 'despite the ubiquity of corn production in large areas of the Irish landscape, there are no surviving Irish paintings that foreground this – it did not meet the expectations of the Irish colonial stereotype': Dunne, 'Auto-Exoticism and the Irish Colonial Landscape'.

CHAPTER 8

Mămăligă was nevertheless eaten by King Carol I on an official trip to Moldavia to officiate the inauguration of a statue of the medieval prince Stephen the Great in Iași, in 1883.[18] It was also included as a characteristic Romanian dish in the 'Cabaret Roumain' set up at the World Exhibition in Paris in 1889.[19]

Good writers know how to make small details count, and a reference to mămăligă in an early Romanian historical novel from the time of independence is worth mentioning. Bucharest-based writer Nicolae Filimon's *Ciocoii vechi și noi* (Upstarts Old and New), published in 1863, but set fifty years earlier, in 1814, during the last years of the so-called Phanariot regime, tells the story of Dinu Păturică, a typical Wallachian social climber from the period, who starts his career as pipe-bearer to a Phanariot boyar but manages to rise to a higher position by exploiting the favours of his master's mistress, Duduca. When his master sends him on a mission to inspect his rural estates, Dinu is threatened by a group of bandits. But through the intervention of one of his entourage, he is persuaded to sit down to eat lamb, 'spit-roasted bandit-style' with his potential attackers in the open countryside, a dish 'that would outdo any kebabs prepared at the Prince's table'. Among the accompaniments to this initially intimidating but ultimately sumptuous repast, with which the upstart Dinu seems to be completely unfamiliar, the bandits serve onions, boiled eggs, fresh butter, wine from Cernătești, and mămăligă. It is telling that, in this feast so vividly invoked by Filimon, mămăligă is considered characteristic bandit food. In reality, as we have seen, the Phanariot princely courts had been no stranger to mămăligă—but a

8.1 Theodor Aman, Mămăligă Gathering, c. 1870

---

18 *Curierul*, 19 June/1 July 1883, repr. in Papuc, 'Inaugurarea statuii', 276–77. King Carol did not eat mămăligă in the Moldavian capital, but in a pavilion erected to accommodate his visit to Mount Stănișoara, Neamț county, on his return trip from the inauguration. It was served by shepherds at an altitude of 1480 metres. A piece of the mămăligă was preserved at *Curierul*'s editorial office in Iași.
19 Minea, 'Roma Musicians, Folk Art and Traditional Food', 165.

writer from the middle of the nineteenth century is already inscribing it as the food of the outsider.[20]

The most explicit thematization of maize in nineteenth-century literature comes not in a work published at the time but in a tale composed by the author Ion Creangă, entitled *Povestea pulei* (The Tale of the Cock) or *Povestea poveștilor* (The Tale of Tales). In this story, which was read to a meeting of the Iași-based *Junimea* (Youth) literary society in 1876 but not published until 1939, a peasant Ion is sowing maize in his field when he is accosted by St. Peter, who asks him what he is sowing. When the foul-mouthed peasant abusively replies that he is sowing cocks, the Saint sees to it that the maize plants bear forth not ears of corn but large, bulging and rosy penises. An old woman arrives on the scene. When the peasant explains his predicament ('how am I to swallow cocks instead of corn?') the woman is at first shocked, but then advises him, in return for a portion of cocks, to bring them to market and sell them. Her strategy comes good and the peasant successfully sells some of his phallic surplus to a widowed gentlewoman. The gentlewoman, who unlike the peasant never swears but nevertheless wants the cocks, pays a large sum for them, justifying the purchase to herself on hearing from the peasant that they are a creation of St. Peter. She keeps it in a silver box lined with cotton and sprinkled with aromatic essences, in the manner of a holy relic, 'something good for one's old age'. Creangă's tale is usually treated as a dirty curiosity of Romanian literature. But it has more anthropological interest for our topic. Besides being one of the few explicit treatments of the sexuality of maize in Romanian culture, *The Story of the Cock* further illustrates the theme of maize's liminality, its position on the boundary between the acceptable and the unacceptable, the desirable and the unspeakable, the profane and the sacred. Being unpublished, Creangă's tale did not circulate widely until recently, and seems to have found few imitators, at least in terms of the eroticization or sacralization of maize in cultural representations.[21] A recent Romanian erotic fiction website draws inspiration from Creangă but makes no mention of maize or mămăligă beyond the intriguing title.[22]

There are a limited number of representations of maize and mămăligă in Romanian artworks of the early twentieth century. In 1905, the state distribution of imported maize to the peasantry formed the subject of a dramatic work, *La împărțitul porumbului* (At the Distribution of Maize) by the neo-Impressionist

---

20 Filimon, *Ciocoii vechi și noi*, 100.
21 Creangă, 'Povestea poveștilor'; in English as Creangă, 'The Tale of the Prick'. On the erotics of maize see especially Fussell, *Story of Corn*, 26.
22 *Mămăliga erotica*.

Ştefan Luchian, which was exhibited in Bucharest in 1905, and was the subject of some controversy, even if maize itself is not represented on the canvas.[23] Also controversial were Iaşi-based artist Octav Băncilă's *Cules de porumb* (Harvesting Maize) and *Pânea noastră cea de toate zilele* (Our Daily Bread), both exhibited in Bucharest in 1914,[24] and described by one reviewer as representing 'an almost brutal realism'.[25] Visiting the exhibition, Interior Minister Vasile Morţun—a former socialist who had defected to the Liberal Party—allegedly told Băncilă that the piece of mămăligă represented in the painting was too large, to which the artist replied that he would make it smaller, in order to represent the true (insufficient) size of the peasant's diet.[26] In 1915, Camil Ressu painted a *Prânz pe câmp* (Field Lunch, 1915), where a mămăligă cauldron figures, but not mămăligă itself.[27] But these are rare exceptions.

In several countries and states around the world—for example, Mozambique, or Philadelphia—maize features prominently in offical heraldry or other symbolic imagery. But in Romania this is not the case. On the official emblem of the Romanian Socialist Republic, for example, there were ears of wheat, alluding to the country's agricultural productivity, but not of maize. Likewise, wheat appears on numerous county shields in Romania—for example, those of Bihor, Călăraşi, Cluj, Dolj, Neamţ, Olt, Satu Mare and Teleorman counties—but maize is absent from them all, featuring only on the shields of a small number of rural communes.[28] This may be partly an effect of the international tradition, in both capitalist and socialist countries, of using sheaves of wheat in heraldry, but is nevertheless telling. In short, while maize and mămăligă served as a national symbol abroad, it became 'othered' or even erased from domestic visual repertoires.

În the absence of more developed literary or visual representations, folklore is an important repository for information about cultural attitudes. The most comprehensive collection of Romanian proverbs dates from the end of the nineteenth century; but its compiler, Iuliu Zanne, incorporated material from the earlier col-

---

23 Jianu, 'Polenta or Mămăligă?', 33.
24 Băncilă, 'Cules de porumb'; idem, 'Pâinea noastra cea de toate zilele'. The originals of these paintings are, sadly, untraceable.
25 Pora, 'Mişcarea artistică', 178.
26 Comarnescu, *Octav Băncilă*, 25–26.
27 Enescu, *Camil Ressu*, 48 (fig. 24).
28 The 'Maize in Heraldry' Wikipedia page lists it on the shields of the following twelve communes: Călăraşi (Botoşani County); Criciova (Timiş); Dragoş Vodă (Călăraşi); Durneşti (Botoşani); Fărăgău (Mureş); Frumoasa (Teleorman); Jegalia (Călăraşi); Peregu Mare (Arad); Rădulești (Ialomiţa); Simnicea (Suceava); Văleni (Olt); Vurpăr (Sibiu).

lections of Iordache Golescu (brother of the aforementioned Constantin), assembled already in the 1840s.[29] From here a remarkably clear division emerges between the image of *mălai*—which nearly always signifies plenty; and mămăligă, which is frequently invoked in derision or shame.

Thus it is said that 'A man's friends are a bag full of money and a sack full of *mălai*' (*prietenul omului este punga cu banii și sacul cu mălaiul*); 'woe to him who has no *mălai*' (*vai, vai de cine n'are mălai*); 'when you have *mălai*, there's no salt' (*când mălai are, sare n'are*, i.e. you'll never have everything at once); 'he says the *mălai* isn't cooked, yet he gobbles at least eight' (*cică mălaiu nu-i copt și el înfulică cât opt*, of an unappreciative yet gluttonous person); 'your *mălai* will be cooking till St. Nicholas's Day' (*coace-te mălai până la Sf. Nicolae*), when you wait on someone who will never deliver; 'it's not the one who eats seven *mălai* cakes that's crazy, but the one who gives them out' (*nu-i nebun cel ce mănâncă șapte mălaie, ci cel ce i le dă*, of someone who goes broke out of excessive generosity), 'to cut a slice of *mălai* into eight' (*a tăia un fir de mălai în opt*, of a cheese-parer). If it rains in May, you'll have *mălai* (*plouă în mai, ai mălai*), while 'the sparrow dreams of *mălai* and the lazy man of the Feast Day' (*vrabia mălai visează și leneșul praznic*). *Mălai* continues to mean life or basic resources even at the end: 'they've lived their life, they've consumed their *mălai*' (*și-a trăit traiul, și-a mâncat mălaiul*); or 'the *mălai*'s getting close to the (bottom of the) knapsack' (*a apropiat mălaiul de traista*), i.e. the money's running out). While neighbouring peoples referred to Romanian *mălai* as to a bad thing,[30] for the Romanians themselves it had relatively positive connotations.

The proverbial history of mămăligă, on the other hand, offers a completely different register. If 'you don't yet know how to eat mămăligă' (*a nu știe încă cum se mănâncă mămăliga*), you are a total beginner; if 'you're good for cutting the mămăligă with' (*bun de tăiat mămăliga*), you're not much good, given that mămăligă can be cut with more or less anything. He who spends more than he earns doesn't even have mămăligă (*cine cheltuiește peste ce câștigă/n'are în casă nici mămăligă*); if you don't have anything at all, you 'looked in the bottom of the sack and all you saw was the mămăligă string' (*mă uitai în fundul pungii/văzui ața mămăligii*). If 'the mămăligă has developed a crust' (*a prins mămăliga coajă*) you have developed airs above your station; a 'raw mămăligă' (*o mămăligă crudă*)

---

29 *Proverbele românilor*, iii:597–61, studied well already by Savin, 'Pentru un studiu lingvistic'; Savin, *Romanian Phraseological Dictionary*, 36–40, 40–45; and Scherf, '"Die Sprache bittet zu Tisch"', 124–25, to which I add some additional sources from *DLR* and other reference works.
30 E.g. Hungarian *Olyan mint az oláh málé* (It's like Romanian mălai), of a bad thing: *Proverbele românilor*, vi:280.

is said of a worthless person; if 'you put it [the fire] on for mămăligă (*a o pune de mămăligă*), you're in a difficult situation; if you're left with the mămăligă string (*ai rămas cu ața de mămăligă*), you've been embarrassed, swindled or made a fool of, in which case you might choose to 'swallow your shame along with mămăligă' (*și-a mâncat rușinea cu mămăligă*). To 'make mămăligă out of somebody' (*a o face pe cineva mămăligă*) is to beat them to a pulp;[31] a lazy or coarse person is a *mămăligar* or *mămăligău* (f. *mămăligăriță*; adj. *mămăligos/-oasă*). It is said of a drunkard that 'his bread doesn't rise in the oven; he makes *mămăliga* in a pot, and eats it bare' (*Bărbatului băutor / nu-i coace pita-n cuptor; / Îi face măliga în oală / și-aceea o mănâncă goală*). It's better to eat bread and salt, and look at the sun, than to eat mămăligă with butter and look at the ground (*Decât să mănânc mămăliga cu unt / și să mă uit în pământ / Mai bine să mănânc pâine cu sare / și să mă uit la soare*). If 'the mămăligă is swelling' (*se îngroasă mămăliga*), the plot is not just thickening, but it is doing so for the worse. Nevertheless, disdain for *mămăliga* should not be total: 'he who spends more than he earns, doesn't even have mămăligă in the house' (*Cine cheltuiește peste ceea ce câștigă / N'are 'n casă nici mămăligă*).[32] But 'don't tread *mămăliga* underfoot, or it will hit you in the stomach' (*nu călca mămăliga în picoare mă, că te-a bate la pîntece*).[33] There is no longing that hits you like the longing for mămăligă (*Ca dor de mămăligă, nici un dor nu te strică*).

The *mălai/mămăligă* dichotomy is perhaps most colourfully illustrated in an early twentieth-century Roma ballad, collected in Hunedoara country by the folklorist Sabin Drăgoi, and published in 1925. In this story, Sir Hot Mălai and Lady Mămăligă travel in a carriage, over Pastry-Bake Hill and Doughnut Dale. They are leaving a 'bad country', where mămăligă is cooked in a pot and stirred with a poker, and entering a 'good country' (their own), in which it is baked in the oven and garnished with whey and butter:

Pe dealul plăcinteloru,	On Pastry-Bake Hill,
Pe valea scoverzeloru	Down Doughnut Dale
Merge domnul mălaiu caldu	Go Sir Hot Mălai
Și cu doamna mămăligă,	And Lady Mămăligă

---

31 I'll make mămăligă out of you [*Am să fac cu tine mămăligă*]': Speranță, 'Povestea poveștilor', 445.
32 Hințescu, *Proverbele românilorŭ*, 31.
33 Lupescu, 'Mămăliga', 3.

> | Amîndoi într'o teligă. | Together in a carriage.
> | — "Unde mergi tu mălai caldu? | — Where are you going, Hot Mălai?
> | "Și cu doamna mămăligă, | And Lady Mămăligă
> | "Amîndoi într'o teligă?" | Together in a carriage?
>
> | — "Eu mă duc în țara mea | — I'm going to my own country
> | "Că asta-i o țară rea, | For this is a bad country,
> | "Că mă bagă în spuzaiu | Where they throw me on hot embers
> | "Și mă bate cu vătraiu; | And thrash me with a poker;
> | "Dar țara mea-i țară bună, | But my country is a good country
> | "Că mă bagă în cuptoru | For they put me in the oven
> | "Și-mi stă pita 'ntr'ajutor. | And the bread-loaf is my ally.
> | "Din cuptor cînd mă scotea, | When they take me from the oven,
> | "Tot prin zară mă trîntea, | They wallop me in whey
> | "Cu untul mă netezea. | And burnish me with butter.
>
> | Pană stă mălaiu 'n spuză, | As the maize-cake cooks on the coals,
> | Opt copii se ling pe buze, | Eight children lick their lips,
> | Unii cu ochii beliți | Some with eyes a-popping
> | Alții cu dinții rănjiți | Others with teeth a-gnashing
> | Vai de mine tu mă'nghiț".[34] | Woe is me, you'll swallow me whole.

The battle between a 'bad country', where mămăligă is fired on embers and thrashed with a poker, and a 'good country', where it is baked in the oven and garnished with dairy products, is, as in earlier sources, not just picturesque. It documents an implicit cultural, and—given that this is a Roma ballad—possibly even racial hierarchy. Mămăligă stands, not for the first time, on the border between two social realms.

In Romanian folktales too, mămăligă is sometimes codified as a Roma particularity. Such tales often begin with a 'once upon a time' formula, and in one such tale, the action is set in the time 'when the Gypsy was eating mămăligă with butter

---

[34] Drăgoi, *303 colinde*, 189–90). The motif of *mălai* or *mămăligă* running away over hill and dale dates at least from the 1870s (Crăiniceanu, *Igiena țeranului*, 233 n.1), while the characters Domnul Mălai Cald and Doamna Mămăligă appear in songs noted in Arad county in the 1890s (Alexici, *Texte*, 118–20); and in Bihor county in the 1910s (Bartók, *Cântece poporale românești*, cited by Giosanu, 'Diete tradiționale', 181 n39).

and licking his fingers until he picked up his tongs' (*când mânca țiganul mămăliga cu unt de-și lingea degetele pân-apuca cleștele*), signalling his traditional profession as a blacksmith. As Cioancă remarks, while such a figure of speech invokes an ahistorical, legendary time, it also references real social conditions—the time between eating and working is impossibly short.[35] In other folktales, Roma fortune-tellers ask for 'a pot of cabbage or a piece of mămăligă' in payment for their services. The heroes of such tales also sometimes eat mămăligă, with wine, cheese, cream, lentil gravy, onions or other accompaniments.[36]

The theme of mămăligă as a potentially stigmatic or dangerous dish on social and ethnic boundaries is also central to one of the few contemporary works of fiction to give it prominence, the 1999 novel by Swiss-Romanian writer Aglaja Veteranyi, *Warum die Kind in der Polenta kocht* (Why the Child is Cooking in the Polenta), which won several prizes in Germany and was translated into at least a dozen languages. The story is narrated from the point of view of an (unnamed) child, in prose that is grammatically simple but complexly allusive in its imagery. Part of an emigrant family of mixed Romanian and Roma ethnicity working as circus performers, the child narrator describes life on the road and in hotels in 'a foreign country', recognizable as Switzerland, and the tensions between her parents, who display signs both of brutality and tenderness, as they eventually split up and find different partners: they achieve respectability but not happiness. Her experiences are rendered in plain and often visceral metaphors. Food is a particularly strong signifier in the book and to the narrator, 'my mother's cooking smells the same everywhere in the world, but it tastes different in foreign countries because of the melancholy'.[37] The image of the child cooking in the polenta may represent an answer to the questions the narrator poses about the violence inherent in her condition as a human being living on multiple borders: between daughter and father, between childhood and adulthood, between poverty and respectability, between Roma and Romanian ethnicity, between Romania and abroad.

---

35   Cioancă, 'Pentru o poetică a imaginarului', 65.
36   Cioancă, 'Pentru o poetică a imaginarului', 67, 72.
37   Veteranyi, *Why the Child*, 10.

Conclusion
The Land is Waiting

When maize first reached southeastern Europe, a century or so after it first crossed the Atlantic, the region was already a 'crossroads of Empire'. We find mămăligă in relatively out-of-the-way locations, in sources which are very frequently about something else. There is little or no evidence either that the plant came from Ottoman centres of power, or that the making of mămăligă resulted from any government policy or princely decree. Establishing exactly when or how it arrived is a near impossible task. But when princes, chroniclers and legislative bodies first noticed maize at the end of the seventeenth century, and started to tax it or regulate its cultivation, it must already have been widespread.

The 'imperial tectonics' of maize became even more evident in the eighteenth century. This was a period both of continued conflict and of increased economic competition between Habsburgs, Ottomans and Russians. Representatives of all three of these empires took an interest in the material resources of these lands. They also all displayed a disdainful attitude towards maize, and took little interest in encouraging its cultivation. In particular, the Habsburgs' conquest of Hungary and Transylvania, and their brief but significant period of rule over Little Wallachia (1718–1739), were of huge importance for the subsequent course of the region's history. But although this led to some of the earliest documentation of mămăligă, Habsburg influence on maize cultivation was initially in a negative direction. Just as in the Ottoman case, imperial disdain for the crop may have encouraged its increased use. In Moldavia and Wallachia, meanwhile, the initiative almost certainly lay with the local inhabitants. Maize continued to be the preserve of people of modest social status, but soon began to be cultivated on boyar and monastery lands in increasingly large quantities.

During the last years of the eighteenth century, elites clearly became increasingly aware of maize's uses and economic value, and it played a role in the rise of noted boyar clans, who went on to become major figures in modern Romanian political history. The governments of Moldavia and Wallachia developed a more regular bureaucratic and fiscal apparatus and began 'policing' maize in a way that they had not done before. The plant came to the attention of authorities whether they liked it or not: in some respects, it was maize that gave rise to policy rather than the other way around. Around 1800, imperial governments began to understand its importance at moments of crisis such as war and famine. In this process they became dependent on local actors, who, partly as a result of their familiarity with local conditions, gained the capital and authority both to change their lifestyle and accumulate further power over land and peasants. We can also speculate on the relationship between maize cultivation, sedentarization and population growth, as well as between maize and the intensification of peasant labour dues.

After the revolt of 1821, in which maize played a very significant role, the principalities of Moldavia and Wallachia were reorganized on modern, quasi-liberal and quasi-capitalist principles. Territorial frontiers were secured, feudal property rights confirmed, arable cultivation expanded significantly, and goods made open to export. The switch to export capitalism did not take place overnight, but was part of a gradual process over several decades. At least up until their unification in 1859, the principalities continued to trade mainly with the Habsburg and Ottoman empires. International crises and wars, particularly the Great Famine in Ireland and the Crimean War, had a significant impact on west European and especially British economic engagement with the region. During the late nineteenth century, there was considerable development of export infrastructure in the form of railways, ports and roads. But techniques of agricultural production changed to a much lesser extent.

The story of Romania is a story of political independence, but also of economic dependency, and maize was very relevant to this process. In this period, cereal cultivation and export came to completely dominate the Romanian landscape and economy to an extent that it had not done before. This led to the peasant uprisings of 1888 and 1907, the latter of which was the largest single act of peacetime violence in the country's modern history.

While avoiding a mămăligocentric approach, my interpretation seeks to highlight several features of the role of maize in triggering the revolts. These include analysis of the distribution of maize cultivation and the effect of crop failures; the importance of the hated 'maize tax' introduced by the government in 1905; and, during the revolt, the propensity to burn maize as a form of symbolic protest. All of these conjunctures have been previously known. But analysing them together and in greater detail than before shows partly cyclical, partly conjunctural, and partly symbolic explanations, all in close relation to maize.

Some elements of the overall agrarian development of Romanian lands in the eighteenth and nineteenth centuries bear comparison with broader global processes. Seven decades ago, in what is still one of the few explicit attempts to discuss maize and colonialism in the region in the form of a historical typology, Traian Stoianovich outlined a scenario wherein independent notables coerced declining pastoral communities into agricultural work, resulting in the spread and commercialization of this crop in the southern Balkans. Unusually but provocatively, Stoianovich suggested maize and cotton as the characteristically colonial crops of the late Ottoman Balkans.[1]

While initially offering the prospect of freedom, maize, like other staple cereals elsewhere in the proto-industrializing world, came to exercise a tyranny over the people who came to depend on it.[2] More recent work in global environmental history has stressed the importance of the development of large-scale plantation cultures across different continents during the period that this book covers. Judith Carney, for example, has called this 'a watershed event in human-mediated history', and that 'emphasis on large-scale cultivation of a single exotic crop coupled with reliance on enslaved labor distinguishes the plantation as an epochal transformative institution.'[3] The subject is not widely discussed in Romania today, and almost never with a specific focus on maize. However, comparison of Romanian economic development with that of other countries around the world is not a recent academic trend, but was undertaken by members of the local elite themselves in the nineteenth century. In 1875, for example, the famous Romanian writer Vasile Alecsandri wrote that the great landowners of Moldavia—of whom he was one, so he knew what he was talking about—'resemble the colonists of Australia'.[4] Similarly, in 1893, an author on agrarian matters considered that Romania's landowning elites

---

1 Stoianovich, 'Land Tenure', 405–6. Also on the level of suggestion: Boomgaard and 't Hart, 'Globalization', 16; Kaller-Dietrich, 'Mais', 19.
2 Parker, *Global Crisis*, 19.
3 Carney, 'Subsistence in the Plantationocene'.
4 Alecsandri, Letter to his daughter, 1875, in Vulcănescu, *București – Paris*, 46, citing Bogdan, *Autrefois et aujourd'hui*, 119. On discourses of colonization in nineteenth-century Romania, see Sorescu, *Visions of Agency*, 56–109.

'have the same disdain for the peasantry as the Europeans for the Congolese'.[5] And an American doctoral student writing in the 1970s concluded that Romania

> was specializing in cereal production just as Cuba was concentrating on sugar production, Malaya on rubber, Columbia on coffee, West Africa on cocoa, and Western Europe on manufactured goods. In essence, Rumania... had become an economic colony of the advanced parts of Western Europe as a result of the international division of labor.[6]

Similarities undoubtedly existed between the development of maize cultivation in Romania and the scenarios invoked by these authors. To think about the spread of mămăligă as the archetypal food of the people of Romania and the Balkans in relation to more global processes is not to demean the particularities of the local dish, still less to put readers of this book off their food. Rather, it can help us understand its logic better. After all, mămăligă was eaten not just in Carpathian valleys and Danubian plains, but also on the slave plantations of Maryland, as Frederick Douglass vividly recounted.[7]

However, it is the historian's task to attend not only to similarities when making comparisons, but also to differences, as no two scenarios ever unfold in the same way,[8] and the transplantation of historiographical models from the Atlantic onto the Balkans may even itself be an act of intellectual colonialism if it is undertaken without a proper understanding of the workings of the societies to which they are applied. What happened on the lower Danube was, I hope to have shown, *both* similar *and* different. To give just one example of difference, plantations as developed by Europeans in the Americas involved settlement of territory, importation of crops and enslaved labourers as a wholesale operation. While in Moldavia and Wallachia some elements of all these phenomena are present, they unfolded in quite different ways.

Paradoxically, it was the gradual emancipation and unification of Wallachia and Moldavia into an independent and territorialized state which led to the large-

---

5   Filotti, *Chestia agrară* (1893), 65, quoted by Wood, *Agrarian Problem*, 65.
6   Tucker, *Rumanian Peasant Revolt*, 70.
7   'We were not regularly allowanced. Our food was coarse corn meal boiled. This was called *mush*. It was put into a large wooden tray or trough, and set down upon the ground. The children were then called, like so many pigs, and like so many pigs they would come and devour the mush; some with oyster-shells, others with pieces of shingle, some with naked hands, and none with spoons. He that ate fastest got most; he that was strongest secured the best place; and few left the trough satisfied.' Douglass, *Narrative*, 27.
8   Bloch, *L'étrange défaite*, 150; cf. Bloch, *Apologie pour l'histoire*, 13.

scale extension of maize cultivation using labour which was nominally free but practically enserfed. Taken as a whole, the new state's agrarian economy can be described as a monoculture, given the extent to which the country's territory was increasingly given over to cereal farming, which came to constitute over ninety percent of overall agricultural production in the country. According to one scholar, Romania was 'a paradigmatic example of a monocultural, grain-exporting, world-market-oriented, population-impoverishing state'.[9] But maize, unlike its main rival, wheat, served a roughly equal task of feeding the population and providing a cash product for exportation. The zoning of produce in the period before and after Romanian independence was part and parcel of the country's integration into new imperial networks of extraction of raw materials.[10] The size and location of the country, and the global changes in directions of trade and population in the late nineteenth century, placed Romania in an increasingly disadvantageous position globally.

The making of mămăligă did not of course come to an end in 1907. Despite the pessimism of early twentieth-century medics and social analysts who at times sought to blame all the country's misfortunes on it, maize continued to be a dominant crop throughout the twentieth century, and mămăligă the standard food of the majority of the population.[11] In the 1970s, in terms of production in proportion to surface area, Romania was still the maiziest country in the world, just as it had been at the beginning of the century.[12] To trace the place of maize through twentieth-century Romania—from the Great Union to the Great Crash, from the food supply chains of the two World Wars to collectivization and late socialist hardship, from the Revolution of 1989 to the country's position since 2007 as a European Union member state—would take up another volume, well beyond the capabilities of this writer. An excellent recent study, taking a consumer-based approach, has shown that the replacement in Romania of mămăligă with white bread took place only extremely gradually, and was by no means complete by the 1980s. Scrob also makes clear that the slow decline of mămăligă consumption did not necessarily result in the decline of maize cultivation, which was instead diverted towards ani-

---

9   Welzk, *Nationalkapitalismus versus Weltmarktintegration*, 6.
10 This was to some extent a broader regional phenomenon: while in Macedonia and Bulgaria, cereal cultivation declined in favour of cotton and tobacco, in Romania cereals dominated and other crops were neglected. Cf. Lapavitsas and Cakiroglu, *Capitalism*, 76–80.
11 Mitrany, *Land and the Peasant*, 294–306; Humlum, *Zur Geographie*, 135–59; Belderok et al., *Bread-Making*, 336.
12 Giurescu, 'Plants of American Origin', 270. Today it is the fourth – after the USA, Serbia and Argentina – in terms of maize production per head of population.

mal feed, contributing to the establishment of a more meat-based diet among the rural population.[13]

In an article published in 1983, American anthropologist Steven Sampson made reference to mămăligă as a metaphor for conditions in Romania under late socialism. Addressing the question of the apparent lack of protest or revolt against the Ceaușescu regime, Sampson subtitled his contribution 'why the mămăligă doesn't explode'. In his analysis, Sampson was critical of those who claimed to locate the alleged passivity of the Romanian population in a so-called 'Balkan mentality', deriving from traditions of foreign imperial rule. Showing that such explanations rely on falsely positing an unchanging inherited tradition, Sampson pointed out that 'what appears to be a "tradition" may in fact be a result of modernization'. He also denied that late socialist society was 'stagnant', insisting rather on the agency of citizens in the form of subtle adjustments to behaviour in relation to authority.[14] In this way, Sampson rightly critiqued the simplistic invocation of long-term historical legacies in social-scientific research, and hinted at a potentially different approach to understanding Romania's pre-national past.

This trend has almost certainly continued in the twenty-first century, characterized by urbanization and large scale-migration of the rural population. At the same time, however, maize production has increased considerably in recent years, and it is once again a very prominent article in Romania's foreign exports.[15] As I send this book to press, maize has again become a matter of some political urgency given the devastating impact of the Russian invasion of Ukraine on the harvest from that country. A significant number of African and Asian countries, where maize is still a food source and not primarily used for fodder, have come to depend on Black Sea maize. While much of the discussion in western countries has focused on energy supply, food security is still an issue, and Romania remains a key link in this chain.[16]

As for mămăligă, in the third millennium it features less in the political science literature about the country, and more in the cultural configuration of the country. We began by mentioning documentaries and feature films produced locally. It figures now in English-language cultural artefacts, in cookbooks such as

---

13 Scrob, *From Mămăligă to Bread*. See also Petrovici and Ritson, 'Food Consumption Patterns' and Zugravu *et al.*, 'Food, Nutrition, and Health in Romania'.
14 Sampson, 'Muddling Through in Rumania', 166–69.
15 Export values doubled from 600 million Euros in 2012 to 1.24 billion Euros in 2019: Anon, 'Value of Maize'.
16 Engel, 'Africa and the Russian Aggression'; Levitt and McCullough, 'Global Food Price Fears'.

Irina Georgescu's beautifully-illustrated *Carpathia*, or in the food documentary about Romania made in 2008 by celebrity chef and globetrotter Anthony Bourdain, where the national cuisine is described as 'the result of five hundred years of non-consensual sex with invading armies'.[17] Bourdain's blasé thumbnail characterization of Romanian food history is of course a prime example of the western traveller's cultural-historical reductionism, as well as of his masculinity. His flippant aside nevertheless hinted, however crudely, at a deeper past that deserved serious attention.

---

17   Bourdain, 'Anthony Visits Romania'.

Appendix
Words and Things

There are three main terms for maize in Romanian, according to region. The modern standard word, *porumb*, is principally attested in Wallachia. In Moldavia, the more ususal term is *păpușoi*, while in the western regions of Transylvania and the Banat, it is *cucuruz*. Some of these terms are easily explained and uncontroversial, whereas others have given rise to hundreds of pages of commentary.

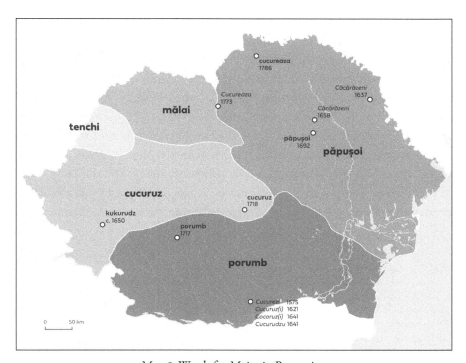

Map 8: Words for Maize in Romanian

APPENDIX

My focus is mainly historical, referring particularly to the period when maize and the word for it first appear. In many early sources, a lack of context means that the referent cannot be accurately determined. In general I am less interested in establishing single meanings or 'deep' origins, than in supplementing an understanding of the context and frameworks in the period when maize became an established crop. In fact the story of these and other words can be approached not as a question of fitting them into standard categories, but of understanding how they cross them, and thereby illustrate aspects of intercultural communication in early modern southeastern Europe.

Cucuruz

A regionalism in modern Romanian, *cucuruz* is a variant of the most commonly used word for maize throughout eastern Europe and Eurasia. In Bosnian, Serbian and Croatian it is *kukuruz*; in Slovene *koruza*; in Magyar *kukorica*; in Czech *kukuřice*; in Slovak *kukurica*; in Ukrainian *kukurudza*; in Polish *kukurydza*; in Russian *kukuruza*. *Kukurutz* is a familiar term in the German spoken in Austria and Bavaria. From Russian it was borrowed into many Caucasian and Central Asian languages. The standard word for maize in Madang province on the northeastern coast of Papua New Guinea, where it was introduced in the nineteenth century by Russian imperial explorer Nikolai Miklouho-Maclay, is *gugurus*.[1] Understandably, therefore, many scholars have sought to explain this popular word.

The earliest attestations referring explicitly to maize occur in several languages within a short interval in the late seventeenth and early eighteenth centuries, all in a relatively circumscribed area of the Habsburg-Ottoman border region: Romanian (*kukurudz*, c.1650; *cucuruz*, 1718);[2] Serbian-Croatian (*kukuruza* c. 1670, *kukuruz*, 1704);[3] Magyar (*kukoricza*, 1691, *kukuricza*, 1692);[4] and the Latin or German used by Habsburg authorities to survey villages inhabited by south Slavs or Romanians (*kukuruz*, 1697; *kukuriz*, 1702; *kukuruza*, before 1736; German *Cucu-*

---

1 Bourke, 'History of Agriculture in Papua New Guinea', 18 n.8.
2 c. 1650: Anon, *Dictionarium valachico-latinum*, 96. 1718: *Însemnări de demult*, 116.
3 c. 1670: *kukuruza*, applied both to buckwheat (fagopyrum, frumentum saracenicum) and maize (frumentum indicum, *mays* dictum), in Bellostenecz, *Gazophylacium*, 580, 686. 1704: *Rječnik*, v:765. Further attestations from 1727: Mihajlović, *Građa*, i:318–19.
4 Thököly, *1691–1692-iki levelesköynve*, 105 (*kukoricza*), 130 (*kukuricza*); *kukoricza* in an undated annotation in Magyar, in Anon, *Dictionarium valachico-latinum*, 133 (facsimile at 370; see editor's comments at 8, 177).

rutz, 1718).⁵ This is where we would expect to find it: as argued in Chapter 1, the Ottoman-Habsburg border is where and when *cucuruz* bursts onto the international stage, and it is also where soldiers and bureaucrats were there to record it.

Some scholars have made tantalizing, if tenuous, attempts to locate it on the Adriatic coast, in Kotor in 1531 or even in Zadar in 1190.⁶ Sounder is the attestation of a village near the Danube, south of Bucharest (today Cucuruzu, Giurgiu county, Romania), first as Cucurezi in 1575, and then from 1621 as Cucuruzi.⁷

Opinions on the word's origin are many: the most thorough available collation of scholarship on the problem lists nearly thirty contributions without achieving exhaustivity.⁸ We may add, for example, historian Nicolae Iorga, who suggested *buburuz* (a folk-term for ladybird in Romanian) as a possible source, on account of its appearance, an idea less outlandish than it appears at first sight, given the accepted entomological origins of closely-related terms.⁹ Slavist Roman Jakobson believed it to be 'one of numerous Balkan-Slavic botanical names derived from reduplication and excessive suffixation from *kur* "rooster, cock, penis"'.¹⁰

Collating these theories, and setting aside the more fanciful among them,¹¹ three merit critical commentary. The first is that it comes from Ottoman Turkish.

---

5 Latin *kukuruz, kukuriz*, 1697–1702: Smičiklas, *Dvijestogodišnjica oslobodjenja Slavonije*, ii:*passim*; *kukurucz*, 1721: Ilea *et al.*, 'Documente', 423; *kukuruza*, before 1736: Balassa, 'Die südslawisch-ungarischen Beziehungen', 87. German *Cucurutz*, 1718: Stoianovich, 'Le maïs', 1027. In Transylvanian German dialects, the term *kukuruz* appears only in the south of the province: Feßler, 'Zur Namengebung', 140.

6 Piper *et al.*, *Kukuruz*, and Zirojević, *Istočna-zapadna sofra*, 77 find a certain Radonja Raosaljić 'dicto Chuchuruz' at Kotor, 1531. Mažuranić, *Prinosi*, 555, invoked 'Cucurruz', allegedly a slave purchased by Stana, abbess of St. Mary's convent, Zadar, 1190; cf. Šimundić, 'Der Eigenname "Kukuruz"', 66. The document supporting this claim, published in the nineteenth century, could not be found at the beginning of the twentieth. See *Codex diplomaticus*, ii:249. Kukur as a personal name, c. 1300: *Monumenta serbica*, 63 (also Kukor, 59).

7 Giurescu, *Istoria Românilor*, ii:549 also posited a 'Cucuruzeni' in Moldavia. However, both this village (in Cârligătură county, attested from 1658), and another of the same name (in Orhei county, from 1637), are consistently spelt Căcărăzeni in early sources. Possibly from *căcărază* 'animal droppings', also a personal and collective name.

8 *Balgarski etimologichen rechnik*, iii:109–11.

9 Iorga, 'Ancienneté', 187. Cf. *căpușă* 'beetle, fruit head' > *căpșun* 'strawberry'; or, conversely, Bulgarian *kalinka* 'ladybird' < *kalina* 'guelder rose'.

10 Jakobson, 'While Reading', 611–12; thanks to Cristian Gașpar for this reference.

11 von Lippmann, 'Geschichte des Mais', 337, suggested *cucurrucho*, a south American sugar product of poor quality. Popescu, '"Colomba" e "mais"', 237–38, apparently seduced by the refrain of an internationally popular Mexican song at the time of writing ('*Cu-cu rru-cu-cu paloma*'), claimed it was a bird word of Spanish American origin (*cucuru*). Kupzow, 'Histoire du maïs', 44, pictured Italian maritime traders telling Balkan Slavs of a fabled Mexican goddess Kukuitz; while Pascu, 'Le maïs', 462, put his money on a Punjabi word *kukri* or *khukhuri*, which he claimed entered Romanian via Turkish. The derivation from an unattested Greek word *kuku-(o)ruza* 'cucumber rice' proposed by Cooper, 'Russian *Kukuruza*', 54–60 is no less fanciful.

APPENDIX

This was perhaps an understandable assumption in standard works of an older generation, given the general tendency to ascribe 'Turkish' origins to maize, which I questioned in Chapter 1.[12] However, it was challenged years ago, and has recently been thoroughly demolished.[13] Stachowski's philological demonstration is in tune with the historical record, insofar as the word appears to be virtually absent from Ottoman Turkish before the nineteenth century.[14]

A second is that *cucuruz* originally meant 'pine cone', and that the term was adopted for the maize cob by analogy with its appearance. This is attractive at first sight, and has been accepted by more scholars than just those wanting to prove that the Carpathian pine forests were the cradle of the Romanian language.[15] The naming of maize after terms for pine cones is quite widely attested in other languages.[16] However, this sense does not appear until quite late (in the form *cucurează*, in the Bukovina region, in 1786).[17] The first mention in the form *cucuruz*, a few years later, seems to suggest that the pine-cone meaning is not the primary one.[18] It may attest to a general sense of fruit head or cluster, applied to the pine cone only in a localized area.[19] The theory that it is a descendant of a Mediterranean, pre-Indo-European stratum is implausible.[20]

A third approach is to argue that the stem word is not *kuk-*, as might be expected, but *-kur*. This is a perfectly common type of word formation, for example *veveritsa* 'squirrel', where the stem is *-ver*, and there is a good case for *mămăligă* (q.v.).[21] On

---

12 Historians: Braudel, *Civilisation matérielle*, i:124; Fussell, *Story of Corn*, 16. Philologists: Skok, *Etimologijski rječnik*, i: s.v.; Mihajlović, *Građa*, i:318.
13 Kholiolchev, 'Za proizhoda na *kukuruz*', 463–64; Stachowski, *Names of Cereals*, 24–25.
14 Nişanyan, *Sözlük*, s.v., gives 1816 as the first usage. For a slightly earlier one, from Wallachia in 1794, see p. 61 above.
15 Pascu, 'Studii filologice', 423–24; Puşcariu, 'Besprechung', 111; Titkin, 'Zu rum. *porumb*', 715; Sala, 'Denumirea porumbului', 185; Kholiolchev, 'Za proizhoda na *kukuruz*', 464–65; Guţia, '*Cucuruz*', 309–11; Giurescu, *Probleme controversate*, 125.
16 For comparative data see Franconie, 'Things from the New World', 44.
17 Joseph II, *Orânduiala de pădure*, 527–28, 532–33. Kukuraza, a mountain (today Cucureasa, Bistriţa-Năsăud county), in Joseph II, *Călătoria* (1773), 662–63, and Hurmuzaki, *Documente*, vii: 489 (1781); Cucureaza (c. 1800), satirical name of a character in a poem by L'viv-based Romanian writer Ion Budai-Deleanu.
18 Klein, *Dictionarium valachico-latinum*, 325, not only listed *cucuruz de brad* after *cucuruz* 'maize', and with a qualifier, but felt the need to gloss it with another term (*shneapan*).
19 Sorbala, 'Originea', 169 n13, finds *cucuruz de strugure* 'bunch of grapes', in Maramureş. *Etymolohichnyĭ slovnyk*, iii:111 claimed a Ukrainian origin (< *kokorudka*) for the pine-cone sense. Scheludko, 'Rumänische Elemente', 138, was of the reverse opinion.
20 Stoianovich, 'Le maïs', 1037–38; see the reservations of Wagner, *Dizionario*, i:417, and Cioranescu, *Diccionario*, 258.
21 Zaimov, 'Nazvaniyata', 121, derives the interesting Bulgarian word *mumuruz* 'maize' from *mura* 'berry'.

this basis, Stachowski, who did much valuable work critiquing the 'Turkish' theory, posited a Slavic stem *-kor 'bent'. However, 'bent' is not a particularly plausible name for maize, and it does nothing to explain the ending -uz.[22]

Advocates of kuk- on the other hand, can point to its historical productivity in Balkan languages. Researchers can go down practically innumerable Greek, Slavic and Romance rabbit holes,[23] but the best explanation may be from Albanian kokërrëz/kokërrzë, a suffixated form of kokërr 'berry, grain'.[24] Although the question requires further research, there are multiple reasons for proposing kokërrëz/-zë as the most likely origin. The first attestation in Romanian is in the form Cucurezi, and the suffix -ëz is venerable in Albanian too.[25] There is an established close relationship between Albanian and Romanian vocabulary, including common words for beans,[26] brambles,[27] buds,[28] currants,[29] fruit pits,[30] grapes,[31] peas[32] and plums[33] which do not appear in neighbouring languages. The exact nature of the Albanian-Romanian relationship is best described as 'it's complicated', and some of these words may be the product of a common substrate, whether Romance or 'autochthonous'.[34] For example, the fact that Romanian cereal words of Latin origin also appear in Albanian is no proof that they came via that language.[35] But others so clearly bear the mark of Albanian morphology as to be hard to explain in any other way. Cucuruz also resembles numerous old-attested Romanian words for insects, birds, and other playful terms,

---

22   Stachowski, *Names of Cereals*, 25.
23   E.g. Greek κόκκος 'grain, granule', κόκορας 'rooster', κουκι 'broad bean', κουκουναρι 'pine cone', etc; BCS kuk 'hip', kuka 'hook', kukac 'insect', kukavica 'cuckoo', kukolj 'corncockle', Bulgarian kukul 'puppet, doll', kukura 'fool', kukuriak 'hellebore' &c: Romanian cuc 'hill', cucui 'crest of feathers', cocor 'crane', &c.
24   kokë 'head' + suffixes -ërr, -ëz/zë. < Latin coccum as per Orel, *Albanian*, 390, not < Proto-Slavic *kor, as per Stachowski, *Names of Cereals*, 25. Densusianu, 'Notes', 75, considered kokë to be one of 'a list of quite numerous Albanian forms introduced into Romanian during the Middle Ages'. These suffixes are generally diminutive but kokërr has an established collective sense (grains, fruit in general), as does -ëz: Brîncuș, 'Note etimologice', 25; Vătășescu, 'Evoluția', 134.
25   Xhuvani and Çabej, *Prapashtesat*, 482–83; Kore and Shaba, 'Common Patterns', 341.
26   *bishtajë / păstaie* 'bean pod'
27   *mërqinje / mărăcine* 'bramble', also *gjemb / ghimpe* 'thorn'
28   *mugull / mugur* 'bud'
29   *kokëzë / coacăză* 'currant'
30   *sumbull / sâmbure* 'pit, kernel'
31   *strydhur / strugure* 'grape'
32   **mādzula / mazăre* 'pea'
33   *kokërrduçe* 'gall, oak apple' / *corcoduşă* 'mirabelle plum'
34   The Romanian view in Boerescu, *Elementele de substrat*; different perspectives in Orel, *Albanian*.
35   *grâu* 'wheat'; *grâne* 'grains'; *mei* 'millet'; cf. Alb. *grurë, grunë, meli*.

some present in Albanian too.³⁶ In any case, if maize, or the word for it, really did travel surreptitiously from the Adriatic to the Danube under the passport name *kokërrëz/-zë*, and started a new life as *cucuruz*, it would not have been alone.

Mălai

Mălai is attested as a cereal name from 1588,³⁷ but it appears much earlier in personal names in both Moldavia (1493) and Wallachia (1525), and as a village name throughout the region (Transylvania 1453, Moldavia 1487, Wallachia 1556). As villages were named after notable people, and people after notable plants, *mălai* was clearly a thing of importance in the local economy and culture. But what kind exactly?

Although in modern standard Romanian, *mălai* means cornmeal, in older usage it referred most frequently to millet. *Mălai* could cover quite a wide range of referents—the plant, the grains, sowings or fields thereof, or flour, meal, cake made therefrom. The suffix *-ai* indicates volume but can accommodate all these senses quite comfortably.

Mălai comes most probably either from Latin *milium* 'millet',³⁸ or from a general term for milling, meal, flour, related to English *meal*, German *Mehl*, &c.³⁹ A combination of these last two senses is also possible.⁴⁰

Mămăligă

Mămăligă is first attested in early sixteenth-century Wallachia, but as a place name. It appears as a personal name somewhat later. As a dish made with maize, it is first mentioned in Brașov in 1718, and in Oltenia from 1723.

Nobody has quite clarified the origin of the word, which is part of its charm. People look elsewhere, claiming a link with Italian *meliga* 'polenta'⁴¹ or Bulgarian *mamul* 'ear of corn'.⁴² But these words are not satisfactorily explained in the respective source languages either. There is a party for *mamă* 'mother, breast, children's

---

36 *buburuză/buburez* 'ladybird'; *bumbărează* 'woman's bottom'; *căcărează/căcărez* 'sheep droppings'; *ceciliz* 'slow worm'; *chichiriză* 'tick'; *curculez* 'ladybird'; *huhurez/ciuhurez* 'tawny owl'; *titirez* 'spindle base, spinning top'.
37 Galata monastery accounts, in *Documente Iași*, i:52–53, alongside wheat, barley, oats, buckwheat and rye.
38 Avram, 'Etimologia cuvăntului *mălai*'; cf. Alb. *meli*.
39 Titkin, *Rumänisch-Deutsches Wörterbuch*, ii, s.v.; Giuglea, 'Crâmpeie', 601.
40 Boerescu, *Etimologii*, 214–15.
41 Cihac, *Dictionnaire*, ii:185; Mladenov, *Etimologicheski rechnik*, 228; *Etymolohichnyĭ slovnyk*, iii:376.
42 Pascu, *Sufixele românești*, 249; Stoianovich, 'Le maïs', 1034; Sorbala, 'Originea', 171.

food',⁴³ and another for *mălai* 'millet, meal'.⁴⁴ Speakers' understandings of the word might have been influenced by both these senses. But, as we have seen, they might have been influenced by a lot of other things too. The combination of a mushy semantics and a sonorous phonology seems appropriate for a dish with such a powerful spoken and unspoken history.

The ending *-igă* is not especially common in mainstream vocabulary, and does not carry any specific connotations.⁴⁵ A small group of words suggesting a meaning of 'ring' is probably coincidental.⁴⁶ However, it is much more common in personal names, where it often has a playful, familiarizing sense, often an adaptation of the very common suffix *-ică*.⁴⁷ In one linguist's apt phrase, *-igă* is 'the product of systemic pressure'.⁴⁸ She was referring to quite technical aspects of sound formation in Romanian, but it describes the political history of the dish pretty well too.

Păpusoi

This is the most common term for maize in Moldavia, and has given rise to much less dispute. The first mentions (1692) seem to refer unequivocally to maize. The standard explanation is from *păpușă* 'doll, puppet' denoting the ear, after a presumed visual resemblance.

However, with reference to maize, *păpușă* often refers not to the fully grown ear but to the young bud.⁴⁹ A meaning from *papă* 'food' is not impossible. While usually diminutive, the suffix *-uș* can also indicate mass or growth.⁵⁰ A different meaning of *păpușă* is 'bunch, sheaf'—of cord or fibre, but also, in some of the earliest attestations, of figs or grapes.⁵¹

---

43 Șaineanu, *Dicționar*, 376; Capidan, 'Elemente românești', 153. Pușcariu, in a note on Capidan, suggested Latin *ma(m)milla* 'breast', with the suffix *-ică* > *-igă*. Cf. Jianu, 'Polenta', 29.
44 Iorga, *Istoria românilor prin călători*, i:280.
45 Carabulea, 'Valorile sufixelor', 256; Hasan, 'În legătură', 52.
46 *verigă* 'chain link', *cârlig* 'hook', *bârliga* (of a cow) 'to swish one's tail'; *covrig* 'dough ring, pretzel'.
47 Baliga, Bașaliga, Bârliga, Bâzdiga, Beligă, Bidiga, Boligă, Bubuligă, Budrigă, Buligă, Cârliga, Câțiga, Citiriga, Ciumuligă, Ciupuliga, Cotiga, Covrigă, Digă, Doniga, Drigă, Durigă, Furnigă, Galiga, Ghiga, Ghiriga, Ghivirigă, Hădărigă, Ianoșligă, Maligă, Mănigă, Ojiga, Oniga, Paliga, Papariga, Pariga, Părpăligă, Peciniga, Pipirigă, Piștrigă, Pițigă, Pițirigă, Rariga, Rasiga, Rebiga, Reșigă, Smeriga, Ștefănigă, Tătăligă, Țăpigă, Țiligă, Țițirigă, Țuligă, Țuțurigă.
48 Hasan, 'În legătură', 53; cf. Oancă, 'Sufixul antroponimic *-ega*', 252.
49 *DLR*, 8-i: 278. Cf. *căpușă* 'bud', Bulgarian *kapushka* 'baby grape'.
50 *albuș, gălbenuș* 'egg white, yolk', *cenușă* 'ash', *rumeguș* 'sawdust'; *pănușă* 'maize husk' &c. On this aspect see Carabulea, 'Sufixul *-uș(ă)*', 206.
51 Attested 1688: *DLR* 8-i:278, or much earlier if, as *DERS*, xvii suggests, a village Păpușari (1525) is unlikely to refer to puppeteers. Hence Ukrainian, Russian *papusha* 'wad, sheaf, bale' (esp. of tobacco);

The noun suffix *-oi* has numerous different functions in Romanian. It can distinguish objects as large,[52] animals as male,[53] and people usually in a disparaging sense.[54] But although maize has been called all these things in the international cultural imaginary,[55] these may not have been *păpuşoi*'s primary associations. Applied to organic matter, *-oi* indicates mass or amount,[56] or has an agentive sense: garlic is called *usturoi* in Romanian because it produces a sting.[57] So whether *păpuşă* is a puppet, a bud, a bunch of fruit or fibre, or something to eat, *păpuşoi* is an amount or source thereof.

Porumb

The standard term for maize in modern Romanian, *porumb*, is agreed by nearly all scholars to derive from *porumb* 'pigeon' after the apparent shape of the ear. Of Latin origin,[58] this word is attested from the sixteenth century.

However, older than *porumb* 'maize' is *porumbă* 'sloe', a berry which grows on a *porumb(ar)* or blackthorn bush (*prunus spinosa*).[59] In a glossary composed around 1700, the Slavic word *černičie*, a type of berry bush, is glossed in Romanian as 'wild plum or *porumb* which produces large *porumbe*'.[60]

The blackthorn is a very old plant in southeastern Europe, giving rise to many place names. It is therefore highly unlikely that it was named after maize.[61] A better explanation is that it was named for the grey-blue 'pigeon' colour of its berries,[62] and

---

see *Etymolohichnyĭ slovnyk*, iv:286; Vasmer, *Wörterbuch*, ii:307, 314 (not vice versa, as per Pascu, 'Le maïs', 465).

52 *buboi* large boil, *butoi* large barrel, *oloi*, large pot.
53 *cotoi* tomcat, *răţoi* drake, *vulpoi* male fox, &c. See Pascu, *Sufixele*, 110.
54 *bulgăroi, ciocoi, ţărănoi*, derogatory ethnic or social labels.
55 *-oi*'s Italian cousin *-one*, whereby grain (*formento*) became maize (*formentone*), has similar augmentative-pejorative meanings: see Abegg-Mengold, *Die Bezeichnungsgeschichte*, 96.
56 *cosoi* (leather) material for sewing; *lătunoi* timber sawn from the edge of a tree trunk; *muşuroi* anthill, mound of earth; *puroi* pus; *puhoi, şiroi, şuvoi* torrent, &c.
57 < *ustura*, vb. 'to sting'; cf. *ardei* capsicum (< *arde*, to burn).
58 < *palumbēs* 'wood pigeon', cf. Alb. *pëllumb*.
59 First in various personal and place names (e.g. Porumbreni, Porumbaru), then as *porumberk* (Evliya Çelebi [c.1660], in *Călători străini*, vi:723); *porumbrea eghiptenească* (acacia); *porumblă* (prunum sylvestre); *porumblă sau măceasă* (spineolus) (Corbea, *Dictiones* [c.1691], 7, 413, 479); *porumbrer* (Cantemir, *Istoria ieroglifică* [c.1704], 194). Cf. (yet again) Alb. *kullumbri* 'blackthorn'.
60 'Černičie: prun sălbatec sau porumb ce face porumbe mari': Glosar slavo-român, in *Chrestomathie roumaine*, i:356; dated to 1704 or earlier by M. Georgescu, 'Cea mai veche listă', 19.
61 Its blossom indicating the time to plant maize, according, for example, to Ionescu-Şişeşti, 'Porumbul', 40.
62 *porumb, porumb(r)iu* (adj.) 'blue-grey'; cf. *porumbac* 'dappled, speckled'. See Titkin, 'Zu rum. *porumb*'.

that maize in turn was named after it. That a word for a familiar berry might have influenced the naming of an unfamiliar grain is a thought worth entertaining. It also accords with the historical evidence presented in Chapter 1, that maize was initially perceived and used not as an arable crop but as a forest fruit or garden plant.

Tenchi

A localized term for maize used in western Transylvania, *tenchi* derives from Magyar *tengeri*. *Tengeri* means 'sea [wheat]' (*tengeri búza* in early sources) and is a common word for maize in Magyar in the same region, and in northeastern Hungary. Attested from 1590, *tengeri búza* does not appear to be borrowed from any Latin or German term, and has led to some speculation that early users of maize in Hungary and Transylvania understood maize to have come from 'overseas'.[63]

---

63   Balassa, 'Der Maisbau', 105; idem, *A magyar kukorica*, 90–92.

APPENDIX

Table 1. Some place and personal names, c. 1450–1800

Cucuruz

Name/locality	Date	Source
Căcărază, Giurgea	1487	*DRH* A, iii:15
Huhurezi, Wallachia	1487, 1535	*DRH* B, i:193, iii:332
Buburuz, Buburuzeni	1546	*Surete și izvoade*, xviii:215–17; *DIR* A *XVI*, i:488
Cucuruzi [Giurgiu], as		
Cucurezi	1575	*DRH* B, vii:279
Cucuruz	1621, 1646, 1647	*DIR* B *XVII*, iv:26; *DRH* B, xxxi:302; xxxii:203
Cucuruzi	1641, 1648, 1649	*DRH* B, xxviii:62; xxxiii:139, 214; xxxiv:119
Cocoruzi	1641, 1649	*DRH* B, xxviii:62; xxxi:309
Cucurudzu	1641	*DRH* B, xxviii:385
Căcăraza, Cârstea	1584	Pușcariu, *Date istorice*, i:168, ii:14
Căcăraz(ă), Ionașco	1623, 1624	*DRH* A, xviii:99, 243
Cucur, Radu, witness	1636	*DRH* B, xxv:356
Căcărăzeni [Orhei]	1637–1658	*Documente Orhei*, 79, 88, 99; *DRH* A, xxiv:91; xxviii:410, 416
Hotarul cucuresc [Prahova]	1650, 1653	*DRH* B, xxxv:222, 235; xxxviii:107
Cucurici's well [Prahova]	1654	*DHR* A, xxxix:416
Căcărăzeni [Cârligătura]	1658, 1662	*Uricariul*, xvi:207; *Ispisoace și zapise*, 3–ii:31

Mălai

Name/locality	Date	Source
Malaesd [Hunedoara]	1453	Csánki, *Földrajza*, v:109
Mălăești [Iași]	1487	*DRH* A, iii:10[64]
Mălai	1493	*DRH* A, iii:263
Duma Mălăescul	1493	*DRH* A, iii:291
Malai family	1507	*DIR* A *XVI*, i:56
Malai șetrar	1517	*DIR* A *XVI*, i:112
Margire a lui Malai	1522	*DIR* A *XVI*, i:196, 199, 206, 208
Grand Postelnic Mălai	1525	*DRH* B, ii:435, 444, 446, 447, 453
Malaia, Gypsy woman	1525	*DRH* B, ii:449
Malai, Niagu	1528, 1546	*DIR* A *XVI*, i:236, 489
Malai, boyar	1529	*DRH* B, iii:126
Mălaia	1544	*DRH* B, iv:186
Mălăești	1556	*DRH* B, v:78; xi:170, 277
Mălai ceasnic	1563	*DRH* A, vi:538, 543, 546, 549, 552
Mălăiești [Roman]	1574	*DRH* A, vii:70
Mălai of Horețca	1586	*Studii și documente*, v:396

---

64 Later translation.

Mămăligă

Name/locality	Date	Source
Mamaliga [Wallachia]	1520, 1525	*DRH* B, ii:393, 449
Mamaleț [Moldavia]	1609	*Studii și documente*, v:11
Mămălata [Moldavia]	1661	*Ispisoace și zapise*, 3, pt. i:176
Mămăligâ, Vlad [Brașov]	1700	*Documente Șchei*, i:7
Mamalyiga [village, Moldavia]	1705	*Călători străini*, viii:242
Mămăligă, Toader sin Gavriil [Moldavia]	1718	Giurescu, 'Înțelesul', 304
Mămăligă, Viștea de Jos [Transylvania]	1726	Pașca, *Nume de persoane*, 274
Mămăligă, Toader [Moldavia]	1741	*Documente Iași*, v:16
Mămăligă, Chiril [Alba]	c. 1750	Anon, 'Deisis'
Mămăligani (*Memeliganÿ*) [Alba]	1760	Ciobanu, 'Statistica', 627
Mămăligă, Neculai [Iași]	1768	*Documente Iași*, vi:746
Mămăligă, Ianeș [Transylvania]	1785	Densușianu, *Revoluțiunea*, 223

Păpușoi

Name/locality	Date	Source
Păpușari	1525, 1562, 1566, 1613	*DRH* B, ii:461, v:276; vi:11; *DIR* B XVII, ii:195
Iftimie Popușoi	1743	*Uricariul*, xxi:414

Porumb

Name/locality	Date	Source
Porumbok [Sibiu]	1466, 1473	*Urkundenbuch*, vi:239; *DRH* B, i:238
Porumbul [Ilfov]	c.1514–1519	*DRH* B, ii:261
Porumbreani [Giurgiu]	1560	*DRH* B, v:180[65]
Porumbul, a serf	1634	*DRH* B, xxiv:540
Porumbul Vornic, boyar	1638	*DRH* A, xxiv: 222, 239, 378
Poromb, scribe	1639–1640	*DRH* A, xxv, 216
Porumbriu, buys land	1639	*DRH* A, xxv:242
Porumb, a gypsy	1641	*DRH* B, xxviii:152
Porumbreni [Giurgiu]	1641–1655	*DRH* B, xxviii:300; xxxi:304, 309; xxxii:203, 211; xxxiii:214; xxxiv:4, 120; xxxvi:20; xxxix:204, 546; xl:150
Vasilie Porumbarul	1645	*DRH* B, xxx:195
Radu Porumbu	1649	*DRH* B, xxxiv:122
Porumbul, witness	1650	*DRH* B, xxxv:25
Porumb, sells land	1654	*DRH* B, xxxix:356
Porumbu, sells land	1655	*DRH* B, xl:207
Stanciu Porumb	1658	*Documente București*, 118

---

65 Later translation.

Glossary

Before 1866, units of measurement in use in Moldavia and Wallachia, especially the *kile* and the *oka*, were of Ottoman origin, but their size differed greatly from standard Ottoman usage. There was also great local variation. This, and the nature of sources, mean that any attempt to calculate yields of maize or even calories resulting from early mămăligă consumption should be made with extreme caution. Further details can be found in Stoicescu, *Cum măsurau strămoșii*; and (for Wallachia) Olaru, *Writs and Measures*, 249–307.

In the text, I use forms recognizable to international scholarship. If the local form differs, I give it in brackets here.

Abbreviations:
Fr. – French, Gk. – Greek; Hu. – Magyar; Lat. – Latin; Pol. – Polish; Sl. – Slavic; Tk. – Ottoman Turkish

arzmahzar – collective petition to the Ottoman Porte (< Tk., Arabic *'arḍ maḥḍar*)
beșli-aga (beșleagă) – captain of Ottoman mercenaries in Moldavia and Wallachia (< Tk. *beșlü-ağa*)
caimacam – interim ruler of Moldavia or Wallachia (< Tk. *kaymakam*, Arabic *ḳāʾim maḳām*)
cetvert – a unit of capacity; here, approx. 210 litres (< Sl. 'quarter')
çiftlik (ciflâc) – larger arable farm, characteristic of late Ottoman Balkans (< Tk. *çiftlik*)
cubulus – unit of capacity in central Europe, from 48–125 litres depending on location / period (< Latin)
divan – court assembly or council (Tk. *divan* < Arabic *diwan*)

161

ekonomos (econom) – treasurer of an Orthodox monastery (< Gk. οικονόμος)
firman – decree of the Sultan (Tk. *ferman* < Persian *farman*)
hegumen (egumen) – head of an Orthodox monastery; abbot (< Gk. ηγούμενος)
ispravnik (ispravnic) – county official, sheriff (< Sl. *ispravnik* 'lawmaker')
kapan – weighing office at the central grain market in Istanbul; by extension, the city's grain trade/supply (< Tk. *kapan* < Arabic *kaban*, weighing device)
kile (chilă, pl. chile) – Ottoman unit of measurement; in Wallachia, approx. 680 litres; in Moldavia, approx. 430 litres (< Tk. *kile* < Arabic)
kiler (cheler) – Ottoman term for Moldavia and Wallachia as sources of grain (< Tk. 'storehouse' < Gk. κελλάριον < Lat. *cellarium*)
korets (coreț) – unit of capacity; in Moldavia, approx. 90–125 litres (< Pol. *korzec*)
merță – unit of capacity, approx. 200 litres (< Pol. *mierczyk*, or Hu. *merce*)
Metropolitan (Mitropolit) – leading Orthodox Church hierarch, equivalent to archbishop (< Gk. Μητροπολίτης)
mumbașir – Ottoman grain procurer (< Tk. *mübașir* 'bailiff', Arabic *bāșara*)
mutasarrıf – governor of a province (< Tk., Arabic)
narh (nart) – fixed price for purchase/requisitioning of goods (< Tk., < Persian *narh*)
oka (oca) – unit of capacity; for grain, usually approx. 1.28 litres in Wallachia, 1.52 litres in Moldavia (< Tk. *okka*, Arabic *ukiyya*, Ancient Gk. ούγκια 'ounce')
ort – low-value coin (Pol. *ort*)
pandur – frontier soldier in Hungary, Croatia-Slavonia, Wallachia (< Hu. *pandur*)
pasha (pașa) – lord, regional governor (< Tk. *pașa*)
pogon – unit of land measurement; approximately 0.5 hectares/1 acre (Sl. *pogon*)
Porte – the Ottoman central government, after the Palace gate where decisions were announced (< Fr. *Sublime Porte*, translating Tk. *Bâb-ı 'Âli* 'exalted gate' < Arabic)
postelnic – a boyar rank in Moldavia and Wallachia, chamberlain (< Sl. *postel* 'bed')
raki (rachiu) – distilled spirit made from fruit or grain (Tk. *rakı* < Arabic *arak*)
raya (raia) – 'flock', taxpaying non-Muslims in the Ottoman Empire (< Tk. *reaya* < Arabic *ra'iya*)
skete (schit) – a monastic community or residence subordinate to a monastery (< Gk. Σκήτη)
spătar – a boyar rank in Moldavia and Wallachia (< Gk. σπαθάριος 'sword-bearer')
stambol, pl. stamboale – an Istanbul *kile*, unit of measurement in Moldavia; approx. 37 litres (< *Stambol* 'Istanbul')
stolnic – a boyar rank in Wallachia, approx. seneschal, high steward (< Sl. *stol* 'table')

takrir – Ottoman diplomatic document (< Tk., Arabic *taqrīr* 'reiteration, clarification')

vakıf (vacuf) – protected endowment or foundation in Muslim societies (< Tk., Arabic *waqf*)

zaherea – tribute payable to the Ottoman Porte (< Tk. *zahire*, Arabic *ẓaḫīra*)

zapciu – bailiff, collector of tribute (< Tk. *zabtiye*, Arabic *ḍabṭiyyah* 'policeman')

zapis – letter, contract (< Sl. *zapis*)

zlot – an old coin/unit of currency (< Pol. *złoty*)

Mămăligography

A magyar törvényhatóságok jogszabályainak gyüjteménye, ed. S. Kolosvári, K. Óvári. 5 vols. Budapest, 1885–1904.
Abegg-Mengold, Colette *Die Bezeichnungsgeschichte von Mais, Kartoffel und Ananas im Italienischen. Probleme der Wortadoption und -adaption*. Bern, 1979.
Achim, Viorel *The Roma in Romanian History*, trans. R. Davies. Budapest – New York, 1998.
Acsády, Ignácz *A magyar jobbágyság története*. Budapest, 1908.
Acte fiscale din Țara Românească, 1701–1820. Document collection, 'Nicolae Iorga' Institute of History, Bucharest, forthcoming.
Acte judiciare din Țara Românească, 1775–1781, ed. G. Cronț, A. Constantinescu, A. Popescu, T. Rădulescu, C. Tegăneanu. Bucharest, 1973.
Acte și fragmente cu privire la istoria romînilor, ed. N. Iorga. 2 vols. Bucharest, 1895–1896.
Adăniloaie, N. *Răscoala țăranilor din 1888*. Bucharest, 1988.
Adas, Michael 'From Avoidance to Confrontation: Peasant Protest in Precolonial and Colonial Southeast Asia', *Comparative Studies in Society and History* 23:2 (1981), 217–47.
Ağir, Seven 'The Evolution of Grain Policy: The Ottoman Experience', *Journal of Interdisciplinary History* 43:4 (2013), 571–98.
Ağir, Seven 'The Evolution of Grain Procurement Practices in Ottoman Macedonia, 1774–1838', *Journal of the Ottoman and Turkish Studies Association* 7:1 (2020), 110–45.
Aksan, Virginia 'Feeding the Ottoman Troops on the Danube, 1768–1774', *War and Society* 13:1 (1995), 1–14.
Aksan, Virginia 'Whatever Happened to the Janissaries? Mobilization for the 1768–1774 Russo-Ottoman War', *War in History* 5:1 (1998), 23–36.
Aksan, Virginia 'Whose Territory and Whose Peasants? Ottoman Boundaries on the Danube in the 1760s', in *The Ottoman Balkans, 1750–1830*, ed. F. Anscombe. Princeton, NJ, 2006, 61–86.
Album literar gastronomic. Bucharest, 1981.
Alecsandri, Vasile 'My Mission to London' [1878], trans. E. D. Tappe, *Slavonic and East European Review* 27:69 (1949), 536–45.
Alecsandri, Vasile 'Surugiul' [1860], in idem, *Opere*, vol. 5: *Teatru*. Bucharest, 1977, 71–77.
Alexandrescu-Dersca Bulgaru, Marie-Mathilde 'L'approvisionnement d'Istanbul par les Principautés roumaines au XVIIIe siècle: Commerce ou requisition?', *Revue des mondes musulmans et de la Méditerranée*, nr. 66 (1992), 73–78.
Alexici, G. *Texte din literatura poporană română*. Budapest, 1899.
Aman, Theodor 'Țigăncuși la mămăligă', unsigned, undated (?1870). Theodor Aman Museum, Bucharest, inv. no. 58. Repr. b/w vignette, in *Centenar – Theodor Aman*. Bucharest, 1991, 220.
Analele parlamentare ale României, 1831–1852. 17 vols. Bucharest, 1890–1914.

Amedoski, Dragana 'Introduction of Rice Culture in the Central Balkans (15th and 16th Century)', in *State and Society in the Balkans Before and After Establishment of Ottoman Rule*, ed. S. Rudić, S. Aslantaş. Belgrade, 2017, 235–55.

Anderson, E. N. *Everyone Eats. Understanding Food and Culture*. New York – London, 2005.

Andreescu, O., and L. Rogozea, 'Aetiology Theories about Pellagra at the End of the Nineteenth Century and Early Twentieth Century in the Vision of Romanian Doctors', *Bulletin of the Transylvania University Braşov, 6th ser.: Medical Sciences* 6(55):2 (2013), 93–98.

Andreozzi, Daniele 'L'aggravio dei dazi: Norme, mercato e concorrenze nei circuiti del grano della Trieste settecentesca', in *La polizia de' grani*, ed. A. Clemente, S. Russo. Catanzaro, 2019, 53–71.

Andrews, Jean 'Diffusion of Mesoamerican Food Complex to Southeastern Europe', *Geographical Review* 83:2 (1993), 194–204.

Andron, Ioan-George 'Calamități naturale și epidemii în Brașov și Țara Bârsei în secolele al XVIII-lea și al XIX-lea', *Țara Bârsei*, n.s., 3(14):3 (2004), 15–34.

Anon, *Dictionarium valachico-latinum* [c. 1650], ed. Gh. Chivu. Bucharest, 2008.

Anon, 'Deisis'. Tempera on wood, Alba county, c. 1740–1760. Collection of the Orthodox Archbishopric, Alba Iulia, Romania. Online catalogue entry at http://museikon.ro/romana-3/arte-plastice.html#viewitem/57B8791C5A8240B29936EBE04A8A6194 [accessed 14 Oct 2021].

Anon, *Vollständige Geschichte des itzigen Krieges zwischen Oesterreich, Rußland und der ottomanischen Pforte von 1788*. 2 vols. Vienna, 1789.

Anon, 'Ueber eine der ersten Ursachen der Brodtheurung in Siebenbürgen', *Siebenbürgische Quartalschrift* 1:1 (1790), 122–37.

Anon, 'Foaie pe care este însemnat porumbul ce l-a dat la țigani', Bucharest, 1834. National Archives of Romania, Fond Mănăstirea Zlătari, online at http://sclavia-romilor.gov.ro/items/show/2044 (accessed 22 March 2022)

Anon, 'Commerce de la Moldavie et de la Valachie', *Le Sémaphore de Marseille* 12:3248 (27 March 1839), 3.

Anon, 'The Irish Crisis', *Edinburgh Review*, no. 85 (January 1848), 229–320.

Anon, 'Logica țăranului', *Calicul* 9:1 (1889), 24.

Anon, 'Bucate bune', *Vatra* 1:19 (1894), 602.

Anon, *Les bons plats roumains*. Bucharest, 1937.

Anon, *Savory Romanian Dishes and Choice Wines*, trans. Anon. Bucharest, 1999.

Anon, 'Value of Maize or Corn Exported from Romania from 2012 to 2020', https://www.statista.com/statistics/762883/maize-corn-export-value-romania/

Anthing, Frederick *History of the Campaigns of Count Alexander Suworow Rymnikski*, trans. Anon. 2 vols. London, 1799.

Ardeleanu, Constantin ' Russian-British Rivalry Regarding Danube Navigation and the Origins of the Crimean War, 1846–1853', *Journal of Mediterranean Studies* 19:2 (2010), 165–86.

Ardeleanu, Constantin 'Military Aspects of the Greek War of Independence in the Romanian Principalities: The Battle of Galați (1821)', in *Greeks in Romania in the Nineteenth Century*, ed. G. Harlaftis, R. Păun. Athens, 2013, 141–66.

Ardeleanu, Constantin *International Trade and Diplomacy at the Lower Danube. The Sulina Question and the Economic Premises of the Crimean War (1829–1853)*. Brăila, 2014.

Ardeleanu, Constantin *The European Commission of the Danube, 1856–1948. An Experiment in International Administration*. Leiden – Boston, 2020. [Balkan Studies Library, 27].

Aricescu, C. D. *Istoria revoluțiunii române dela 1821*. Craiova, 1874.

Arion, Virgil *Pagini din timpul răscoalelor țărănești*. Vălenii-de-Munte, 1912.

Asachi, Gheorghe, 'Înturnarea plăieșului din Anglia' [1850], in idem, *Opere*, 2 vols. Chișinău, 1991, ii: 64–80.

Aslan, Margareta 'Turkish Flavours in the Transylvanian Cuisine', in *Earthly Delights*, ed. A. Jianu, V. Barbu. Leiden – Boston, 2018, 99–126.

Avram, Andrei 'Etimologia cuvântului *mălai* și o problemă de fonetică istorică a limbii române', *Studii și cercetări lingvistice* 38:2 (1987), 120–25.

Axenciuc, Victor *Evoluția economică a României. Cercetări statistico-istorice, 1859–1947*. 3 vols. Bucharest, 1992–2000.

Aydın, Mahir 'On the Shores of Danube: Neighbourhood between Wallachia and Vidin', in *Turkey & Romania*, ed. F. Nitu, C. Ionita, M. Ünver, Ö. Kolçak, H. Topaktaş. Istanbul, 2016, 145–63.

Bacalbașa, Constantin *Dictatura gastronomică. 1501 feluri de mâncări*. 2nd edn. Bucharest, 1935.

Badea, M., C. Fotino, D. Hurezeanu, M. Iosa, and V. Niculae, 'Wallachia', in *The Great Romanian Peasant Revolt of 1907*, ed. I. Ilinciou. Bucharest, 1991, 98–155.

Bălan, Maria 'Contribuții la istoria învățămîntului din Oltenia în secolul al XVIII-lea', *Studii și materiale de istorie medie* 6 (1973), 289–95.

Balassa, I. 'Der Maisbau in Ungarn', *Acta Ethnographica Academiae Scientiarum Hungaricae* 5:1–2 (1956), 103–79.

Balassa, Iván *A magyar kukorica. Néprajzi tanulmány*. Budapest, 1960.

Balassa, Iván 'Die südslawisch-ungarischen Beziehungen im Maisbau', *Ethnologia Slavica* 7 (1975), 85–104.

Balgarski etimologichen rechnik, 2nd edn. Sofia, 2012, vol. 3.

Băncilă, Octav 'Cules de porumb', *Luceafărul* 13:7 (1914), 192.

Băncilă, Octav 'Pâinea noastră cea de toate zilele', *Luceafărul* 13:7 (1914), 193.

Barbu, Violeta 'The "Emperor's Pantry": Food, Fasting and Feasting in Wallachia (17th-18th Centuries)', in *Earthly Delights*, ed. A. Jianu, V. Barbu. Leiden – Boston, 2018, 217–70.

Bărbulescu, Constantin '"The Peasant's Food Is Only the Polenta": The Hygiene of Rural Peoples' Nourishment in Romania in the Medical Discourse of the Second Half of the 19th Century through the Beginning of the 20th Century', *Studia Universitatis Babeș-Bolyai, Historia* 59:2 (2014), 83–109.

Bărbulescu, Constantin *Physicians, Peasants and Modern Medicine. Imagining Rurality in Romania, 1860–1910*, trans A. Jianu. Budapest – New York, 2018.

Bărbulescu, Constantin 'O simbioză perfectă. Ion Ionescu de la Brad și țăranii', *Archiva Moldaviae* 12 (2020), 89–144.

Bardili, Johann *Reisebeschreibung von Pultawa durch das Desert Dzike Pole nach Bender und durch die Wallachey und Moldau nach Teutschland*. N.p., 1714.

Bartha, Júlia 'Points of Connection Between Turkish and Hungarian Dietary Culture', in *World of Similar Tastes*, ed. M. Hoppál, M. Öcal Oğuz, E. Ölçer Özünel. Ankara, 2016, 45–68.

B[awr, F. W. von] *Mémoires historiques et géographiques sur la Valachie*. Frankfurt – Leipzig, 1778.

Bejenaru, Ionel 'Județul Botoșani la ora răscoalei. 100 de ani de la Marea Răscoală din 1907. Montaj de documente inedite', *Acta Moldaviae Septentrionalis* 5–6 (2006–2007), 221–28.

Belasco, Warren and Phil Scranton, eds. *Food Nations. Selling Taste in Consumer Societies*. New York, 1992.

Belderok, B., J. Mesdag and D. A. Donner, *Bread-Making Quality of Wheat. A Century of Breeding in Europe*. Dordrecht, 2000.

Bellostenecz, Joannes *Gazophylacium seu latino-illyricorum onomatum aerarium [...] nunc primum peculiariter illyrorum commodo apertum*. Zagreb, 1740.

Benda, Borbála 'Obiceiuri alimentare pe domeniile aristocratice și evoluția lor în secolul al XVII-lea', *Caiete de antropologie istorică* 5:1–2 (nr. 8–9) (2006), 31–54.

Benda, Borbála *Étkezési szokások a magyar főúri udvarokban a kora újkorban*. Szombathely, 2014.
Bentham, Jeremy *Correspondence*, vol. 3: *1781–1788*. London, 1971.
Berceanu, Maria 'Reformele lui Constantin Mavrocordat, început al modernizării administrative în Moldova. Un studiu de caz: Ținutul Bacău', *Cercetări istorice*, n.s., 32 (2013), 211–48.
Berciu-Drăghicescu, A. and Dinică Ciobotea, 'Viața economică a Țării Românești în epoca lui Constantin Brâncoveanu', *Revista Arhivelor* 54(70):4 (1993), 373–93.
Bethlen, Miklós *Önéletírása*, 2 vols. Budapest, 1955.
Bethlen, Miklós *Autobiography*, trans. B. Adams. London, 2004.
Bibliografia românească veche (1508–1830), 4 vols. Bucharest 1903–1944.
Bielski, Marcin *Sprawa rycerska* [1569], excerpts ed. & trans. B. P. Hasdeu, *Archiva Românească* 1:2 (1865), 161–70.
Bilgin, Arif 'From Artichoke to Corn: New Fruits and Vegetables in the Istanbul Market (Seventeenth to Nineteenth Centuries', in *Living the Good Life*, ed. E. Akçetin, S. Faroqhi. Leiden, 2018, 257–82.
Blaszczyk, Arkadiusz and Stefan Rohdewald, eds. *From Kebab to Ćevapčići. Foodways in (Post-) Ottoman Europe*. Wiesbaden, 2018.
Bleibtreu, Karl *Ein Freiheitskampf in Siebenbürgen. Kulturhistorischer Roman*. Jena, n.d. [c. 1900].
Bloch, Marc *L'étrange défaite. Témoignage écrit en 1940*. Paris, 1990.
Bloch, Marc *Apologie pour l'histoire, ou métier de l'historien*. 2nd edn. Paris, 1952.
Bodale, Arcadie M. 'Informații documentare privind alimentația în Țara Moldovei (secolele XV-XVIII)', in *Alimentație și demografie în Moldova*, ed. L. Pîrnău, G. Bilavschi, L. Bejenaru, V.-M. Groza. Cluj-Napoca, 2021, 45–63.
Bodea, Cornelia C. 'Contribuții documentare privind răscoala țăranilor din 1988', *Studii* 11:2 (1958), 155–94.
Bodea, Cornelia 'Préoccupations économiques et culturelles dans les textes transylvains des années 1786–1830', in *La culture roumaine à l'époque des Lumières*, ed. R. Munteanu, 2 vols. Bucharest 1982, i:227–61.
Boerescu, Pârvu *Elementele de substrat (autohtone) ale limbii române*. Bucharest, 2014.
Boerescu, Pârvu *Etimologii românești controversate. Ipoteze și soluții*. Bucharest, 2017.
Bogdan, Ioan 'Sămile mănăstirilor de țară din Moldova pe anul 1742', *Buletinul Comisiei Istorice a României* 1 (1915), 217–79.
Bohatcová, Mirjam 'Prager Drucke der Werke Pierandrea Mattiolis aus den Jahren 1558–1602', *Gutenberg-Jahrbuch* 60 (1985), 167–85.
Boomgaard, Peter and Marjolein 't Hart, 'Globalization, Environmental Change, and Social History: An Introduction', *International Review of Social History* 55 (2010), Supplement, 1–26.
Born, Ignaz von *Briefe über mineralogische Gegenstände, auf seiner Reise durch das Temeswarer Bannat, Siebenbürgen, Ober- und Nieder-Hungarn*. Leipzig, 1774.
Born, Ignaz von *Travels through the Bannat of Temeswar, Transylvania, and Hungary, in the Year 1770*, trans. R. E. Raspe. London, 1777.
Boteanu, G. 'Din mizeriile vieții', *Revista literară* 9:27 (1888), 371.
Bourdain, Anthony 'Anthony Visits Romania'. *Kitchen Confidential* Documentary Series (2008). Online at https://www.dailymotion.com/video/x3annea (accessed 14 January 2021).
Bourke, R. Michael 'History of Agriculture in Papua New Guinea', in *Food and Agriculture in Papua New Guinea*, ed. R.M. Bourke, T. Harwood. Canberra, 2009, 10–26.
Brad Chisacof, Lia 'Turkish Known or Unknown During the 18th Century in the Romanian Principalities?', in *Turkey & Romania*, ed. F. Nitu, C. Ionita, M. Ünver, Ö. Kolçak, H. Topaktaş. Istanbul, 2016, 259–70.
Brandes, Stanley 'Maize as a Culinary Mystery', *Ethnology* 31:4 (1992), 331–36.

Brandolini, A. and A. Brandolini, 'Maize Introduction, Evolution and Diffusion in Italy', *Maydica* 54 (2009), 233–42.
Brătianu, Iane, Oancea Brătianu, and Iordache Brătianu, 'Zapis', 2 June 1728, Museum of Viticulture and Pomiculture, Goleşti, Romania: online at http://clasate.cimec.ro/detaliu.asp?k= A328C449E92847DD915377E8C9B4F853
Braudel, Fernand *Civilisation matérielle et capitalisme (XVe–XVIIIe siècle)*, t. I. Paris, 1967.
Bredt, Heinz W. 'Beiträge zur Erforschung und Entwicklung des Kartoffelanbaues im Burzenland, in Siebenbürgen und in Rumänien', *Zeitschrift für Siebenbürgische Landeskunde* 23:2 (2000), 237–50.
Bright, Richard *Travels from Vienna through Lower Hungary*. Edinburgh, 1818.
Brîncuş, Grigore 'Note etimologice', *Studii și cercetări de lingvistică* 12:1 (1961), 25–27.
Brown, Edward *A Brief Account of Some Travels in Hungaria, Servia, Bulgaria, Macedonia, Thessaly, Austria, Styria, Carinthia, Carniola and Friuli*. London, 1673.
Brown, Edward *An Account of Several Travels Through a Great Part of Germany*. London, 1677.
Brunner, Walter 'Frühe Nachrichten über Maisanbau in der Steiermark', *Blätter für Heimatkunde* 68 (1994), 5–15.
Budai-Deleanu, Ion *Opere*. 2 vols. Bucharest, 1974–1975.
Budinszky, Johann *Die Bukowina zu Anfang des Jahres 1783*, ed. J. Polek. Chernivtsi, 1894.
Bulat, T.G. 'O poruncă domnească din 1820', *Arhivele Olteniei* 5:25–26 (1926), 211.
Burger, Johann *Vollständige Abhandlung über die Naturgeschichte, Cultur und Benützung des Mais oder türkischen Weizens*. Vienna, 1809.
Burke, Peter 'Cultural Frontiers of Early Modern Europe', *Przegląd Historyczny* 96:2 (2005), 205–16.
Burtt-Davy, Joseph *Maize. Its History, Cultivation, Handling and Uses, With Special Reference to South Africa*. London, 1914.
Burzo, Dan Cătălin 'Culinaria. O bibliografie a bucătăriei românești', https://llll.ro/culinaria/ [accessed 20 November 2021]

Caillat, J.-M. *Voyage médical dans les provinces danubiennes*. Paris, 1854.
Călători străini despre Țările Române, 10 vols. Bucharest, 1966–2001.
Călători străini despre Țările Române în secolul al XIX-lea, 11 vols. Bucharest, 2004–2020.
Calciu, Laurențiu (dir.) *The Land is Waiting* (2004) https://www.imdb.com/video/vi250741785.
Calic, Marie-Janine *The Great Cauldron. A History of Southeastern Europe*, trans. E. Janik. Cambridge, MA – London, 2019.
Campenhausen, Freiherr von *Bemerkungen über Russland*. Leipzig, 1807.
de Candolle, Alphonse *Géographie botanique raisonnée, ou exposition des faits principaux et des lois concernant la distribution géographique des plantes de l'époque actuelle*. 2 vols. Paris, 1855.
Cantacuzino, Alexandru *America vis-à-vis cu România*. Bucharest, 1876.
Cantemir, Dimitrie *Istoria ieroglifică* [c. 1704]. Bucharest, 1883. [*Opere*, vol. 6].
Cantemir, Dimitrie *Descriptio Moldaviæ* [c. 1715]. Bucharest, 1973.
Capidan, Th. 'Elemente românești în limba albaneză', *Dacoromania* 7 (1931–1933), 151–54.
Carabulea, Elena, 'Sufixul -*uș(ă)*', in *Formarea cuvintelor în limba română*, ed. A. Graur. Bucharest, 1970, 199–212.
Carabulea, Elena 'Valorile sufixelor diminutivale substantivale', *Studii și cercetări de lingvistică* 26:3 (1975), 255–67.
Caracaş, Constantin *Topografia Țării Românești* [1828], trans. G. Sion. Bucharest, 2018.
Caragiali, Costache 'Doi coțcari sau păziți-vă de răi ca de foc' [1849], in *Primii noștri dramaturgi*, ed. A. Niculescu. Bucharest, 1960, 257–86.
Carmen Sylva, 'Vengeance. Récit de mœurs roumaines', *Revue des Deux Mondes*, 3d ser., 110:4 (1892), 848–76.

Carney, Judith A. 'Subsistence in the Plantationocene: Dooryard Gardens, Agrobiodiversity, and the Subaltern Economies of Slavery', *Journal of Peasant Studies* 48:5 (2021), 1075–99.
Carney, Judith A., and Richard Nicholas Rosomoff, *In the Shadow of Slavery. Africa's Botanical Legacy in the Atlantic World*. Berkeley – Los Angeles – London, 2009.
Carraretto, Maryse *Histoires de maïs. D'une divinité amérindienne à ses avatars transgéniques*. Paris, 2005.
Cărtărescu, Mircea 'Mierte fierte, scoici prăjite', in *Intelectuali la cratiță*, ed. I. Pârvulescu. Bucharest, 2012, 59–66.
Cassin, Barbara, Emily Apter, Jacques Lezra and Michael Wood, eds. *Dictionary of Untranslatables. A Philosophical Lexicon*. Princeton, NJ, 2014.
Cazacu, Matei *The Story of Romanian Gastronomy*, trans. L. Beldiman. Bucharest, 1999.
Cazacu, P. 'Locuințele sătenilor', *Viața românească* 1:10 (1906), 540–51.
Căzan, Ileana 'Princes roumains créditeurs de la Cour de Vienne. Michel le Brave et ses descendants', *Historical Yearbook* 5 (2008), 41–52.
Cereș, Irina 'Exportul de mărfuri din Principatul Moldova în Imperiul Rus la sfârșitul sec. al XVIII-lea – începutul sec. al XIX-lea', *Tyragetia*, n.s. 9:2 (2015), 79–90.
Cernovodeanu, Paul 'An Unpublished British Source Concerning International Trade through Galați and Brăila, 1837–48', *Southeastern Europe* 4:1 (1977), 32–47.
Cernovodeanu, Paul 'Comerțul Țărilor Române în secolul al XVII-lea', *Revistă de istorie* 33:6 (1980), 1071–98.
Cernovodeanu, Paul and Beatrice Marinescu, 'British Trade in the Danubian Ports of Galatz and Braila between 1837 and 1853', *Journal of European Economic History* 8:3 (1979), 704–41.
Chaplin, Joyce E. *Subject Matter. Technology, the Body, and Science on the Anglo-American Frontier, 1500–1676*. Cambridge, MA, 2001.
Chelcu, Cătălina 'Mărturii despre pedepsirea celor ce "s-au făcut cătane" în domnia lui Mihai Racoviță', *Anuarul Institutului de Istorie 'A.D. Xenopol'*, 51 (2014), 73–79.
Chelcu, Cătălina 'Legal and Tax Systems in Moldavia (late 16th century – 17th century): The Case of the Dedicated Monasteries', *Tyragetia*, n.s., 11:2 (2017), 41–50.
Chelcu, Marius 'Merchants from Iași in their Trade with Transylvania in Documents between the 17th-18th Centuries', *Anuarul Institutului de Istorie 'G. Barițiu'*, *Series Historica*, Supliment I (2015), 399–407.
Chen, Shuo and James Kai-sing Kung, 'Of Maize and Men: The Effect of a New World Crop on Population and Economic Growth in China', *Journal of Economic Growth* 21 (2016), 71–99.
Chenot, Adam *Tractatus de peste*. Vienna, 1766.
Cherniwchan, Jevan and Juan Moreno-Cruz, 'Maize and Precolonial Africa', *Journal of Development Economics* 136 (2019), 137–50.
Chirot, Daniel *Social Change in a Peripheral Society. The Creation of a Balkan Colony*. New York, 1976.
Chirot, Daniel and Charles Ragin, 'The Market, Tradition and Peasant Rebellion: The Case of Romania in 1907', *American Sociological Review* 40:4 (1975), 428–44.
Chivu, Gh. 'Studiu filologic', in Anon, *Dictionarium valachico-latinum*. Bucharest, 2008, 7–35.
Chivu, Gh. '*Dictionarium Valachico-Latinum*: The First Original Bilingual Lexicon in Romanian', *Diacronia* 14 (2021), 1–5.
Chivu, Iulian *Cultul grâului și al pâinii la români*. Bucharest, 1997.
Chrestomathie roumaine / Chrestomatie română, ed. M. Gaster, vol. 1. Leipzig – Bucharest, 1891.
Chronicon Fuchsio-Lupino-Oltardinum, ed. J. Trausch. 2 vols. Brașov, 1847–1848.
Cihac, A. de *Dictionnaire d'étymologie daco-romane*. 2 vols. Frankfurt, 1870–1879.
Cioancă, Costel 'Pentru o poetică a imaginarului (II). Bucătăria și bucatele basmului fantastic românesc', *Meridian critic* 29:2 (2017), 63–76.

Ciobanu, Nadejda and Veronica Brote, *Pe urmele renumitei bucătării românești*. Bucharest, 1971.
Ciobanu, Virgil 'Statistica românilor ardeleni din anii 1760–1762', *Anuarul Institutului de Istorie Națională* 3 (1924–1925), 616–700.
Cioranescu, Alejandro *Diccionario etimológico rumano*. Tenerife, 1958–1965.
Ciorba, Ioan 'Alimentația de criză din timpul marii foamete din Transilvania dintre anii 1813–1817', *Caiete de antropologie istorică* 5:1–2 (nr. 8–9) (2006), 271–79.
Ciorba, Ioan 'Drama celorlalți în ochii noștri: Reflectarea marii foamete irlandeze de la mijlocul secolului al XIX-lea în presa românească', *Crisia* 44 (2014), 57–73.
Ciubotaru, Iuliu 'Așezămintele agrare moldovenești (1766–1832)', *Anuarul Institutului de Istorie și Arheologie 'A.D. Xenopol'* 5 (1968), 87–120.
Ciure, Florentina 'Contribuția negustorilor străini din Transilvania la dezvoltarea comerțului exterior al Țărilor Române în a doua jumătate a secolului al XVI-lea', in *Negustorimea în Țările Române*, ed. C. Luca. Galați, 2009, 33–61.
Claflin, Kyri W. and Peter Scholliers, eds. *Writing Food History. A Global Perspective*. London – New York, 2012.
Clusius, Carolus *Rariorum aliquot stirpium historia*. Antwerp, 1583.
Codex diplomaticus Regni Croatiae, Dalmatiae et Slavoniae, vol. 2, ed, T. Smičiklas. Zagreb, 1904.
Codru Drăgușanu, Ion *Peregrinulu transelvanu*. Sibiu, 1865.
Coe, Sophie D. *America's First Cuisines*. Austin, TX, 1994.
Colquhoun, Robert 'An Account of the Market Prices of the several Sorts of Corn, Grain, Flour & other Articles, the Raw Produce of Agriculture at Bucharest during the Quarter ending on the 31st of March 1848', UK National Archives, FO 78/744, f. 183 [Copy kindly supplied by James Morris].
Colson, Félix *De l'état présent et de l'avenir des Principautés de Moldavie et de Valachie*. Paris, 1839.
Columbeanu, Sergiu *Grandes exploitations domaniales en Valachie au XVIIIe siècle*, trans. R. Crețeanu. Bucharest, 1974.
Columbeanu, Sergiu 'Contribuții la istoria marinei și navigației în România, 1829–1866', *Muzeul Național* 2 (1975), 445–52.
Comarnescu, Petru *Octav Băncilă*. Bucharest, 1972.
Comșa, Ecaterina Dr. S. *Buna menajeră sau carte de bucate. Cea mai practică și mai bogată dintre toate cărțile de bucate scrise până azi în limba română* [1902]. 4th edn. Bucharest, 1925.
Constantinescu, Ioana 'Date noi privind agricultura Moldovei în perioada 1829–1833', *Terra Nostra* 2 (1971), 45–55.
Constantinescu, Ioana *Arendășia în agricultura Țării Românești și a Moldovei până la Regulamentul organic*. Bucharest, 1985.
Constantinescu, Ioana 'Climă, agricultură și societate în Țara Românească și Moldova sub fanarioți', *Revista de istorie* 42:3 (1989), 259–72.
Constantinescu, N. *Dicționar onomastic romînesc*. Bucharest, 1963.
Constantinescu, N. N., ed. *Romania's Economic History from the Beginnings to World War II*, trans. I. Popescu, M. Fata. Bucharest, 1994.
Constantiniu, Florin 'Situația clăcașilor din Țara Românească în perioada 1746–1774', *Studii* 12:3 (1959), 71–109.
Constantiniu, Florin and Șerban Papacostea, 'Les réformes des prémiers Phanariotes en Moldavie et en Valachie. Essai d'interprétation', *Balkan Studies* 13:1 (1972), 89–118.
Cooper, Brian 'Russian *Kukuruza* and Cognates: A Possible New Etymology', *Slavonica* 4:1 (1997), 46–63.
Corbea, Teodor *Dictiones latinæ cum valachica interpretatione* [c. 1691–1698], ed. A.-M. Gherman. Cluj-Napoca, 2001.

Cornea, Paul 'Le paradis des affamés: Le motif du "Pays de Coccagne"', *Caietele Echinox*, nr. 10 (2006), 352–57.
Corespondența lui Dimitrie Aman, negustor din Craiova (1794–1834), ed. N. Iorga. Bucharest, 1913.
Corfus, Ilie *Agricultura Țării Românești în prima jumătate a secolului al XIX-lea*. Bucharest, 1969.
Corfus, Ilie *Agricultura în Țările Române 1848–1864*. Bucharest, 1982.
Costache, Stefania *At the End of Empire. Imperial Governance, Inter-Imperial Rivalry and 'Autonomy' in Wallachia and Moldavia (1780s–1850s)*. PhD diss., University of Illinois, 2013.
Cotoi, Călin *Inventing the Social in Romania, 1848–1914: Networks and Laboratories of Knowledge*. Leiden, 2020. [Balkan Studies Library, 28].
Covey, Herbert C. and Dwight Eisnach, *What the Slaves Ate*. Santa Barbara, CA, 2009.
Crăiniceanu, Gheorghe *Igiena țĕranuluĭ român*. Bucharest, 1895.
Craven, Elizabeth, Lady *A Journey Through the Crimea to Constantinople, in a Series of Letters*. London, 1789.
Creangă, Ion *Amintiri din copilărie* [1881], in Creangă, *Opere*. Bucharest, 1953.
Creangă, Ion 'Povestea poveștilor' [1876], online at https://ro.wikisource.org/wiki/Povestea_pove%C8%99tilor [accessed 23 January 2022]
Creangă, Ion 'The Tale of the Prick', trans. A.I. Blyth, *Plural* 26:2 (2005), online at https://www.icr.ro/pagini/the-tale-of-all-tales-the-tale-of-the-prick [accessed 23 January 2022]
Cronica Ghiculeștilor, ed. and trans. N. Camariano, A. Camariano-Cioran. Bucharest, 1965.
Cronicarii greci care au scris despre români în epoca fanariotă, ed. C. Erbiceanu. Bucharest, 1888.
Cronicele României, ed. M. Kogălniceanu, 3 vols. Bucharest, 1874.
Cronici turcești privind Țările Române, ed. and trans. M. Guboglu. 3 vols. Bucharest, 1966–1981.
Crosby, Alfred W. 'Maize, Land, Demography and the American Character', *Revue française d'études américaines*, nr. 48–49 (1991), 151–62.
Crosby, Alfred W. *The Columbian Exchange. Biological and Cultural Consequences of 1492* [1973], 30th anniversary edn. Westport, CN, 2003.
Csánki, Dezső *Magyarország történelmi földrajza a Hunyadiak korában*. 5 vols. Budapest, 1890–1913.
Csetri, Alexis 'Débuts de la science agricole en Transylvanie: János Fridvaldszky', *Cahiers d'histoire économique et sociale* 9 (1978), 229–54.
Cushing, Nancy 'The Mysterious Disappearance of Maize: Food Compulsion and Food Choice in Colonial New South Wales', *Food, Culture & Society* 10:1 (2007), 109–30.

Dalby, Andrew '"It is in Truth an Island": Impressions of Food and Hospitality in 19th-century Transylvania', in *Earthly Delights*, ed. A. Jianu, V. Barbu. Leiden – Boston, 2018, 405–25.
Dan, Mihail and Samuel Goldenberg, 'Le commerce balkano-levantin de la Transylvanie au cours de la seconde moitié du XVIe siècle et au début du XVIIe siècle', *Revue des études sud-est européennes* 5:1–2 (1967), 87–117.
Dannenfeldt, Karl H. *Leonhard Rauwolf. Sixteenth-Century Physician, Botanist and Traveler*. Cambridge, MA, 1968.
D'Atri, Stefano '*Per conservare la città tributtaria et divota*: Ragusa (Dubrovnik) and the 1590–91 Crisis', *Dubrovnik Annals* 14 (2010), 71–98.
Davidova, Evguenia *Balkan Transitions to Modernity and Nation-States through the Eyes of Three Generations of Merchants (1780s-1890s)*. Leiden – Boston, 2012. [Balkan Studies Library, 6].
Dekaprelevich, L.L. 'Iz istorii kultury kukuruzy v SSSR', *Materialy po istorii sel'skogo khoziaistva i krest'ianstva SSSR. Sbornik IV*. Moscow, 1960, 366–413.
Del Chiaro, Anton-Maria *Istoria delle moderne rivoluzioni della Valachia*. Venice, 1718.

Deletant, Dennis *Communist Terror in Romania. Gheorghiu-Dej and the Police State, 1948–1965*. London, 1999.

Demény, Ludovic 'Introducerea unor plante noi în agricultura Transilvaniei în secolul al XVII-lea', *Revista de istorie* 42:12 (1989), 1245–55.

Densuşianu, Nicolae *Revoluţiunea lui Horea în Transilvania si Ungaria: 1784–1785*. Bucharest, 1884.

Densusianu, Ov. 'Notes de lexicographie roumaine', *Romania* 33:129 (1904), 71–86.

DERS: Dicţionarul elementelor româneşti din documentele slavo-române, 1374–1600, ed. G. Bolocan. Bucharest, 1981.

Desjardins, Anne E. and Susan A. McCarthy, *Milho, makka, and yu mai. Early journeys of Zea mays to Asia*. Bellesville, MD, 2004.

Detchev, Stefan 'Dress, Food, and Boundaries. Politics and Identity (1830–1912): The Bulgarian Case', *New Europe College* Europa *Program Yearbook* (2006–2007), 19–44.

Dionisie Eclesiarhul, *Hronograful Ţării Româneşti (1764–1815)*. Bucharest, 1987.

DIR A XVI = Documente privind istoria Romîniei, Veacul XVI. A: Moldova, 4 vols. Bucharest, 1952–1953.

DIR A XVII = Documente privind istoria Romîniei, Veacul XVII. A: Moldova, 5 vols. Bucharest, 1952–1957.

DIR B XVII = Documente privind istoria Romîniei, Veacul XVII. B: Ţara Romînească. 4 vols. Bucharest, 1951–1954.

Disraeli, Benjamin 'Speech to House of Commons, Corn Importation Bill – Adjourned Debate (Third Night), 15 May 1846', in Hansard, vol. 86 (1846), column 661.

Djuvara, Neagu *Le pays roumain entre Orient et Occident. Les Principautés danubiennes au début du XIXe siècle*. Paris, 1989.

DLR = Dicţionarul limbii române, 13 vols. Bucharest, 1913–2000.

Dobrogeanu-Gherea, Constantin *Neoiobăgia. Studiu economico-sociologic al problemei noastre agrare*. Bucharest, 1910.

Documente bârlădene, ed. I. Antonovici. 5 vols. Huşi–Bârlad, 1911–1926.

Documente bucovinene, ed. T. Bălan. 5 vols. Cernăuţi, 1937–1939.

Documente 1821 = Documente privind istoria Romîniei. Răscoala din 1821, 5 vols. Bucharest, 1959–1962.

Documente 1907 = Documente privind marea răscoală a ţăranilor din 1907. 5 vols. Bucharest, 1977–1987.

Documente Bucureşti = Documente privitoare la istoria oraşului Bucureşti, 1594–1821, ed. G. Potra. Bucharest, 1961.

Documente Callimachi = Documente privitoare la familia Callimachi, ed. N. Iorga. 2 vols. Bucharest, 1901–1902.

Documente Iaşi = Documente privitoare la istoria oraşului Iaşi, ed. I. Caproşu. 10 vols. Iaşi, 1999–2007.

Documente Orhei = Documente privitoare la târgul şi ţinutul Orheiului, ed. A. V. Sava. Bucharest, 1944.

Documente privind relaţiile agrare în veacul al XVIII-lea. 2 vols. Bucharest, 1961–1966.

Documente privitoare la economia Ţării Româneşti, 1800–1850, ed I. Cojocaru, 2 vols. Bucharest, 1958.

Documente putnene, ed. A. Sava. 2 vols. Focşani, 1929; Chişinău, 1931.

Documente Şchei = Documente privitoare la trecutul romînilor din Şchei, ed. S. Stinghe. 5 vols. Braşov, 1901–1906.

Documente turceşti privind istoria României, ed. M. Guboglu. 3 vols. Bucharest, 1974–1986.

Đorđević, Vlastimir *Kukuruz*. Belgrade, 1956.

Dorondel, Ștefan and Stelu Șerban, 'A Missing Link: The Agrarian Question in Southeastern Europe', *Martor* nr. 19 (2014), 7–30.

Douglass, Frederick *Narrative of the Life of Frederick Douglass, an American Slave*. Dublin, 1846.

Drace-Francis, Alex 'Cultural Currents and Political Choices: Romanian Intellectuals in the Banat to 1848', *Austrian History Yearbook* 36 (2005), 65–93.

Drace-Francis, Alex *The Traditions of Invention. Romanian Ethnic and Social Stereotypes in Historical Context*. Leiden – Boston, 2013. [Balkan Studies Library, 10]

Drăgoi, Sabin V. *303 colinde cu text și melodie*. Craiova, n.d. [1925].

Dragomir, Cosmin *Curatorul de zacuscă*. Bucharest, 2021.

DRH A = *Documenta Romaniae Historica*, A: *Moldova*. 38 vols. Iași, 1975–2006.

DRH B = *Documenta Romaniae Historica*, B: *Țara Românească*. 40 vols. Bucharest, 1966–2018.

Dudnicenco, Nicolae 'Băuturile alcoolice în Țara Moldovei (sec. XVI-XVIII)', *Buletin științific. Revistă de etnografie, științele naturii și muzeologie* 21:34 (2014), 172–82.

Dunne, Tom 'Auto-Exoticism and the Irish Colonial Landscape', in *Networks, Narratives and Nations*, ed. M. Brolsma, A. Drace-Francis, K. Lajosi, E. Maessen, M. Rensen, J. Rock, Y. Rodríguez Pérez, G. Snel. Amsterdam, 2022, 275–84.

Dursteler, Eric R. 'Bad Bread and the "Outrageous Drunkenness of the Turks": Food and Identity in the Accounts of Early Modern European Travelers to the Ottoman Empire', *Journal of World History* 25:2-3 (2014), 203–28.

Duzinchevici, Gh. 'Contribuții la istoria legăturilor comerciale romîno-polone în secolul al XVIII-lea', *Revista istorică* 21:7–9 (1935), 225–32.

Earle, Rebecca *The Body of the Conquistador. Food, Race and the Colonial Experience in Spanish America, 1492–1700*. Cambridge, UK – New York, 2012.

Earle, Rebecca *Feeding the People. The Politics of the Potato*. Cambridge UK – New York, 2020.

Edroiu, Nicolae 'Economic Literature of the 1780–1820 Period and Romanian Society', in *Enlightenment and Romanian Society*, ed. P. Teodor. Cluj-Napoca, 1980, 40–54.

Ehrler, Johann Jakob *Banatul de la origini pînă acum (1774)*, trans. C. Feneșan. Bucharest, 1982.

Eidelberg, Philip 'Vasile Kogălniceanu and Rumanian Conservative Populism (1900–1921)', *Rumanian Studies* 3 (1973–1975), 77–92.

Eidelberg, Philip Gabriel *The Great Rumanian Peasant Revolt of 1907. Origins of a Modern Jacquerie*. Leiden, 1974.

Erbiceanu, Constantin *Istoria Mitropoliei Moldaviei și a Sucevei și a Catedralei Mitropolitane din Iași*. Bucharest, 1888.

Enescu, T. *Camil Ressu*. Bucharest, 1958.

Engel, Ulf 'Africa and the Russian Aggression against Ukraine – A Blog Series, Part 3: What is the Economic Fallout of Russia's War in Ukraine for Africa?', *Universität Leipzig Research Centre Global Dynamics*, 11 March 2022, online at https://recentglobe.hypotheses.org/1035?fbclid=IwAR19E1DYAyD55h37vVNyqm--OUF__Zcbq-KBmNmeI_hz37VgVPpapsJhXZw#fn1

Epure, Violeta-Anca 'Alimentația locuitorilor din Principatele Române în viziunea consulilor și voiajorilor francezi din perioada prepașoptistă', *Cercetări istorice*, n.s., 35 (2016), 145–61.

Eschholz, T.W., P. Stamp, R. Peter, J. Leipner, and A. Hund 'Genetic Structure and History of Swiss Maize (*Zea mays L. ssp mays*) landraces', *Genetic Resources and Crop Evolution* 57:1 (2010), 71–84.

Etymolohichnyĭ slovnyk ukraïns'koï movy. 6 vols to date. Kyiv, 1982–2012.

Fabian, Steven 'Locating the Local in the Coastal Rebellion of 1888–1890', *Journal of Eastern African Studies* 7:3 (2013), 432–49.

Faroqhi, Suraiya *The Ottoman Empire and the World Around It*. London, 2005.
Faroqhi, Suraiya 'Trading Between East and West. The Ottoman Empire of the Early Modern Period', in *Well-Connected Domains*, ed. P. Firges, T. Graf, C. Roth, G. Tulasoğlu. Leiden – Boston, 2014, 15–36.
Fekete, Albert 'Late Renaissance Garden Art in the Carpathian Basin', *Landscape & Environment* 14:2 (2020), 10–28.
Felea, Alina 'Cofeturi, "dulceață de Myrobolau", "zahăr candel", miere de prigon: dulciurile în alimentația populației din Țara Moldovei în secolul al XVII-lea – începutul secolului al XIX-lea' in *Alimentație și demografie în Moldova*, ed. L. Pîrnău, G. Bilavschi, L. Bejenaru, V.-M. Groza. Cluj-Napoca, 2021, 125–47.
de Feller, François-Xavier *Itinéraire, Ou Voyages de Mr. L'Abbé de Feller en diverses parties de l'Europe*, 2 vols. Liège-Paris, 1823.
Felix, Iacob '*Zea L.*', in *Enciclopedia română*, ed. C. Diaconovich. 3 vols. Sibiu, 1904, iii:1265–66.
Feneșan, Costin *Administrație și fiscalitate în Banatul imperial, 1716–1778*. Timișoara, 1997.
Feneșan, Cristina *Vilayetul Timișoara, 1552–1716*. Timișoara, 2014.
Feßler. Helga 'Zur Namengebung der aus Amerika eingeführten Kulturpflanzen Kartoffel, Mais und Tomate im Nordsiebenbürgisch-Sächsischen', *Zeitschrift für Siebenbürgische Landeskunde* 12:2 (1989), 130–43.
Filitti, Ioan C. *Domniile române sub Regulamentul organic 1834–1848*. Bucharest, 1915.
Filimon, Nicolae *Ciocoii vechi și noi, sau ce naște din pisică șoarici mănîncă* [1862]. Bucharest, 1964.
Finan, John J. 'Maize in the Great Herbals', *Annals of the Missouri Botanical Garden* 35:2 (1948), 149–91.
Finzi, Roberto *'Sazia assai ma dà poco fiato'. Il mais nell'economia e nella vita rurale italiane. Secoli XVI-XX*. Bologna, 2009.
Flamm, Heinz 'Die Pellagra', *Wiener klinische Wochenschrift* 133:S1 (2021), 1–21.
Flandrin, Jean-Louis and Massimo Montanari, eds. *Histoire de l'alimentation*. Paris, 1996.
Florea, Pavel-Mircea 'Câteva considerații privind introducerea culturii porumbului în Țările Române', *Studii de istorie economică și istoria gândirii economice* 3 (1998), 46–57.
Florescano, Enrique *Precios del maíz y crisis agrícolas en Mexico (1708–1810)*. Mexico City, 1969.
Florescu, Radu R. 'The Rumanian Principalities and the Origins of the Crimean War', *Slavonic and East European Review* 43:100 (1964), 46–67.
Fodor, Pál 'Hungary Between East and West: The Ottoman Turkish Legacy', in *More modoque*, ed. P. Fodor, G. Mayer, M. Monostori, K. Szovák, L. Takács. Budapest, 2013, 399–419.
Fotić, Aleksandar, 'The Introduction of Coffee and Tobacco to the Mid-West Balkans', *Acta Orientalia Academiae Scientiarum Hungaricae* 64:1 (2011), 89–100.
Foust, Clifford M. *Rhubarb. The Wondrous Drug*. Princeton, NJ, 1992.
Franconie, Hélène 'Things from the New World in the European Dialects', *Food and Foodways* 9:1 (2000), 21–58.
Frank Johnson, Alison 'Europe without Borders: Environmental and Global History in a World after Continents', *Contemporary European History* 31:1 (2022), 129–41.
Freedman, Paul, ed. *Food. The History of Taste*. London, 2007.
Freedman, Paul, Joyce E. Chaplin, and Ken Albala, eds. *Food in Time and Place. The American Historical Association Companion to Food History*. Berkeley, CA, 2014.
Frivaldszky, János 'Egy kétszázötven éves gazdaságpolitikai reformjavaslat', *Jászsági évkönyv* (2012), 110–25.
Fuchs, Leonhart *De historia stirpium commentarii insignes*. Basel, 1542.
Furnică, Dumitru Z., ed. *Din istoria comerțului la români, mai ales băcănia. Publicațiune de documente inedite, 1593–1855*. Bucharest, 1908.

Furnică, Dumitru Z., ed. *Documente privitoare la comerțul românesc, 1473–1868*. Bucharest, 1931.
Fussell, Betty 'Translating Maize into Corn: The Transformation of America's Native Grain', *Social Research* 66:1 (1999), 41–65.
Fussell, Betty *The Story of Corn*. Albuquerque, NM, 1999.

Gabaccia, Donna R. *We Are What We Eat. Ethnic Food and the Making of Americans*. Cambridge, MA – London, 1998.
Gandev, Christo 'L'apparition des rapports capitalistes dans l'économie rurale de la Bulgarie du nord-ouest au cours du XVIIIe siècle', *Études historiques à l'occasion du XIe Congrès International des Sciences Historiques*. Sofia, 1960, 207–20.
García, María Elena *Gastropolitics and the Specter of Race. Stories of Capital, Culture, and Coloniality in Peru*. Berkeley, CA, 2021.
Garić Petrović, Gordana 'Maize Cultivation in Serbia: A Historical Perspective', *Istorijski časopis* 68 (2019), 261–79.
Garoflid, Constantin *Agricultura veche. Condițiile economice, tehnice și sociale ale agriculturii mari din stepa de răsărit înainte de expropriere*. Bucharest, 1943.
Gatejel, Luminita 'Overcoming the Iron Gates: Austrian Transport and River Regulation on the Lower Danube, 1830s–1840s', *Central European History* 49:2 (2016), 162–80.
van Gelder, Esther *Tussen hof en keizerskroon. Carolus Clusius en de ontwikkeling van de botanie aan Midden-Europese hoven (1573–1593)*. PhD diss., University of Leiden, 2011.
Genealogia Cantacuzinilor, ed. N. Iorga. Bucharest, 1902.
Gentilcore, David *Pomodoro! A History of the Tomato in Italy*. New York, 2010.
Gentilcore, David *Food and Health in Early Modern Europe. Diet, Medicine and Society, 1450–1800*. London, 2015.
Georgescu, Irina *Carpathia. Food from the Heart of Romania*. London, 2020.
Georgescu, Magdalena 'Cea mai veche listă cu nume românești de plante', *Limba română* 30:1 (1981), 13–21.
Ghita, Ina Irina 'Altering Cooking and Eating Habits during the Romanian Communist Regime by Using Cookbooks', *Encounters in Theory and History of Education* 19 (2018), 141–62.
Ghorbani, Abdolbaset, Jan J. Wieringa, Hugo J. de Boer, and Henk Porck, 'Botanical and Floristic Composition of the Historical Herbarium of Leonhard Rauwolf Collected in the Near East (1573–1575)', *Taxon* 67:3 (2018), 565–80.
Ginnaio, Monica, 'Pellagra in Late Nineteenth Century Italy: Effects of a Deficiency Disease', *Population* 66:3–4 (2011), 583–609.
Giosanu, Eva 'Diete tradiționale: Prepararea și conservarea alimentelor', *Anuarul Muzeului Etnografic al Moldovei* 2 (2002), 165–200.
Giuglea, George 'Crâmpeie de limbă și viață străveche românească', *Dacoromania* 3 (1922–1923), 561–628.
Giurescu, Constantin C. *Istoria românilor*, vol. 3, part ii. Bucharest, 1946.
Giurescu, Constantin C. 'Înțelesul topicului "Parîng": Date despre agricultura românească din Carpați în Evul Mediu', in *Omagiu lui Alexandru Rosetti la 70 de ani*. Bucharest, 1965, 303–6.
Giurescu, Constantin C. 'Plants of American Origin in the Carpatho-Danubian Area', *Nouvelles études d'histoire* 5 (1975), 269–75.
Giurescu, Constantin C. *A History of the Romanian Forest*, trans. E. Farca. Bucharest, 1977.
Giurescu, Constantin C. *Probleme controversate în istoriografia română*. Bucharest, 1977.
Golescu, Dinicu *Însemnare a călătoriei mele* [1826]. Bucharest, 1915.
Golescu, Dinicu 'Learning from Enlightened Europe', trans. A. Drace-Francis in *Orientations*, ed. W. Bracewell. Budapest – New York, 2009, 101–7.

Gonța, Alexandru I. 'Începutul industriei alcoolului in Moldova feudală', *Anuarul Institutului de Istorie 'A.D. Xenopol'* 8 (1971), 145–57.
Gonța, Alexandru I. 'Producția de cereale și animale în Moldova între 1812–1821 și furniturile trimise la Înalta Poartă', *Terra Nostra* 3 (1973), 233–42.
Good, David F. *The Economic Rise of the Habsburg Empire, 1750–1914*. Berkeley, 1984.
Gradeva, Rossitsa 'War and Peace along the Danube: Vidin at the End of the Seventeenth Century', *Oriente Moderno* 81:1 (2001), 149–75.
Gradeva, Rossitsa 'The Ottoman Balkans: A Zone of Fractures or a Zone of Contacts?', in *Zones of Fracture in Modern Europe*, ed. A. Bues. Wiesbaden, 2005, 61–75.
Gray, Peter 'The Triumph of Dogma: Ideology and Famine Relief', *History Ireland* 3:2 (1995), 26–34.
Grigoruța, Sorin 'Scrisori din vremea ciumei', *Anuarul Institutului de Istorie 'A. D. Xenopol'* 56 (2019), 63–75.
Griselini, Francesco *Lettere odeporiche*. Milan, 1779.
Guboglu, M. *Catalogul documentelor turcești*. 2 vols. Bucharest 1960–1965.
Guția, Ioan 'Cucuruz "maïs" dans l'Europe Centrale', *Verhandlungen des Zweiten Internationalen Dialektenkongress*, 2 vols. Wiesbaden, 1967 [*Zeitschrift für Mundartforschung*, Beihefte, N.F. 3], i:302–18.

Hacquet[, Balthasar] *Hacquet's neueste physikalisch-politische Reisen in den Jahren 1788. und 1789. durch die Dacischen und Sarmatischen oder Nördlichen Karpathen*. 4 vols. Nuremberg, 1790–1796.
Hale-Dorrell, Aaron *Khrushchev's Corn Crusade. The Industrial Ideal and Agricultural Practice in the Era of Post-Stalin Reform, 1954–1964*. PhD diss., University of North Carolina, 2014.
Halikowski-Smith, Stefan 'In the Shadow of a Pepper-centric Historiography: Understanding the Global Diffusion of Capsicums in the Sixteenth and Seventeenth Centuries', *Journal of Ethnopharmacology* 167 (2015), 64–77.
Hasan, Finuța 'În legătură cu etimologia sufixelor -ac, -ec, -ic, -oc, -uc și -ag, -eg, -ig, -og, -ug', in *Studii și materiale privitoare la formarea cuvintelor în limba română*, vol. 6. Bucharest, 1972, 45–54.
Hasdeu, B. P. 'Originile agriculturei la români', *Columna lui Traian* 5:3 (1874), 48–53.
Hatt, Gudmund 'The Corn Mother in America and in Indonesia', *Anthropos* 46:5–6 (1951), 853–914.
Haupt, Georges 'B: Dans les Pays du Danube et à la mer Noire', part of Traian Stoianovich and Georges Haupt, 'Le maïs arrive dans les Balkans', *Annales: Histoire, sciences sociales* 17:1 (1962), 87–93.
d'Hauterive, Comte *Mémoire sur l'état ancien et actuel de la Moldavie*. Bucharest, 1902.
Hehn, Victor *Wanderings of Plants and Animals from Their First Home*, trans. Anon, ed. J.S. Stallybrass. London, 1885.
Heister, Carl von *Ethnographische und geschichtliche Notizen über die Zigeuner*. Königsberg, 1842.
Heppner, Harald *Österreich und die Donaufürstentümer, 1774–1812. Ein Beitrag zur habsburgischen Südosteuropapolitik*. Graz, 1984.
Herlihy, Patricia 'A Report on the Commerce of Moldavia and Wallachia in 1840', *Revue des études sud-est européennes* 12:1 (1974), 121–37.
Hilliard, Sam Bowers *Hog Meat and Hoecake. Food Supply in the Old South, 1840–1860*. Carbondale, IL, 1972.
Hințescu, J. C. *Proverbele românilorŭ*. Sibiu, 1877.
Hitchcock, Tim 'Historical Agency in a World of Consumers: Simon Schama and the Hamburger of History', *Xenopoliana* 11:1–2 (2003), 82–95.

Hitchins, Keith *Rumania 1866–1947*. Oxford, 1994.
Hitchins, Keith *The Romanians 1774–1866*. Oxford, 1996.
Ho, Ping-Ti 'The Introduction of American Food Plants into China', *American Anthropologist*, n.s., 57:2 (1955), 191–201.
Hodgyai, Mátyás 'Ínséges évek Biharban 1814–1817 között', *Történelmi szemle* 1–2 (1991), 59–69.
Hoffmann, Richard C. 'Frontier Foods for Late Medieval Consumers: Culture, Economy, Ecology', *Environment and History* 7:2 (2001), 131–67.
Howard, Douglas A. *A History of the Ottoman Empire*. Cambridge, 2017.
Hrabak, Bogumil *Izvoz žitarica iz Osmanljiskog carstva u XIV, XV i XVI stoleću. Udeo Dubrovčana u prometu 'Turskim' žitom*. Priština, 1971. [Zajednica naučnih ustanova Kosova. Studija, 20]
Humlum, Johannes *Zur Geographie des Maisbaus. Ursprung, Verbreitung, heutige Ausdehnung des Maisbaus und seine Bedeutung für den Welthandel. Anforderungen des Maises an das Klima, mit besonderem Hinblick auf Rumänien*. Copenhagen, 1942.
Hurezeanu, Damian *Problema agrară și lupta țărănimii din România la începutul secolului al XX-lea*. Bucharest, 1961.
Hurezeanu, D., and M. Iosa, 'Social, Economic and Political Condition of the Peasants in the Early 20th century', in *The Great Romanian Peasant Revolt of 1907*, ed. I. Ilincioiu. Bucharest, 1991, 9–41.
Hurmuzaki, *Documente = Documente privitoare la istoria românilor culese de Eudoxiu Hurmuzaki*. 22 vols. Bucharest, 1876–1943.

Iancovici, Sava 'Unele documente inedite despre Tudor Vladimirescu', *Studii* 13:5 (1960), 121–46.
Ilea, Ana, Gheorghe Mudura, and Veronica Covaci, 'Documente. Conscrierea domeniului Beiuș la anul 1721', *Crisia* 10 (1980), 353–452.
İnalcık, Halil 'The Emergence of Big Farms, Çiftliks: State, Landlords and Tenants', in *Landholding and Commercial Agriculture in the Middle East*, ed. Ç. Keyder, F. Tabak. Albany, NY, 1991, 17–34.
Ingigian, Hugas 'Mărturii armenești despre Români: Valahia și Moldova', trans. H. Dj. Siruni, *Analele Academiei Române. Memoriile secțiunii istorice*, 3d series, 9 (1928–1929), 255–316.
Însemnări de demult, ed. I. Corfus. Iași, 1975.
Ionescu, Ion *Agricultura română în judetiulu Mehedinți*. Bucharest, 1868.
Ionescu, Ion *Escursiune agricolă în Câmpia Dobrogei*. Bucharest, 1879.
Ionescu, Ion and Ion Ghica, *Corespondența între Ion Ionescu de la Brad și Ion Ghica, 1846–1874*, ed. V. Slăvescu. Bucharest, 1943.
Ionescu-Șișești, Gh. *Cultura porumbului*. Bucharest, 1955.
Ionescu-Șișești, Gh. 'Porumbul în economia mondială', in *Porumbul*, ed. T. Săvulescu. Bucharest, 1957, 39–73.
Iordache, Anastasie 'Oltenia', in *Marea Răscoală a țăranilor din 1907*. Bucharest, 1967, 445–522.
Iordachi, Constantin *Liberalism, Constitutional Nationalism, and Minorities. The Making of Romanian Citizenship, c. 1750–1918*. Leiden – Boston, 2019. [Balkan Studies Library, 25]
Iordachi, Constantin 'The Phanariot Regime in the Romanian Principalities, 1711/1716–1821', in *The Routledge Handbook of Balkan and Southeast European History*, ed. J. Lampe, U. Brunnbauer. London, 2020, 35–41.
Iorga, N. 'Un boier oltean la Karlsbad in 1796–1797', *Analele Academiei Române. Memoriile secțiunii istorice*, 2d ser., 29 (1906–1907), 215–31.
Iorga, N. 'Scrisori inedite ale lui Tudor Vladimirescu din anii 1814–1815', *Analele Academiei Române. Memoriile secțiunii istorice*, 2d ser., 37 (1914–1915), 121–60.

Iorga, N. 'Vechimea culturii porumbului la noi', *Revista istorică* 6:7–9 (1920), 170–75.
Iorga, N. 'Ancienneté de la culture du maïs en Roumanie', trans. C. Cerkez. *Académie Roumaine. Bulletin de la section historique* 9:1–2 (1921), 185–90.
Iorga, N. *Istoria comerțului românesc*, 2 vols. Bucharest, 1925.
Iorga, N. 'Documente urlățene', *Buletinul Comisiei Istorice a României* 5 (1926), 177–315.
Iorga, N. *Istoria românilor prin călători*, 4 vols. Bucharest, 1928.
Iorga, N. 'Un martur german al timpurilor de prefacere românești', *Revista istorică*, 25:4–6 (1939), 141–46.
Iosa, Mircea 'Comerțul cerealier și piața de cereale din România la sfîrșitul secolului al XIX-lea și începutul secolului al XX-lea', *Revista de istorie* 42:3 (1989), 247–58.
İslamoğlu, Huri and Suraiya Faroqhi, 'Crop Patterns and Agricultural Production Trends in Sixteenth-Century Anatolia', *Review (Fernand Braudel Center)* 2:3 (1979), 400–436.
Ispisoace și zapise, ed. Gh. Ghibănescu. 6 vols. Iași, 1906–1931.
Istrati, Corneliu 'Cu privire la exportul de grîne din Moldova în anii 1830–1831', *Anuarul Institutului de Istorie și Arheologie 'A.D. Xenopol'* 10 (1973), 199–215.
Ittu, Gudrun-Liane, Constantin Ittu, and Ioan Bondrea, *Din istoria bucătăriei fine de la Renaștere până în zilele noastre. Repere sibiene*. Sibiu, 2019.
Izvoare și mărturii referitoare la evreii din România. 3 vols. Bucharest, 1988–1999.

Jackson, John *A Journey from India, towards England, in the Year 1797*. London, 1799.
Jakobson, Roman 'While Reading Vasmer's Dictionary', *Word* 11:4 (1955), 611–17.
Jakubowski, Melchior 'The Introduction of the Potato in Eastern Europe: State or Peasant Initiative?' *Eighteenth-Century Studies* 54:3 (2021), 651–65.
Jensen, J.H. and Gerhard Rosegger, 'Transferring Technology to a Peripheral Economy. The Case of Lower Danube Transport Development, 1856–1928', *Technology and Culture* 19:4 (1978), 675–702.
Jesner, Sabine 'The Physician Adam Chenot: Reshaping Plague Control in the Austrian Cordon Sanitaire', *Banatica* 25 (2015), 283–300.
Jianu, Angela '"The Taste of Others": Travellers and Locals Share Food in the Romanian Principalities (19th Century)', in *Earthly Delights*, ed. A. Jianu, V. Barbu. Leiden – Boston, 2018, 426–58.
Jianu, Angela 'Polenta or Mămăligă? British Perceptions of a South-East European Dish', *Petits Propos Culinaires*, no. 114 (June 2019), 28–36.
Jianu, Angela and Violeta Barbu, eds. *Earthly Delights. Economies and Cultures of Food in Ottoman and Danubian Europe, c. 1500–1900*. Leiden – Boston, 2018. [Balkan Studies Library, 23].
Jones, Michael Owen *Corn. A Global History*. London, 2017.
Jormescu, C. and I. Popa-Burcă, *Harta agronomică a României*. Bucharest, 1907.
Joseph II, *Călătoria Împăratului Iosif al II-lea în Transilvania la 1773 / Die Reise Kaiser Josephs II. durch Siebenbürgen im Jahre 1773*, ed. I. Bozac, T. Pavel. Cluj-Napoca, 2006.
Joseph II, *Orânduiala de pădure* [1786], trans. V. Balș, repr. în Ovidiu Bâtă, 'Evoluția legislației silvice din Bucovina (II)', *Analele Bucovinei* 18:2 (2011), 515–49.

Kakar, M. Hasan *The Consolidation of the Central Authority in Afghanistan under Amir 'Abd Al-Rahman, 1880–1896*. MPhil Thesis, University of London, 1966.
Kălbova, V. and G. Staikov *Tsarevitsa*. Sofia, 1957.
Kaller-Dietrich, Martina 'Mais – Ernährung und Kolonialismus', in *Mais. Geschichte und Nutzung einer Kulturpflanze*, ed. D. Ingruber, M. Kaller-Dietrich. Frankfurt – Vienna, 2001, 13–33.
Kármán, Gábor and Lovro Kunčević, eds., *The European Tributary States of the Ottoman Empire*. Leiden – Boston, 2013.

Katsiardi-Hering, Olga and Maria A. Stassinopoulou, eds. *Across the Danube. Southeastern Europeans and Their Travelling Identities (17th-19th C.)*. Leiden – Boston, 2016.
Kartodirdjo, Sartono *The Peasants' Revolt of Banten in 1888. Its Conditions, Course and Sequel. A Case Study of Social Movements in Indonesia*. The Hague, 1966.
Katić, Tatjana *Tursko osvajanje Srbije 1690. godine*. Belgrade, 2012.
Kellogg, Frederick *The Road to Romanian Independence*. West Lafayette, IN, 1995.
Kemmerer, Donald L. 'The Pre-Civil War South's Leading Crop, Corn', *Agricultural History* 23:4 (1949), 236–39.
Kholiolchev, Khristo 'Za proizhoda na *kukuruz* (*kukurica*) "tsarevitsa *Zea Mays*"', *Izvestiya na Instituta za Bălgarski Ezik* 11 (1964), 459–68.
Kia, Mehrdad *Daily Life in the Ottoman Empire*. Santa Barbara, CA, 2011.
King, Charles *The Black Sea. A History*. Oxford, 2004.
Kiple, Kenneth F. and Kriemhild Coneè Ornelas, eds. *The Cambridge World History of Food*, 2 vols. Cambridge, 2000–2008.
Kisbán, Eszter 'Maisnahrung im Karpatenbecken', in *Festschrift Matthias Zender*, ed. E. Ennen, G. Wiegelmann, 2 vols. Bonn, 1972, i:264–80.
Klein, Samuel *Dictionarium valachico-latinum*, ed. L. Gáldi. Budapest, 1944.
Klemun, Marianne 'Globaler Pflanzentransfer und seine Transferinstanzen als Kultur-, Wissens- und Wissenschaftstransfer der frühen Neuzeit', *Berichte zur Wissenschaftsgeschichte* 29:3 (2006), 205–23.
Koch, Krisztina Kormosné *The Distinctiveness of Hungarian Gastronomy*. Debrecen, 2015.
Kogalnitchan, Michel de *Esquisse sur l'histoire, les mœurs et la langue des Cigains*. Berlin, 1837.
Kogălniceanu, Mihai *Opere*, v: *Oratorie III*. 5 parts. Bucharest, 1984–2004.
[Kogălniceanu, Mihai and Costache Negruzzi], *200 de rețete cercate de bucate* [1841]. Cluj, 1973.
Kogălniceanu, Vasile M. *Chestiunea țărănească*. Bucharest, 1906.
Kohl, J.G. *Hundert Tage auf Reisen in den österreichischen Staaten*. Dresden – Leipzig, 1842.
Kołodziejczyk, Dariusz 'Twisted Ways of Commodities in the Early Modern Era and the Positioning of Poland on the Map of Colonialism', *European Review* 26:3 (2018), 441–47.
Komlos, John 'The New World's Contribution to Food Consumption during the Industrial Revolution', *Journal of European Economic History* 27:1 (1998), 67–82.
König, Theodor *Lebens- und Reisebilder aus Ost und West*. Breslau, 1852.
Kontler, László *A History of Hungary*. Basingstoke, UK – New York, 2002.
Kore, Mimoza and Violeta Shaba, 'Common Patterns of Word Formation in Balkan Languages: The Case of Diminutive Suffixes', *Asian Journal of Social Sciences & Humanities* 2:2 (2013), 338–44.
Köröškeny, Vijekoslav, ed. *Uputa u gospodarstvo po XIV. njemačkom nagradjenom izdanju "Schlipf's Populäres Handbuch der Landwirtschaft" obzirom na naše okolnosti priredili i nadopunili*. Zagreb, 1904.
Kosáry, Domokos *Culture and Society in Eighteenth-Century Hungary*, trans. Z. Béres. Budapest, 1987.
Kovács, Nándor Erik 'The Legal Status of the Danubian Principalities in the 17th Century as Reflected in the *Şikayet Defteris*', *Güney-Doğu Avrupa Araştırmaları Dergisi* 25:1 (2014), 1–24.
Kreuter, Peter Mario 'Zuckerwerk und zehn Bouteillen Wein: Was uns Reise- und diplomatische Berichte über das kulinarische Leben in den Donaufürstentümern mitteilen können', in *Culinaria balcanica*, ed. Th. Kahl, P.M. Kreuter, C. Vogel. Berlin, 2015, 185–202.
Kreuter, Peter Mario 'Attempts of Austrian Redesign of the Administration of Lesser Wallachia between 1718 and 1739', *Yearbook of the Society for 18th Century Studies on South Eastern Europe* 2 (2019), 131–40.

Kupzow, A. J. 'Histoire du maïs (suite et fin)', *Journal d'agriculture tropicale et de botanique appliquée* 15:1–3 (1968), 42–68.

Lack, H. Walter 'Lilac and Horse Chestnut: Discovery and Rediscovery', *Curtis's Botanical Magazine* 17:2 (2000), 109–41.
Landais, Benjamin 'Enregistrer l'ethnicité au XVIIIe siècle: l'identification des migrants ottomans à la frontière habsbourgeoise', *Revue d'histoire moderne et contemporaine* 66:4 (2019), 89–120.
Lang, George *The Cuisine of Hungary*. Harmondsworth, UK, 1985.
Langer, William L. 'American Foods and Europe's Population Growth 1750–1850', *Journal of Social History* 8:2 (1975), 51–66.
Lapavitsas, Costas and Pinar Cakiroglu, *Capitalism in the Ottoman Balkans. Industrialization and Modernity in Macedonia*. London – New York, 2019.
Latham, A. J. H. *Rice. The Primary Commodity*. London, 1998.
Laudan, Rachel *Cuisine and Empire. Cooking in World History*. Berkeley, CA, 2013.
Launay, Robert 'Maize avoidance? Colonial French Attitudes towards Native American Foods in the Pays des Illinois (17th–18th century)', *Food and Foodways* 26:2 (2018), 92–104.
Lazăr, Gheorghe 'The Food Trade in 18th-century Wallachia', in *Earthly Delights*, ed. A. Jianu, V. Barbu. Leiden – Boston, 2018, 311–38.
LeDonne, John P. 'Geopolitics, Logistics, and Grain: Russia's Ambitions in the Black Sea Basin, 1737–1834', *International History Review* 28:1 (2006), 1–41.
Lee, Jonathan L. *Afghanistan. A History from 1260 to the Present*. London, 2018.
Lefebvre, Thibault *Études diplomatiques et économiques sur la Valachie*. Paris, n.d. [1858].
Legea pentru Regularea Proprietăței Rurale (Legea no.1014/1864), online at https://lege5.ro/gratuit/heztqmzy/legea-nr-1014-1864–pentru-regularea-proprietatei-rurale [consulted 3 May 2021]
Levi, Giovanni 'The Diffusion of Maize in Italy: From Resistance to the Peasants' Defeat', in *Global Goods and the Spanish Empire, 1492–1824*, ed. B. Aram, B. Yun Casalilla. Basingstoke, 2014, 100–115.
Lévi-Strauss, Claude *Le Totémisme aujourd'hui*. Paris, 1962.
Levitt, Tom and Chris McCullough, 'Global Food Price Fears as Ukraine Farmers Forced to Reduce Crop Planting', *Guardian*, 2 April 2022, online at https://www.theguardian.com/environment/2022/apr/02/global-food-price-fears-as-ukraine-farmers-forced-to-reduce-crop-planting
Lesicon Roma'nescu-Latinescu-Ungurescu-Nemțescu / Lexicon Valachico-Latino-Hungarico-Germanicum. Buda, 1825.
Liiceanu, Gabriel 'De la mămăligă cu pâine la prepeliță reconstituită', in *Intelectuali la cratiță*, ed. I. Pârvulescu. Bucharest, 2012, 153–70.
Lim, T. K. *Edible Medicinal and Non-Medicinal Plants*, vol. 5: *Fruits*. Dordrecht, 2013.
Limona, E., and D. Limona, 'Aspecte ale comerțului brașovean în veacul al XVIII-lea. Negustorul aromîn Mihail Țumbru', *Studii și materiale de istorie medie* 4 (1960), 525–64.
von Lippmann, Edmund O. 'Zur Geschichte des Mais' [1892], in idem, *Abhandlungen und Vorträge zur Geschichte der Naturwissenschaften*. Leipzig, 1907, 335–38.
Livadă-Cadeschi, Ligia 'Financing Social Care in the Romanian Principalities in the Eighteenth and Nineteenth Centuries', *Analele Universității din București. Seria Științe Politice*, nr. 1 (2013), 37–50.
Livesey, James *Provincializing Global History. Money, Ideas, and Things in the Languedoc, 1680–1830*. New Haven, CT – London, 2020.
Lowood, Henry 'The New World and the European Catalog of Nature', in *America in European Consciousness, 1493–1750*, ed. K.O. Kupperman. Chapel Hill, NC – London, 1995, 295–323.

Luca, Cristian 'Greek and Aromanian Merchants, Protagonists of the Trade Relations between Transylvania, Wallachia, Moldavia and the Northern Italian Peninsula (Second Half of the 17th–First Half of the 18th Century)', *Transylvanian Review* 19:S4 (2010), 313–36.
Lukinich, Imre 'Egy erdélyi kereskedelmi társaság terve 1703–ból', *Századok* 48:6 1914), 464–76.
Lupaş, I. 'Date privitoare la activitatea lui Radu Tempea', *Ţara Bârsei* 4:3 (1932), 195–99.
Lupescu, Mihai 'Bucătăria ţăranului: mămăliga', *Şezătoarea* 5:1 (1898), 3–7.
Lupescu, Mihai *Din bucătăria ţăranului român* [1915]. Bucharest, 2000.
Lusignan, Sauveur *Reise nach der Türkei und einem Theil der Levante*. Hamburg, 1789.

McCann, James C. *Maize and Grace. Africa's Encounter with a New World Crop, 1500–2000*. Cambridge, MA, 2005.
McGowan, Bruce *Economic Life in Ottoman Europe. Taxation, Trade and the Struggle for Land, 1600–1800*. Cambridge, 1981.
McGowan, Bruce 'The Age of the *Ayans*, 1699–1812', in *An Economic and Social History of the Ottoman Empire*, ed. H. İnalcık, D. Quataert. 2 vols. Cambridge, 1994, ii:637–758.
McNeill, J. R. *The Mountains of the Mediterranean World. An Environmental History*. Cambridge, 1992.
McNeill, William H. *Europe's Steppe Frontier, 1500–1800*. Chicago, 1964.
McNeill, William H. 'American Food Crops in the Old World', in *Seeds of Change. A Quincentennial Commemorative*. Washington DC, 1991, 43–59.
Maftei, Maria 'Consideraţii privind comerţul cu cereale din Basarabia prin porturile Ismail şi Reni (anii 1812–1856)', *Tyragetia*, n.s., 1(16):2 (2007), 211–16.
Makkai, László, ed. *I. Rákóczi György birtokainak gazdasági iratai (1631–1648)*. Budapest, 1954.
Malcolm, Noel *Agents of Empire. Knights, Corsairs, Jesuits and Spies in the Sixteenth-Century Mediterranean World*. London, 2015.
Mămăliga erotica: https://mamaligaerotica.com/ [Accessed 18 October 2021]
Mandelblatt, Bertie 'Foods and Diets', in *The Princeton Companion to Atlantic History*, ed. J.C. Miller. Princeton, NJ, 2015, 204–7.
Mann, Stuart E. *An Historical Albanian-English Dictionary*. London, 1948.
Manning, Anne *The Interrupted Wedding. A Hungarian Tale*. London, 1864.
Marea răscoală a ţăranilor din 1907. Bucharest, 1967.
Marie, Queen of Rumania *My Country*. London - New York - Toronto, 1916.
Marin, Irina *Peasant Violence and Antisemitism in Early Twentieth-Century Eastern Europe*. Basingstoke, 2018.
Marin, Sanda *Carte de bucate* [1936]. 9th edn. Bucharest, 1943.
Marinescu, Florin 'The Trade of Wallachia with the Ottoman Empire between 1791 and 1821', *Balkan Studies* 12:2 (1981), 289–319.
Matković, Petar 'Dva talijanska putopisa po balkanskom poluotoku iz XVI. vieka', *Jugoslavenska Akademija Znanosti i Umjetnosti* 10 (1878), 201–56.
Matthioli, Petr Ondřej *Herbář jinak bylinář velmi užitečný*, trans. T. Hájek z Hájku [1562]. Facsimile edn., Prague, 1982.
Matthioli, Petrus Andrea *New Kreüterbuch, mit den allerschönsten und artlichsten Figuren aller Gewechß, dergleichen vormals in keiner sprach nie an tag kommen*, trans. G. Handsch. Prague, 1563.
Maurer, Maria *Carte de bucate* [1849], ed. S. Lazăr. Bucharest, 2019.
Mayer, Matthew Z. 'The Price for Austria's Security: Part I – Joseph II, the Russian Alliance, and the Ottoman War, 1787–1789', *International History Review* 26:2 (2004), 257–99.
Mayer, Milan *Die Landwirtschaft der Königreiche Kroatien und Slavonien*. Leipzig, 1908.
Mazower, Mark *The Balkans. A Short History*. London, 2000.

Mažuranić, Vladimir *Prinosi za hrvatski pravno-povjestni rječnik*. Zagreb, 1908–1922.
Mehmet, Mustafa 'Acţiuni diplomatice la Poarta în legătură cu mişcarea revoluţionară din 1821', *Studii* 24:1 (1971), 63–76.
Mémoires et projets de réforme dans les Principautés Roumaines, 1769–1830, ed. V. Georgescu. Bucharest, 1970.
Merişescu, Tache *Tinereţile unui ciocoiaş* [c. 1840], ed. C. Vintilă-Ghiţulescu. Bucharest, 2019.
Messedaglia, Luigi *Notizie storiche sul mais. Una gloria veneta. Saggio di storia agraria*. Venice, 1924.
Messer, Ellen 'Maize', in *The Cambridge World History of Food*, ed. K. Kiple, K. Coneè Ornelas. 2 vols. Cambridge, 2000–2008, i:97–112.
Mézes, Ádám 'Georg Tallar and the 1753 Vampire Hunt. Administration, Medicine and the Returning Dead in the Habsburg Banat', in *The Magical and Sacred Medical World*, ed. É. Pócs. Newcastle, 2019, 93–136.
Mézes, Ádám *Doubt and Diagnosis: Medical Experts and the Returning Dead of the Southern Habsburg Borderland (1718–1766)*. PhD diss., Central European University, 2020.
Mihăescu, Petre E. *Tutunul în trecutul Ţării Româneşti şi al lumii întregi*. Bucharest, 1931.
Mihail, Gh. *Soia*. Bucharest, 1904.
Mihail, Zamfira 'Pâinea în cultul ortodox şi semnificaţia sa în viaţa laicilor', *Revista de etnografie şi folclor* 38:5 (1993), 465–71.
Mihăilescu, Vintilă 'En quête de la *sarma*. Essai sur les attentes sociales', *Revue du MAUSS* 25:1 (2005), 428–51.
Mihajlović, Velimir *Građa za rečnik stranih reči u predvukovskom periodu (od vremena pre Velike seobe do Vukovog rječnika 1818. godine)*. 2 vols. Novi Sad, 1972–1974.
Mihordea, Vasile *Maîtres du sol et paysans dans les principautés roumaines au XVIIIe siècle*, trans. R. Creţeanu. Bucharest, 1971.
Mikes, Kelemen *Török országi levelek*. Szombathely, 1794.
Mikes, Kelemen *Letters from Turkey*, trans. B. Adams. London, 2000.
Mikhail, Alan *Nature and Empire in Ottoman Egypt. An Environmental History*. Cambridge, 2011.
Milică, Ioan 'Nume de plante şi nume de locuri', *Philologica Jassyensia* 10:2 (2014), 61–68.
Minea, Cosmin 'Roma Musicians, Folk Art and Traditional Food from Romania at the Paris World Fairs of 1889 and 1900', in *World Fairs and the Global Moulding of National Identities*, ed. J. Leerssen, E. Storm. Leiden, 2021, 144–69.
Mir, C., T. Zerjal, V. Combes, F. Dumas, D. Madur, C. Bedoya, S. Dreisigacker, J. Franco, P. Grudloyma, P. Hao, S. Hearne, C. Jampatong, D. Laloë, Z. Muthamia, T. Nguyen, B. Prasanna, S. Taba, C. Xie, M. Yunus, S. Zhang, M. Warburton, A. Charcosset 'Out of America: Tracing the Genetic Footprints of the Global Diffusion of Maize', *Theoretical and Applied Genetics* 126:11 (2013), 2671–82.
Mîrza, Mihai 'Cheltuielile casei marelui vistiernic Toader Palade, după o samă din anul 1752', *Analele ştiinţifice ale Universităţii 'Alexandru Ioan Cuza' din Iaşi*, n.s., Istorie, 59 (2013), 333–408.
Mitrany, David *The Land and the Peasant in Rumania. The War and Agrarian Reform (1917–1921)*. Oxford, 1930.
Mladenov, Stefan *Etimologicheski i pravopisen rechnik na bălgarskiya knizhoven ezik*. Sofia, 1941.
Mlekuž, Jernej *Burek. A Culinary Metaphor*. Budapest – New York, 2015.
Mlekuž, Jernej 'The Renaissance of Sausage: The Role of Krajnska Sausage in the Contemporary Process of Reconstructing the Slovenian Nation', *Nations and Nationalism* 26:2 (2020), 407–23.
Mocarelli, F. Luca and Aleksander Panjek, eds. *Maize to the People! Cultivation, Consumption and Trade in the North-Eastern Mediterranean (Sixteenth-Nineteenth Century)*. Koper, 2020.

Moga, I. 'Politica economică austriacă și comerțul Transilvaniei în veacul XVIII', *Anuarul Institutului de Istorie Națională* 7 (1936–1938), 86–165.
Montanari, Massimo *The Culture of Food*, trans. C. Ipsen. Oxford, UK – Cambridge, MA, 1994.
Monumenta Comitalia Regni Transylvaniae/Erdély Orszaggyűlési Emlékek, vol. 18 *(1683–1686)*, ed. S. Szilágyi. Budapest, 1895.
Monumenta historica Slavorum meridionalium, vol. 1–i, ed. V. Makuscev. Warsaw, 1874.
Monumenta serbica spectantia historiam Serbiae, Bosniae, Ragusii, ed. F. Miklosich. Vienna, 1858.
Mrgić, Jelena 'A Polyphony of Stories from 17th- and 18th-Century Southeastern Europe', *Godišnjak za društvenu istoriju* nr. 2 (2015), 7–24.
Müller, Konrad *Siebenbürgische Wirtschaftspolitik unter Maria Theresia*. Munich, 1961.
Mungiu, Cristian (dir.) *4 luni, 3 săptămâni și 2 zile* [4 Months, 3 Weeks and 2 Days] (2007) https://www.imdb.com/title/tt1032846/
Mureșan, Florin Valeriu *Satul românesc din nord-estul Transilvaniei la mijlocul secolului al XVIII-lea*. Cluj-Napoca, 2005.
Murgescu, Bogdan 'Der Anteil der rumänischen Fürstentümer am europäischen Viehhandel vom 16. bis zum 18. Jahrhundert', *Scripta Mercaturae* 33:2 (1999), 61–91.
Murgescu, Bogdan 'Romanian Grain Exports and the Treaty of Adrianople (1829)', in *Schnittstellen. Gesellschaft, Nation, Konflikt und Erinnerung in Südosteuropa*, ed. U. Brunnbauer, A. Helmedach, S. Troebst. Munich, 2007, 57–65.
Murgescu, Bogdan *România și Europa. Acumularea decalajelor economice (1500–2010)*. Iași, 2010.
Murgescu, Bogdan *Țările Române între Imperiul Otoman și Europa creștină*. Iași, 2013.
Murphey, Rhoads *Ottoman Warfare, 1500–1700*. London, 1999.
Mutafchieva, Vera *Osmanska sotsialno-ikonomicheska istoriya*. Sofia, 2008 [*Izbrani proizvedeniya* 5].

Nacu, Florin, 'A Survey of Romanian Culinary Heritage in the Second Half of the Nineteenth Century', *Transylvanian Review*, Suppl. 2 (2021), 79–102.
Nadal, Jordi 'The Failure of the Industrial Revolution in Spain, 1830–1914', in *The Fontana Economic History of Europe*, vol. 4: *The Emergence of Industrial Societies*, ed. C. M. Cipolla. Glasgow, 1973, ii:532–626.
Nădejde, Sofiea 'Hrana', *Contemporanul* 3:16 (1884), 601–5.
Nădejde, Sofiea 'Schițe din vieața la țară', *Contemporanul* 5:4 (1886), 289–301.
Nagy, Imola Katalin 'O scurtă istorie a literaturii gastronomice / A Short History of Gastronomic Literature', *Journal of Romanian Literary Studies* 11 (2017), 323–34.
Nagy, Imola Katalin 'Disputed Words of Disputed Territories: Whose is *Kürtőskalács*?', *Acta Universitatis Sapientiae. Philologica* 10:3 (2018) 67–85.
Nasta, Alexander *Der Maisbau in Rumänien*. Leipzig, 1909.
Nasta, Dominique *Contemporary Romanian Cinema. The History of an Unexpected Miracle*. London – New York, 2013.
Neacșu, I. 'Participarea locuitorilor satelor din Oltenia la răscoala din 1821', *Studii* 11:2 (1958), 91–114.
Neale, Adam *Travels through Some Parts of Germany, Poland, Moldavia and Turkey*. London, 1818.
Neamțu, Vasile *La technique de la production céréalière en Valachie et en Moldavie jusqu'au XVIIIe siècle*, trans. A. Marin. Bucharest, 1975.
Neculce, Ion *Letopisețul Țării Moldovei* [c. 1740], ed. G. Ștrempel. Bucharest, 1982.
Neuburger, Mary C. *Ingredients of Change. The History and Culture of Food in Modern Bulgaria*. Ithaca, NY, 2022.
Nişanyan, Sevan *Sözlük*, online at https://www.nisanyansozluk.com/
Notaker, Henry 'Romania, Cooking, Literature and Politics: A Cookbook from Moldova, 1841', *Petits propos culinaires* nr. 35 (1990), 7–22.

Noth- und Hilferuf der Gemeinden des Moldauisch-Campulunger Okols in der Bukowina. Vienna, 1861.

Oancă, Teodor 'Sufixul antroponimic *-ega*', *Limba română* 31:3 (1982), 252–59.
Obradović, Dositej *Ezopove basne*. Leipzig, 1788.
Obradovici, Grigorie trans. *Carte de mână pentru Bine Orânduita Economie, Lucrarea câmpului, şi pentru plămădirea şi pândirea a vitelor şi a păsărilor celor casnice. Spre mare treabă a plugarilor celor rumâneşti*. Buda, 1807.
Oişteanu, Andrei 'Jewish Tavern-Keepers and the Myth of the Poisoned Drinks', in *Earthly Delights*, ed. A. Jianu, V. Barbu. Leiden – Boston, 2018, 478–511.
Oişteanu, Andrei *Moravuri şi năravuri. Eseuri de istorie a mentalităţilor*. Iaşi, 2021.
Olaru, Vasile Mihai *Writs and Measures. Symbolic Power and the Growth of State Infrastructure in Wallachia, 1740–1800*. PhD diss., Central European University, 2014.
Olbrycht, T. and W. Nadwyczawski *Kukurydza*. Warsaw, 1956.
Oliphant, Laurence *The Russian Shores of the Black Sea in the Autumn of 1852*. London, 1854.
O'Neill, Thomas P. 'The Organisation and Administration of Relief, 1845–52', in *The Great Famine*, ed. R. Dudley Edwards, T. D. Williams. Dublin, 1956, 209–61.
Onilov, Tatiana *Generalul Pavel Kiseleff, Principatele Române şi Regulamentele Organice*. PhD diss., Romanian Academy School of Higher Advanced Studies, Cluj-Napoca, 2018.
Orel, Vladimir *Albanian Etymological Dictionary*. Leiden, 1998.
Örenç, Ali Fuat 'Albanian Soldiers in the Ottoman Army During the Greek Revolt at 1821', in *2nd International Balkan Annual Conference* (IBAC 2012), Proceedings, ed. B. Çınar. 2 vols. Tirana, 2012, ii:502–24.
Orraeus, Gustav *Descriptio pestis quae anno MDCCLXX in Jassia, et MDCCLXXI in Moscva grassata est*. St. Petersburg, 1784.
Osterhammel, Jürgen 'Kulturelle Grenzen in der Expansion Europas', *Jahrbuch für Universalgeschichte* 46:1 (1995), 101–38.
Oţetea, Andrei *Tudor Vladimirescu şi mişcarea eteristă în ţările româneşti, 1821–1822*. Bucharest, 1945.
Oţetea, Andrei 'Constrângerea extraeconomică a clăcaşilor la începutul secolului al XIX-lea', *Studii şi referate privind istoria Rômîniei* 2 (1954), 1055–76.
Oţetea, Andrei 'Le second asservissement des paysans roumains (1746–1821)', *Nouvelles études d'histoire* 1 (1955), 299–312.
Oţetea, Andrei 'Le second servage dans les Principautés danubiennes (1831–1864)', *Nouvelles études d'histoire* 2 (1960), 325–46.
Oţetea, Andrei *Pătrunderea comerţului românesc în circuitul internaţional*. Bucharest, 1977.
Otter, Chris *Diet for a Large Planet. Industrial Britain, Food Systems and World Ecology*. Chicago, 2020.

Păcurar, Cristina 'Suntem ceea ce mâncăm: evoluţii privind alimentaţia şi identităţile culinare în spaţiul românesc – o istoriografie a alimentaţiei', *Caiete de antropologie istorică*, nr. 37 (2020), 17–31.
Pakucs-Willcocks, Mária 'The Transit of Oriental Goods through the Customs of Sibiu/Hermannstadt in the Sixteenth and Seventeenth Centuries: An Overview', in *Economy and Society in Central and Eastern Europe*, ed. D. Dumitran, V. Moga. Münster, 2014, 19–30.
Pálffy, Géza *Hungary between Two Empires, 1526–1711*. Bloomington, IN, 2021.
Palmer-Mehta, Valerie and Alina Haliliuc, 'The Performance of Silence in Cristian Mungiu's *4 Months, 3 Weeks, and 2 Days*', *Text and Performance Quarterly* 31:2 (2011), 111–29.
Pamfile, Tudor *Agricultura la români*. Bucharest, 1913.

Panjek, Aleksander 'Tracing Maize in the Slovenian Regions, Sixteenth-Eighteenth Century', in *Maize to the People!*, ed. L. Mocarelli, A. Panjek. Koper, 2020, 87–111.

Pap, Francisc 'Produse agricole la vama Clujului în prima jumătate a secolului XVII', *Terra Nostra* 3 (1973), 345–56.

Papacostea, Șerban 'Contribuție la problema relațiilor agrare în Țara Romînească în prima jumătate a veacului al XVIII-lea', *Studii și materiale de istorie medie* 3 (1959), 233–321.

Papacostea, Șerban *Oltenia sub stăpânirea austriacă, 1718–1739*. Bucharest, 1998.

Papuc, Liviu 'Inaugurarea statuii lui Ștefan cel Mare la Iași – moment de efervescență națională', *Analele Putnei* 7:1 (2011), 219–98.

Parker, Geoffrey *Global Crisis. War, Climate Change and Catastrophe in the Seventeenth Century*. New Haven, CT – London, 2013.

Parvev, Ivan *Habsburgs and Ottomans between Vienna and Belgrade (1683–1739)*. Boulder, CO, 1995.

Pașca, Ștefan *Nume de persoane și nume de animale în Țara Oltului*. Bucharest, 1936.

Pascu, G. 'Studiĭ filologice, VII: Elemente greceștĭ', *Arhiva Societății Științifice și Literare din Iași* 16 (1905), 423–28.

Pascu, G. *Sufixele românești*. Bucharest, 1916.

Pascu, G. 'Le maïs dans les langues romanes et balkaniques', *Homenatge a Antoni Rubió y Lluch*, vol. 1 (Barcelona, 1936), 451–69.

de Paz Sánchez, Manuel 'El trigo de los pobres: La recepción del maíz en el Viejo Mundo', *Batey: Revista Cubana de Antropología Sociocultural* 5:5 (2013), 142–74.

Pedani, Mara Pia *Dalla frontiera al confine*. Venice, 2002.

Penelea, Georgeta *Les foires de la Valachie pendant la période 1774–1848*, trans. M. Costescu. Bucharest, 1973.

Penelea, Georgeta 'Considerații asupra comerțului extern al Țării Românești în epoca reglementară', *Terra Nostra* 3 (1973), 323–31.

Perianu, Radu I. 'Raiaua Brăilei: Noi contribuțiuni', *Revista istorică română* 15:3 (1945), 287–333.

Pešalj, Jovan *Monitoring Migrations: The Habsburg-Ottoman Border in the Eighteenth Century*. PhD diss., University of Leiden, 2019.

Petőfi, Sándor *János Vitéz / John the Valiant* [1844; trans. J. Ridland, 1999]. Bilingual edition at https://www.babelmatrix.org/works/hu/Pet%c5%91fi_S%c3%a1ndor-1823/J%c3%a1nos_Vit%c3%a9z_(teljes)

Petrică, Virginia *Identitate culinară românească din perspectiva călătorilor străini*. Bucharest, 2013.

Petrică, Virginia *Topography of Taste. Landmarks of Culinary Identity in the Romanian Principalities from the Perspective of Foreign Travellers*. Bucharest, 2018.

Petrovici, Dan A. and Christopher Ritson, 'Food Consumption Patterns in Romania', *British Food Journal* 102:4 (2000), 290–308.

Philippides, Daniil *Geografikon tis Roumounias* [1816], trans. N. Bănescu, in 'Viața și opera lui Daniel (Dimitrie) Philippide', *Anuarul Institutului de Istorie Națională* 2 (1923), 156–204.

Philliou, Christine M. 'Communities on the Verge. Unraveling the Phanariot Ascendancy in Ottoman Governance', *Comparative Studies in Society and History* 51:1 (2009), 151–81.

Philliou, Christine M. *Biography of an Empire. Governing Ottomans in an Age of Revolution*. Berkeley, CA, 2012.

Piccillo, Giuseppe *Il glossario italiano-moldavo di Silvestro Amelio (1719). Studio filologico e testo*. Catania, 1982.

Pilcher, Jeffrey M. *Food in World History*. New York – Abingdon, 2006.

Pina-Cabral, João 'Minhoto Counterpoints. On Metaphysical Pluralism and Social Emergence', *HAU: Journal of Ethnographic Theory* 11:1 (2021), 191–201.

Piper, Milorad *et al. Kukuruz*. Belgrade, 1965. Consulted online at https://www.tehnologijahrane.com/knjiga/kukuruz
Pippidi, Andrei *Hommes et idées du sud-est européen à l'aube de l'âge moderne*. Paris – Bucharest, 1980.
Pippidi, Andrei 'Balkan Hinterlands: The Danubian Principalities', in *A Critical Dictionary of the Greek Revolution*, ed. P. Kitromilides, C. Tsoukalas. Cambridge, MA – London, 2021, 19–29.
Pîrnău, Ludmila, George Bilavschi, Luminița Bejenaru, Vasilica-Monica Groza, eds. *Alimentație și demografie în Moldova din Evul Mediu până în epoca modernă. Abordări interdisciplinare*. Cluj-Napoca, 2021.
Platon, Gh. 'Cu privire la pribegirea locuitorilor din Moldova în anul 1834', *Analele științifice ale Universității 'Al. I. Cuza' din Iași*, n.s., Secțiunea 3 (Științe Sociale), 4 (1958), 49–60.
Platon, Gh. *Domeniul feudal din Moldova în preajma revoluției de la 1848*. Iași, 1973.
Poboran, G. *Istoria orașului Slatina*, 2nd edn. Slatina, 1908.
Polónia, Amélia 'Think Globally, Act Locally: Environmental History as Global History in the First Global Age', *Asian Review of World Histories* 3:1 (2015), 59–80.
Popescu, Adina *Casting Bread Upon the Waters. American Farming and the International Wheat Market, 1880–1920*. PhD diss., Columbia University, 2014.
Popescu, Mircea '"Colomba" e "mais" in romeno', *Societas Academica Dacoromana. Acta philologica* 2 (1959), 235–39.
Popovici, Vlad 'Establishment of the Austrian Military Border in Transylvania and Its Short- and Medium-term Effects', *Povijesni prilozi* 37:54 (2018), 291–306.
Popovici-Lupa, N. O. 'Mijloacele prin cari s'ar putea schimba hrana săteanului, înlocuindu-se mămăliga cu pânea', *Buletinul Societății de Științe din București-Romania* 14:3–4 (1905), 319–26.
Pora, I. 'Mișcarea artistică', *Calendarul Minervei pe anul 1915*. Bucharest, 1915, 177–87.
Post, John D. *The Last Great Subsistence Crisis in the Western World*. Baltimore, MD – London, 1977.
Potra, George *Din Bucureștii de altădată*. Bucharest, 1981.
Proverbele românilor, ed. I. A. Zanne. 9 vols. Bucharest, 1895–1903.
Pușcariu, Ioan Cavaler de *Date istorice privitorie la familiele nobile române*. 2 vols. Sibiu, 1892–1895.
Pușcariu, Sextil 'Besprechung: W. Meyer-Lübke, *Romanisches Etymologisches Wörterbuch*', *Zeitschrift für romanische Philologie* 37:1 (1913), 99–114.
Pușcariu, Sextil, note on Capidan, 'Elemente românești', *Dacoromania* 7 (1931–1933), 153.

Rădulescu, Maria 'Raporturi lingvistice bulgaro-române', in *Omagiu lui Iorgu Iordan*. Bucharest, 1958, 715–20.
Radushev, Evgeni Svetlana Ivanova, Rumen Kovachev, 'Introduction' to eidem, eds. *Inventory of Ottoman Turkish Documents about Waqf Preserved in the Oriental Department at the St St Cyril and Methodius National Library, Part 1*. Sofia, 2003, 11–56.
[Raicevich, Ignaz Sfefan] *Osservazioni storiche naturali e politiche intorno la Valachia e Moldavia*. Naples, 1788.
Rapoarte consulare și diplomatice engleze privind Principatele Dunărene, 1800–1812, ed. P. Cernovodeanu. Brăila, 2007.
Rapoarte diplomatice ruse din România (1899–1905), ed. F. Solomon, A. Cușco, G. Șkundin, A. Stâkalin. [= Hurmuzaki, *Documente*, 3d ser., iv]. Bucharest – Brăila, 2020.
Răscoala țăranilor din 1888. Documente, ed. M. Roller. Bucharest, 1950.
Rauwolf, Leonhart *Aigentliche beschreibung der Raiß, so er vor diser zeit gegen Auffgang inn die Morgenländer, fürnemlich Syriam, Judaeam, Arabiam, Mesopotamiam, Babyloniam, Assyriam, Armeniam etc. nicht ohne geringe mühe unnd grosse gefahr selbs volbracht*. N.p., 1582.

Reader, John *Potato. A History of the Propitious Esculent*. New Haven, CT, 2009.
Regueiro y González-Barros, Antonio M. 'La flora americana en la España del siglo XVI', in *America y la España del siglo XVI*, ed. F. de Solano, F. del Pino. 2 vols. Madrid, 1982–1983, 1:205–17.
Regulamentele Organice ale Valahiei și Moldovei. Bucharest, 1943.
Relațiile româno-otomane, 1711–1821. Documente turcești, ed. & trans. V. Veliman. Bucharest, 1984.
Richards, Alan *Egypt's Agricultural Development, 1800–1980*. Boulder, CO, 1982.
Richards, John F. *The Unending Frontier. An Environmental History of the Early Modern World*. Berkeley, CA, 2003.
Riedler, Florian 'The Istanbul–Belgrade Route in the Ottoman Empire', in *The Balkan Route*, ed. F. Riedler, N. Stefanov. Berlin, 2021, 103–20.
Reindl-Kiel, Hedda 'Simits for the Sultan, Cloves for the Mynah Birds: Records of Food Distribution in the Saray', in *Earthly Delights*, ed. A. Jianu, V. Barbu. Leiden, 2018, 50–76.
Rivlin, Helen Anne B. *The Agricultural Policy of Muḥammad 'Alī in Egypt*. Cambridge, MA, 1961.
Rječnik hrvatskoga ili srpskoga jezika, 23 vols. Zagreb, 1880–1976.
Robarts, Andrew *A Plague on Both Houses? Population Movements and the Spread of Disease Across the Ottoman-Russian Black Sea Frontier, 1768–1830s*. PhD diss., Georgetown University, 2010.
Robarts, Andrew *Migration and Disease in the Black Sea Region. Ottoman-Russian Relations in the Late Eighteenth and Early Nineteenth Centuries*. London – New York, 2017.
Roider, Karl 'Nationalism and Colonization in the Banat of Temesvar, 1718–1778', in *Nation and ideology*, ed. I. Banac, J. Ackerman, R. Szporluk. New York 1981, 87–100.
Roman, Louis 'Statistiques fiscales et statistiques démographiques, ou les fausses apparences', *Annales de démographie historique* (1985), 245–80.
Roman, Nicoleta 'Women in Merchant Families, Women in Trade in Mid 19th-Century Romanian Countries', in *Women, Consumption, and the Circulation of Ideas in South-Eastern Europe*, ed. C. Vintilă-Ghițulescu. Leiden – Boston, 2017, 169–99.
Roman, Radu Anton *Bucate, vinuri și obiceiuri românești* [1998]. 2nd edn. Bucharest, 2001.
Roman, Radu Anton *Romanian Dishes, Wines and Customs*, trans. A. Blyth. Bucharest, 2008.
Rosenberger, Bernard 'Cultures complémentaires et nourritures de substitution au Maroc (XVe-XVIIIe siècle)', *Annales* 35:3–4 (1980), 477–503.
Rosetti, Radu *Pământul, sătenii și stăpânii în Moldova*. Bucharest, 1907.
Rosetti, Radu *Pentru ce s'au răsculat țăranii*. Bucharest, 1907.
Rosetti, Theodor 'Despre direcțiunea progresului nostru' [1874], in *Antologia ideologiei junimiste*, ed. E. Lovinescu. Bucharest, 1943, 117–62.
Roth, Klaus 'Türkentrank, Gulyás, Joghurt, Döner: Stereotypen in der europäischen Esskultur', in *Vom Schwarzwald bis zum Schwarzen Meer*, ed. V. Heuberger, G. Stangler. Frankfurt am Main, 2001, 43–55.
Rothenberg, Gunther E. 'The Austrian Sanitary Cordon and the Control of Bubonic Plague: 1710–1871', *Journal of the History of Medicine and Allied Sciences* 28:1 (1973), 15–23.
Rus, Dorin-Ioan 'Weather Anomalies in Transylvania, the Banat and Partium from 1813 to 1818, as reflected in contemporary sources', *Ekonomska i ekohistorija* 16 (2020), 146–66.

Sacerdoțeanu, Aurel 'Acte drăjnene', *Buletinul Comisiei Istorice a României* 13 (1934), 183–98.
Sacher-Masoch, Leopold von *Basil Hymen*. Leipzig, 1882.
Șaineanu, Lazăr *Dicționar universal al limbei române*, 5th edn. Craiova [1925].
Șakul, Kahraman 'The Evolution of Ottoman Military Logistical Systems in the Later Eighteenth Century: The Rise of a New Class of Military Entrepreneur', in *War, Entrepreneurs,*

and the State in Europe and the Mediterranean, 1300–1800, ed. J. Fynn-Paul. Leiden, 2014, 307–27.
Sala, Marius 'În legătură cu denumirea porumbului în limba romînă', *Fonetică și dialectologie* 1 (1958), 181–87.
Sala, Marius 'Sobre las denominaciones rumanas del maíz', *Revista brasileira de filologia* 5:1–2 (1959–1960), 119–27.
Salaberry, Charles-Marie d'Yrumberry, comte de *Voyage à Constantinople*. Paris, 1799.
Salah Harzallah, Mohamed 'Food Supply and Economic Ideology: Indian Corn Relief During the Second Year of the Great Irish Famine', *The Historian* 68:2 (2006), 305–22.
Salzmann, Ariel 'The Age of Tulips: Confluence and Conflict in Early Modern Consumer Culture (1550–1730)', in *Consumption Studies and the History of the Ottoman Empire*, ed. D. Quataert. New York, 2000, 83–106.
Sampson, Steven 'Muddling Through in Rumania (Or: Why the Mamaliga Doesn't Explode)', *International Journal of Rumanian Studies* 3:1–2 (1981–1983), 165–79.
Sassoon, Donald *The Anxious Triumph. A Global History of Capitalism, 1860–1914*. London, 2018.
Savin, Petronela 'Pentru un studiu lingvistic al frazeologiei cerealelor și preparatelor din cereale', *Philologica Jassyensia* 3:1 (2007), 57–64.
Savin, Petronela *Universul din lingură. Despre terminologia alimentară românească*. Iași, 2012.
Savin, Petronela *Romanian Phraseological Dictionary*, trans. I. Boghian. Iași, 2012.
Savin, Petronela 'Bread. From Culture to Phraseological Imaginary', *Philologica Jassyensia* 8:2 (2012), 185–91.
Săvulescu, Traian, ed. *Porumbul*. Bucharest, 1957.
Scheludko, D. 'Rumänische Elemente im Ukrainischen', *Balkan-Archiv* 2 (1926), 113–46.
Scherf, Ioana '"Die Sprache bittet zu Tisch": Zu Lebensmittelbegriffen in rumänischen Redewendungen', in *Culinaria balcanica*, ed. Th. Kahl, P.M. Kreuter, C. Vogel. Berlin, 2015, 113–30.
Schmidt, Peer 'Der Anbau amerikanischer Nahrungspflanzen in Europa (16.-19. Jh.)', *Jahrbuch für Geschichte von Staat, Wirtschaft und Gesellschaft Lateinamerikas* 32 (1995), 57–104.
Schwantz, Friedrich 'Kurtze Erklährung und Bericht über die diesseith des Alth-Flusses gelegene fünff Districte der Kayserlichen Valachey sive Valachiae Cis-Alutanae' (1723), Österreichische Nationalbibliothek, Sammlung von Handschriften und alten Drucken, Cod. Ser. 34, online at https://digital.onb.ac.at/RepViewer/viewer.faces?doc=DTL_6387095&order=1&view=SINGLE.
Scott, James C. *The Art of Not Being Governed. An Anarchist History of Upland Southeast Asia*. New Haven, CT, 2009.
Scott, James C. *Against the Grain. A Deep History of the Earliest States*. New Haven, CT, 2017.
Scrob, Mircea-Lucian *From Mămăligă to Bread as the "Core" Food of Romanian Villagers. A Consumer-Centred Interpretation of a Dietary Change, 1900–1980*. PhD diss., Central European University, 2015.
Senciuc, Olivia 'Istoriografia românească a alimentației: Geneză, surse documentare, direcții și metode de cercetare', *Cercetări istorice*, n.s., nr. 30–31 (2011–2012), 65–81.
Senciuc, Olivia 'Exotic Brew? Coffee and Tea in 18th-century Moldavia and Wallachia', in *Earthly Delights*, ed. A. Jianu, V. Barbu. Leiden, 2018, 127–46.
Șerban, Constantin 'Cîteva date privind producția de cereale din Țara Românească în secolul XVIII', *Terra Nostra* 3 (1973), 255–61.
Șerban, Constantin *Vasile Lupu. Domn al Moldovei, 1634–1653*. Bucharest, 1991.
Sestini, Domenico *Viaggio curioso-scientifico-antiquario per la Valachia, Transilvania e Ungheria fino a Vienna*. Florence, 1815.

Sima al lui Jón, Gr. *Ardeleanul glumeț sau 101 de anecdote poporale*. Sibiu, 1889.
Šimundić, Mate 'Der Eigenname "Kukuruz" im Lichte der Herkunft des betreffende Substantivs', *Балканско езикознание / Linguistique balkanique*, 23:4 (1980), 59–69.
Șincai, Gheorghe *Elementa linguæ Dacoromanæ sive Valachicæ*. Buda, 1805.
Șincai, Gheorghe *Povățuiri cătră Economia de Câmp*. Buda, 1806.
Siruni, H. Dj. *Armenii in viața economică a Țărilor Române*. Bucharest, 1944.
Situația agrară, economică și socială a Olteniei în epoca lui Tudor Vladimirescu. Documente contemporane, ed. N. Iorga, Bucharest, 1915.
Skene, J. H. *The Danubian Principalities. The Frontier Lands of the Christian and the Turk*. 3rd edn., 2 vols.. London, 1854.
Skok, Petar *Etimologijski rječnik hrvatskoga ili srpskoga jezyka*. 4 vols. Zagreb, 1971–1974.
Slavici, Ioan 'Gura satului' [1878], in *Nuvele din popor*, vol. 2. Bucharest, 1881.
Smičiklas, Tade *Dvijestogodišnjica oslobodjenja Slavonije*, 2 vols. Zagreb, 1891.
Smith, Melanie and Márta Jusztin 'Paprika: The Spice of Life in Hungary', in *Spices and Tourism*, ed. L. Joliffe. Bristol, UK – Tonawanda, NY, 2014, 53–71.
Soranzo, Jacopo *Diario del viaggio da Venezia a Costantinopoli, MDLXXV.* Venice, 1856.
Sorbala, Vitale 'Despre originea termenilor *ciocălău, mămăligă* și *cioclej* în limba română', *Studii și cercetări lingvistice* 22:2 (1971), 167–73.
Sorescu, Andrei Dan *Visions of Agency. Imagining Individual and Collective Action in Nineteenth-Century Romania*. PhD diss., University College London, 2018.
Șotropa, Virgil 'Tătarii în Valea Rodnei', *Anuarul Institutului de Istorie Națională* 3 (1924–1925), 255–74.
Speranță, Th. D. 'Povestea poveștilor', *Contemporanul* 2:12 (1882), 444–52.
Sperber, Galia *The Art of Romanian Cooking*. Gretna, LA, 2002.
Stachowski, Kamil *Names of Cereals in the Turkic Languages*. Cracow, 2008 (Studia Turcologica Cracoviensa, 11).
Stahl, Henri H. *Contribuții la studiul satelor devălmașe românești*, 3 vols. Bucharest, 1958–1965.
Stahl, Henri H. *Traditional Romanian Village Communities*, trans. D. Chirot, H.C. Chirot. Cambridge – Paris, 1980.
Stanojević, Milorad L. *Die Landwirtschaft in Serbien*. Halle, 1913.
Ștefănescu, Barbu 'Începuturile introducerii tehnicii moderne în agricultura Bihorului', *Biharea* 9 (1981), 7–38.
Ștefănescu, Barbu 'Considerații asupra nivelului tehnicii agricole din Bihor în secolul al XVIII-lea', *Crisia* 13 (1983), 167–81.
Ștefănescu, Ștefan 'Aspects de la révolution démographique dans les pays roumains à la fin du XVIIIe siècle', *Nouvelles études d'histoire* 6:1 (1980), 310–26.
Steube, Johann Kaspar *Von Amsterdam nach Temiswar. Wanderschaften und Schicksale, 1772–1781* [1791], ed. J. Holz. Berlin, 1984.
Stoianovich, Traian 'Land Tenure and Related Sectors of the Balkan Economy, 1600–1800', *Journal of Economic History* 13:4 (1953), 398–411.
Stoianovich, Traian 'The Conquering Balkan Orthodox Merchant' *Journal of Economic History* 20:2 (1960), 234–313.
Stoianovich, Traian 'Le maïs dans les Balkans', *Annales*, 21:5 (1966), 1026–40.
Stoianovich, Traian 'Russian Domination in the Balkans', in *Russian Imperialism*, ed. T. Hunczak. New Brunswick, NJ, 1974, 198–238.
Stoianovich, Traian *Balkan Worlds. The First and Last Europe*. Armonk, NY – London, 1994.
Stoica de Hațeg, Nicolae *Cronica Banatului*, ed. D. Mioc. 2nd edn. Timișoara, 1981.
Stoicescu, Nicolae *Cum măsurau strămoșii. Metrologia medievală pe teritoriul României*. Bucharest, 1971.

Stoker, Bram *Dracula*. London, 1897.
Stratilesco, Tereza *From Carpathian to Pindus. Pictures of Roumanian Country Life*. London, 1906.
Studii și documente cu privire la istoria românilor, ed. N. Iorga. 31 vols. Bucharest 1901–1918.
Sugar, Peter F. 'Railroad Construction and the Development of the Balkan Village in the Last Quarter of the 19th Century', in *Der Berliner Kongreß von 1878*, ed. R. Melville, H. J. Schröder. Wiesbaden, 1982, 485–98.
Sulzer, Franz Joseph *Geschichte des Transalpinen Daciens*, 3 vols. Vienna, 1781.
Sümegi, Pál, Dávid Molnár, Katalin Náfrádi, Dávid Gergely Páll, Gergő Persaits, Szilvia Sávai, Tünde Törőcsik 'The Environmental History of Southern Transdanubia during the Medieval and the Ottoman Period in the Light of Paleoecological and Geoarchaeological Research', in *"per sylvam et per lacus nimios"*, ed. G. Kovács, C. Zatykó. Budapest, 2016, 46–50.
Surányi, János and György Mándy, *A kukorica*. Budapest, 1955.
Surete și izvoade. Documente slavo-române, ed. Gh. Ghibănescu. 25 vols. Iași, 1906–1933.
Szabo, Franz A. J. *Kaunitz and Enlightened Absolutism, 1753–1780*. Oxford, 1994.
Székely, Maria Magdalena 'Food and Culinary Practices in 17th-century Moldavia', in *Earthly Delights*, ed. A. Jianu, V. Barbu. Leiden - Boston, 2018, 170–216.
Sziksai, Fabricius Balázs *Latin-magyar szójegyzéke 1590-ből*, ed. J. Melich. Budapest, 1906.

Tabak, Faruk 'Agrarian Fluctuations and Modes of Labor Control in the Western Arc of the Fertile Crescent, c. 1700–1850', in *Landholding and Commercial Agriculture in the Middle East*, ed. Ç. Keyder, F. Tabak. Albany, NY, 1991, 135–54.
Tabak, Faruk *The Waning of the Mediterranean, 1550–1870. A Geohistorical Approach*. Baltimore, MD, 2008.
Taki, Victor *Tsar and Sultan. Russian Encounters with the Ottoman Empire*. London – New York, 2016.
Taki, Victor *Russia on the Danube. Empire, Elites and Reform in Moldavia and Wallachia, 1812–1834*. Budapest – New York, 2021.
Tallar, Georg *Visum repertum anatomico-chirurgicum oder gründlicher Bericht von den sogenannten Blutsäugern, Vampier, oder in der wallachischen Sprache* Moroi, *in der Wallachey, Siebenbürgen, und Banat*. Vienna – Leipzig, 1784.
Tappe, E. D. 'John Sibthorp in the Danubian Lands, 1794', *Revue des études sud-est européennes* 5:3–4 (1967), 461–73.
Tappe, E. D. 'T. Wemyss Reid and Rumania', *Slavonic and East European Review* 64:2 (1986), 256–60.
Taylor, Gail Marlow *Putting Down Roots. The Reception of New World Medicinal Plants in Early Modern Germany, 1492–1648*. PhD diss., University of California, Irvine, 2014.
Tatay, Anca Elisabeta 'Imagini din cărțile de economie tipărite la Buda (1810–1823)', *Revista Transilvania*, nr. 5–6 (2013), 19–24.
Tenaillon, Maud Irène and Alain Charcosset, 'A European Perspective on Maize History', *Comptes Rendus Biologies* 334:3 (2011), 221–28.
Teutsch, G. D. *Geschichte der Siebenbürger Sachsen für das sächsische Volk*, 2nd edn. 2 vols. Leipzig, 1874.
Thököly, Imre *Késmárki Tököly Imre naplója 1693– 1694. évekből*, ed. I. Nagy [*Monumenta Hungariae Historica*, 2d ser., 15]. Pest, 1863.
Thököly, Imre *Thököly Imre fejedelem 1691–1692-iki leveleskönyve*, ed. K. Thaly [*Monumenta Hungariae Historica*, 2d ser., 34]. Budapest, 1896.
Thomas, Colin 'The Anatomy of a Colonization Frontier: The Banat of Temešvar', *Austrian History Yearbook* 19:2 (1984), 3–22.

"Those Infidel Greeks". *The Greek War of Independence through Ottoman Archival Documents*, ed. H. Şükrü Ilıcak. 2 vols. Leiden – Boston, 2021.
Titkin, H. *Rumänisch-Deutsches Wörterbuch*, 3 vols. Bucharest, 1903–1925.
Titkin, H. 'Zu rum. *porumb* "Mais"', *Zeitschrift für romanische Philologie* 40 (1920), 713–15.
Todorova, Maria 'The Establishment of British Consulates in the Bulgarian Lands and British Commercial Interests', *Études balkaniques* nr. 4 (1973), 80–88.
Todorova, Maria *Scaling the Balkans. Essays on East European Entanglements*. Leiden – Boston, 2019. [Balkan Studies Library, 24]
Tofan, Constantin 'Venitul cântarului pe teritoriul Moldovei din secolul al XVIII-lea până în prima jumătate a secolului al XIX-lea', *Acta bacoviensia* 6 (2011), 233–54.
Toussaint-Samat, Maguelonne *A History of Food* [1987], trans. A. Bell. 2nd edn. Chichester, 2009.
Tracy, James D. *Balkan Wars. Habsburg Croatia, Ottoman Bosnia, and Venetian Dalmatia, 1499–1617*. Lanham, MD – London, 2016.
Trifu, V. '1907 în poezia populară din Oltenia', *Steaua* 8:3 (1957), 73–78.
Tucker, Jack *The Rumanian Peasant Revolt of 1907. Three Regional Studies*. PhD diss., University of Chicago, 1972.

Uekötter, Frank 'Afterword. Europe's Guinea Pigs: Globalizing the Agricultural History of Southeastern Europe', *Martor* nr. 19 (2014), 175–79.
Ulieriu, Daniela and Doina Popescu, *Trei secole de gastronomia românească. De la muhalebiu și schembea la volovan și galantina*. Pitești, 2018.
Ungureanu, Gh. 'Documente relative la începutul domniei lui Ioan Sandu Sturza Voevod', *Revista Arhivelor* 6:1 (1944), 47–59.
Urbeanu, Adolf *Importanța soeĭ pentru hrana copiilor*. Bucharest, 1905.
Urbeanu, Adolf *Evoluția chestiei soiei în Europa și în România*. Bucharest, 1908.
Urbeanu, Adolf *Neoiobăgia și capitalismul față de hrana populației. Răspuns d-lui C. Dobrogeanu-Gherea*. Bucharest, 1911.
Urechia, V. A. 'Edilitatea sub Caragea', *Analele Academiei Române. Memoriile secțiunii istorice*, 2d ser, 21 (1898–1899), 475–634.
Urechia, V. A. *Istoria românilor*. 14 vols. Bucharest, 1891–1902.
Uricariul, 25 vols., ed. T. Codrescu. Iași, 1853–1894.
Urkundenbuch zur Geschichte der Deutschen in Siebenbürgen, vol. 6: *1458–1473*, ed. G. Gündisch. Bucharest, 1981.
Ursu, N.A. 'Cărți de popularizare a științei traduse de Petru Maior', *Limba romînă* 10:2 (1961), 135–43.

Văcărescu, Ienăchiță *Istoria othomanicească*. Bucharest, 2001.
Văduva, Ofelia *Pași spre sacru. Din etnologia alimentației românești*. Bucharest, 1996.
Văduva, Ofelia *Steps toward the Sacred. From the Ethnology of Romanian Food Habits*, trans. S. Georgescu-Gorjan. Bucharest, 1999.
Van Wijk Roelandszoon, Jacobus *Algemeen aardrijkskundig woordenboek*, Bd. 7. Dordrecht, 1821.
Van Young, Eric *The Other Rebellion. Popular Violence, Ideology, and the Mexican Struggle for Independence, 1810–1821*. Stanford, CA, 2001.
Vanhaute, E., R. Paping, Cormac Ó Gráda, 'The European Subsistence Crisis of 1845–1850: A Comparative Perspective', in *When the Potato Failed*, ed. C. Ó Gráda, R. Paping, E. Vanhaute. Turnhout, 2007, 15–40.
Vaniček, Fr. *Specialgeschichte der Militärgrenze*, 4 vols. Vienna, 1875.
Vantini, Sandra 'L'inserimento del mais nel paesaggio veneto', in *Profumi di terre lontane*, ed. S. Conti. Genoa, 2006, 653–68.

Varga, Zsuzsanna 'The Buda University Press and National Awakenings in Habsburg Austria', in *The Matica and Beyond*, ed. K. Lajosi, A. Stynen. Leiden – Boston, 2020, 11–29.

Vasmer, Max *Russisches etymologisches Wörterbuch*. 3 vols. Heidelberg, 1953.

Vătășescu, Cătălina 'Evoluția lat. *pomus, pomum* în română și albaneză', *Fonetică și dialectologie* 33 (2014), 131–40.

Veichtlbauer, Ortrun *Zwischen Kolonie und Provinz. Herrschaft und Planung in der Kameralprovinz Temeswarer Banat im 18. Jahrhundert*. Vienna, 2016.

Velichi, C. 'Acte covurluiene', *Revista istorică* 23:4–6 (1937), 172–81.

Verdery, Katherine *Transylvanian Villagers. Three Centuries of Political, Economic and Ethnic Change*. Berkeley, CA, 1983.

Verdery, Katherine 'Moments in the Rise of the Discourse on National Identity, I: Seventeenth through Nineteenth Centuries', in *Românii în istoria universală*, 3–i, ed. I. Agrigoroaiei, Gh. Buzatu, V. Cristian. Iasi, 1988, 25–60.

Vernav, Constantinus nobilis a *Rudimentum physiographiæ Moldaviæ*. Buda, 1836.

Verne, Jules *Le château des Carpathes*. Paris, 1892.

Verteuil, Fr. Anthony *The Years of Revolt. Trinidad, 1881–1888*. Port of Spain, 1984.

Veteranyi, Aglaja *Why the Child is Cooking in the Polenta*, trans. V. Kling. Champaign, IL – London, 2012.

Vintilă, Constanța *Changing Subjects, Moving Objects. Status, Mobility, and Social Transformation in Southeastern Europe, 1700–1850*. Paderborn, 2022. [Balkan Studies Library, 31]

Vintilă-Ghițulescu, Constanța *Evgheniți, ciocoi, mojici. Despre obrazele primei modernități românești, 1750–1860*. Bucharest, 2013.

Vintilă-Ghițulescu, Constanța *Patima și desfătare. Despre lucrurile mărunte ale vieții cotidiene în societatea românească, 1750–1860*. Bucharest, 2015.

Vîrtosu, Emil, ed. *Mărturii noi din viața lui Tudor Vladimirescu*. Bucharest, 1941.

Visser, Margaret *Much Depends on Dinner. The Extraordinary History and Mythology, Allure and Obsessions, Perils and Taboos, of an Ordinary Meal*. Toronto, 1986.

Vitcu, Dumitru 'Hotarnica unor moșii ale Mănăstirii Sucevița din anul 1787 (Ibănești, Măgura și Cristinești)', *Anuarul Institutului de Istorie 'A.D. Xenopol'* 50 (2013), 413–32.

Vlăduțiu, Ion *Etnografia românească. Istoric. Cultura materială. Obiceiuri*. Bucharest, 1973.

Vrbanus, Milan 'Ratarstvo u slavonskoj Posavini krajem 17. stoljeća', *Scrinia slavonica* 2 (2002), 202–60.

Vrbanus, Milan 'Proizvodnja pšenice na našičkome području u prva tri desetljeća 18. stoljeća', *Povijesni prilozi* 35:50 (2016), 139–89.

Vulcănescu, Elena *București – Paris via Mircești*. Iași, 2007.

Wagner, Max Leopold *Dizionario etimologico sardo*. 4 vols. Heidelberg, 1957–1964.

Walter, Tilmann, Abdolbaset Ghorbani, and Tinde van Andel, 'The Emperor's Herbarium: The German Physician Leonhard Rauwolf (1535?–96) and His Botanical Field Studies in the Middle East', *History of Science* 60:1 (2021), 130–51.

Warman, Arturo *Corn and Capitalism*, trans. N. L. Westrate. Chapel Hill, NC, 2003.

Welzk, Stefan *Nationalkapitalismus versus Weltmarktintegration? Rumänien 1830–1944*. Saarbrücken – Fort Lauderdale, FL, 1982 [Sozialwissenschaftliche Studien zu internationalen Problemen, 76].

Wemyss Reid, T. 'Rural Roumania', *Fortnightly Review*, n.s., 25:145 (1879), 80–95.

White, Sam *The Climate of Rebellion in the Early Modern Ottoman Empire*. Cambridge, 2012.

Wijnands, Onno 'Tulpen naar Amsterdam: Plantenverkeer tussen Nederland en Turkije', in *Topkapi en Turkomanie*, ed. H. Theunissen, A. Abelmann. Amsterdam, 1989, 97–106.

Wilkinson, William *An Account of the Principalities of Moldavia and Wallachia*. London, 1820.

Wilson, Thomas M., ed. *Food, Drink and Identity in Europe*. Amsterdam, 2006 [European Studies, 22].
Wolf, Andreas *Beiträge zu einer statistisch-historischen Beschreibung des Fürstenthums Moldau*. 2 vols. Sibiu, 1805.
Wolfe, Mikael D. 'The Climate of Conflict: Politico-Environmental Press Coverage and the Eruption of the Mexican Revolution, 1907–1911', *Hispanic American Historical Review* 99:3 (2019), 467–99.
Wood, Peter G. *The Agrarian Problem in Wallachia, 1870–1907*. PhD diss., University of London, 1984.
Woodham-Smith, Cecil *The Great Hunger. Ireland 1845–9*. London, 1956.

Xenopol, A. D. *Istoria Românilor din Dacia Traiană*, vol. 4: *Epoca lui Ștefan cel Mare (1457–1504)* [1896], 3rd edn. Bucharest, n.d.
Xenopol, A. D *Mijloacele de îndreptare ale stării țărănimii române*. Iași, 1907.
Xhuvani, Aleksandër and Eqrem Çabej, *Prapashtesat e gjuhës shqipe* [1962], repr. in Aleksandër Xhuvani, *Vepra*, vol. 1. Tirana, 1980, 419–581.

Yaycioglu, Ali *Partners of the Empire. The Crisis of the Ottoman Order in the Age of Revolutions*. Stanford, CA, 2016.
Yediyıldız, Bahaeddin *Ordu Kazası sosyal tarihi (1455–1613)*. Ankara, 1985.
Yıldız, Aysel and İrfan Kokdaş, 'Peasantry in a Well-protected Domain: Wallachian Peasantry and Muslim *Çiftlik/Kışlaks* under the Ottoman Rule', *Journal of Balkan and Near Eastern Studies*, 22:1 (2018), 175–90.

Zadoks, J. C. 'The Potato Murrain on the European Continent and the Revolutions of 1848', *Potato Research* 51 (2008), 5–45.
Zahariuc, Petronel 'Începutul domniei lui Ioniță Sandu Sturza', in *In honorem Mircea Ciubotaru*, ed. L.-V. Lefter, M.-B. Atanasiu. Iași, 2015, 487–551.
Zaimov, Yordan 'Nazvaniyata na tsarevitsata v bŭlgarski ezik', in *Ezikovedski izsledvaniya v chest na Akademik Stefan Mladenov*. Sofia, 1957, 113–26.
Zhuravleva, Victoria I. 'American Corn in Russia: Lessons of the People-to-People Diplomacy and Capitalism', *Journal of Russian-American Studies* 1:1 (2017), 23–45.
Zirojević, Olga 'Biljni i stočni fond u vreme turske vladavine', *Almanah* 37–38 (2007), 15–18.
Zirojević, Olga *Istočno-zapadna sofra. Mali kulturnoistorijski i kulinarski leksikon*. Belgrade, 2019.
Zugravu, Corina Aurelia, Dana Gafițianu, and Anca Ioana Nicolau, 'Food, Nutrition, and Health in Romania', in *Nutritional and Health Aspects of Food in the Balkans*, ed. A. I. Gostin, D. Bogueva, V. Kakurinov. London, 2021, 227–48.

Illustration Credits

Images

1.1 Emperor Rudolf II as Vertumnus, by Guiseppe Arcimboldo. Prague 1591. Skokloster Castle, Sweden. Image: Wikimedia Commons.

1.2 Prince Michael the Brave. Engraving by Aegidius Sadeler, Prague 1601. Seventeenth-century coloration by Dirk Janszoon van Santen. Herzog Ulrich Anton Museum, Wolfenbüttel, Germany. Image: Virtuelles Kupferstichkabinett.

1.3 Life in Ottoman Hungary. Ferenc Wathay, Songbook, 1604. Hungarian Academy Library, ms. K62, f. 45r. Image from digitized version at http://real-ms.mtak.hu/16749/

1.4 Prince Imre Thököly. Engraving by Jacob Peeters. Antwerp, 1686. Image: Wikimedia Commons.

2.1 Reporting on mămăligă: Friedrich Schwantz von Springfels, Bericht, 1723. Austrian National Library, ms. cod. ser. n. 34. Image reproduced with permission.

2.2 Brătianu brothers, letter of mortgage, Poenărei, Wallachia, 1728. Museum of Viticulture and Pomiculture, Goleşti, Romania, number 9869/833. Image: Europeana.eu

3.1 Peasant house and maize store, by Johan Jakob Ehrler, Banat of Temesvar. 1774. Manuscript G 189/a, Eötvös Loránd University Library and Archives, Budapest, p. 50/c. Reproduced with permission.

3.2 Plan for a cereal warehouse, Galaţi, 1793. Haus-, Hof- und Staatsarchiv, Vienna. AT-OeStA/HHStA StAbt Moldau-Walachei I 8 Walachei, 1793. Reproduced with permission.

3.3 Romanian ploughman, 1808. From Grigorie Obradovici, *Carte de mână*, Buda, 1807. Image: Digital Library, Lucian Blaga Central University Library, Cluj-Napoca.

6.1 Romania and the Boyar, 1861. *Bondarul* (The Drone) satirical magazine. Image: Digital Library, Mihai Eminescu Central University Library, Iaşi.

6.2 Road among Gardens, by Emanoil Panaiteanu-Bardasare. 1882. Iaşi Art Museum. Image: Wikimedia Commons.

6.3 'Mama-Liga de Lux': cigarette paper packaging, c. 1900. Bucharest Municipal Museum. Image reproduced with permission.

Illustration Credits

7.1 Register of maize given as rations to Roma slaves, Monastery of the Goldsmiths' Guild, Bucharest 1834. National Archives of Romania, Fond Mănăstirea Zlătari, online at http://sclavia-romilor.gov.ro/items/show/2044 Image reproduced with permission.

8.1 Mămăligă Gathering, by Theodor Aman. Engraving, 1870. Theodor Aman Museum, Bucharest. Image reproduced with permission.

Maps

Maps by Cezar Buterez. Data credits:

Maps 1, 3, 4, 5: Elevation data from NASA Shuttle Radar Topography Mission (SRTM) (2013). Shuttle Radar Topography Mission (SRTM) Global. Distributed by OpenTopography. https://doi.org/10.5069/G9445JDF.

Map 2: geographic data partially derived from Peter Andorfer (2019). acdh-oeaw/histogis-data: new data + wiki data ids (v4.0), Zenodo. https://doi.org/10.5281/zenodo.3474085

Maps 6 and 7: geographic data from RoHGIS project, 2016–2022

Map 8: Author's attestation data placed on map adapted from Sala, 'Denumirea', Map 1 (original area data from *Atlasul lingvistic romîn*, new series)

Acknowledgements

This book was largely written in lockdown conditions in 2021. I am therefore especially grateful to the following people who generously shared material, read partial drafts, or answered queries no matter how abstruse or tangential: Zoltán András, Constantin Ardeleanu, Stefano d'Atri, Delia Bălăican, Constantin Bărbulescu, Philippe Blasen, Dan Burzo, Cathie Carmichael, Roland Clark, Roxana Coman, Dejan Djokić, Carmina Drace-Francis, Emir Filipović, Aleksandar Fotić, Cristian Gaşpar, Vesna Goldsworthy, Rigels Halili, Ştefania Hîrtopanu, Angela Jianu, Jakob Jung, James Kapaló, Tatjana Katić, Eva Kowalská, Peter Mario Kreuter, Domnica Macri, Martin Maiden, Bogdan Mateescu, Ruben Mendoza, Cătălina Mihalache, Cosmin Minea, Zoran Milutinović, James Morris, Susan Morrissey, Levente Nagy, Ahmed Nuri, Christian Noack, Andrei Oişteanu, Virginia Petrică, Laurenţiu Rădvan, Erik van Ree, Margaret Renwick, Semie Rogers, Nicoleta Roman, Andrei Sorescu, Oana Sorescu Iudean, István Szalma, Antal Szantay, Anca Tatay, Ana-Marija Tkalčić, the late and very much missed Ljubinka Trgovčević, Alexandra Urdea, Bálint Varga, Zsuzsanna Varga, Nóra Veszprémi, Constanţa Vintilă, Milan Vrbanus, Rupert Wolfe Murray.

In January 2021 Manuela Boatcă invited me to present the early kernels of my research at the lecture series of the Graduate Program *Imperien: Dynamischer Wandel, Temporalität und nachimperiale Ordnungen* [Empires: Dynamic Change, Temporality and Postimperial Orders], hosted at the University of Freiburg via Zoom. This was an inspiring invitation for me and helped me especially to think about the interplay between imperial, national and local history. I owe a huge thanks to Manuela for taking an interest in this project when it was at such an incipient stage, as well as to the attendees and participants in the Graduate School. It was the perfect spur to consider the best approach. I also thank my colleagues in

Acknowledgements

the European Studies Department in Amsterdam for tasting a version of the argument in March 2021, and for suggestions and comments made on that occasion.

I owe a large debt to digital libraries, which, whatever their shortcomings, have transformed access to and verification of primary and secondary source material. A good supply of source materials does not produce instant history any more than a regular supply of cornmeal leads to instant mămăligă, and the consumer of digital cornmeal is always in danger of overeating. The hard work is in the stirring: in history this means not just to collect and cite sources but to collate, compare and explain them, and to place them in a broader and hopefully more digestible narrative based on deeper reflection. Readers and reviewers can decide whether or not I have succeeded. But I could not have even attempted this task, especially in 2021, without access to documents available through digitization. Although I used material from dozens of countries, I mention particularly the Bucharest Digital Library (digibuc.ro), the Lucian Blaga University Library of Babeş-Bolyai University, Cluj-Napoca (https://dspace.bcucluj.ro/), the Mihai Eminescu Central Library of the University of Iaşi (http://dspace.bcu-iasi.ro/), and the Digital Library of Cultural Publications hosted by the Romanian National Heritage Institute (biblioteca-digitala.ro).

In the second half of 2021 I was able to visit the following libraries to whose staff I extend my thanks: the University of Amsterdam Library; the British Library; Bucharest University Central Library; the Library of the International Institute for Social History, Amsterdam; the Library of the 'Nicolae Iorga' Institute of History, Bucharest; Leiden University Library; the Linnaeus Society Library, London; and the Library of the Institute of Archaeology, University College London. Being unable to reach the Meertens Instituut Library in Amsterdam, the University and Research Library in Wageningen, the Romanian Academy Library, the Austrian National Library or the National and University Library in Zagreb, I am all the more grateful to librarians there who answered my queries. Thanks also to Ionela Bucşa of the Theodor Aman Museum in Bucharest, to Adrian-Nicolae Furtună of the Research and Documentation Section of the National Centre of Roma Culture, Bucharest, to Ildiko Balogh of the Eötvös Loránd University Library in Budapest, and to staff at the Bucharest Municipal Museum and at the Haus-, Hof- und Staatsarchiv in Vienna for help sourcing, scanning and securing permissions for illustrations.

Also institutionally I thank the Amsterdam School of Regional, Transnational and European Studies (ARTES) for providing funds to pay for maps and illustrations. More broadly I thank colleagues at the New Europe College in Bucharest and at the Rethinking Modern Europe Seminar at the Institute of Historical Research in London, for providing such stimulating intellectual environments for comparative historical thought.

The two scholars commissioned by the Press to evaluate the submitted draft offered expert observations and suggestions for improvement of a kind I could not have got otherwise. A final draft was read by colleagues Dejan Djokić (London/Berlin), Ewa Stańczyk (Amsterdam) and Constanța Vintilă (Bucharest), all three of whom shared their unique knowledge and made valuable comments on both argumentation and sources. Their experienced eyes and critical acumen made a big difference to the final dish.

A huge thanks to Linda Kunos at Central European University Press for taking on this proposal and handling all aspects of the editorial process, and to Cezar Buterez for his excellent maps. It was a pleasure to work with both of them. Doru Panaitescu very kindly let me use his wonderful photograph for the cover.

At various periods I had the pleasure of the company (and food) of Christian, Mariya, and my son John. It cannot have been easy living with a man with a head full of mămăligă. In their very different ways, they all kept my spirits up and provided lively and intelligent friendship and support during the making of this book. My wider family and friends also tolerated my obsession with forbearance. I am fortunate to know and work with so many talented and generous people. It goes without saying that any errors are mine alone.

Index

Abdul Hamid I, Ottoman Sultan 55, 56
Abdul Hamid II, Ottoman Sultan 103
Abdullah bin İbrahim el-Üsküdarî 24n60
acorns 23, 41, 50, 52, 71
Ada Kale island 75
Adas, Michael 101
Adrianople *see* Edirne
Adriatic Sea 6, 17, 22, 151, 154
Africa 4, 6, 14, 17, 26, 69, 101, 144, 146
Ahmed III, Ottoman Sultan 44n62
Ahmed, Pasha of Rusçuk 86
Ahmed Hacı İsmailoğlu, merchant 89n23
Albanians 78, 80; Albanian language, 153; national dances, 76
Aldrovandi, Ulisse 17
Alecsandri, Vasile 3, 143
alcohol 46, 54–55, 99, 116, 117; *see also* beer, wine, raki
Alexandria (Egypt) 17; Patriarchate of, 42
alivenci (sweet maize cakes) 127, 129
Aman, Dimitrie 76
Aman, Theodor 76, 133–34
Amelio, Silvestro 29
America(s) 6–7, 13–15, 23, 144; North, 3, 37; South, 104, 151n11; Central, 128; plantations of, 69; *see also* United States
Anatolia 15–16, 68
Anastasia, nun 51–52
Andronachi, Vorniceasa 51
aniseed 63
Antioch, Orthodox Patriarchate of 42
Arabic 15, 16

Arad county 139n34
Arcimboldo, Giuseppe 18, 19
Argentina 88, 98, 104, 105, 145n12
Argeş county, Wallachia 39, 40, 51, 53, 61n86, 66, 82, 108 n70
Argeş river 39
Armăşoaia, Ţiţa, widow 51
Armenian people, language 26n70, 52, 69
Aromanians 50, 60n78
Arsaki, Apostol 53n34
Arsenie, D., landowner 108n69
Asachi, Gheorghe 91–92
Asia 4, 13–15, 30
Asturias, Miguel Ángel 132
Athos, Mount 42
Atlantic Ocean 14, 30, 144
aubergine *see* eggplant
Auşeu, Bihor county 25n64
Ausilia, Giovanni Maria 41n39
Austrian Empire, Austria-Hungary *see* Habsburg Empire
Bacalbaşa, Constantin 127
Bacalbaşa, Laurenţia 127n70
Bacău, Moldavia 51
Bacău county, Moldavia 40–41, 59n73, 106
Băileşti, Dolj county 107n65
bakers, baking 50, 60, 113, 116, 124, 125, 132, 138–39
Bălăciţa, Mehedinţi county 107n64
Bălceşti, Vâlcea county 108n68
Băleasa, Romanaţi county (today Olt county) 107n66

Index

Balkans 16–19, 30–31, 44, 62, 73, 143–44; as contact zone 8; Christian peoples of, 22, 24, 67–68; 'mentality' of, so-called, 146
Balkan Mountains 85
balmoş (balmos), 113, 126n69, 128n77
Bălnaca (Bálnaca), Bihor county 25n64
Balş, Moldavian boyar 62n92, 73n16
Balş, Romanaţi county (today Olt county) 108n66
Băltaţi, Teleorman county 108n69
Banat of Temesvar 30, 35, 37, 44–45, 58, 64, 67, 71, 115–16, 120n36, 149
Băncilă, Octav 136
Banten province, Java 100
Barbu, Violeta 8
Bărbulescu, Constantin 124
Baring Brothers & Co. (bank) 89
barley 17, 24, 36, 40, 42, 55n51, 58, 61, 63–64, 76, 80, 87–88, 93, 108n69, 110, 117n22, 154n37
Băseni-Stârci (today Stârci, com. Costeşti), Argeş county 108n70
Batia, Olt county 108n67
Bavaria 17, 150
Becicherec Mare *see* Zrenjanin
beans 68, 115, 117, 153
beech, bark 71; nuts 50
beehives, beekeeping 43, 91; *see also* honey, wax
beer 66
Belgrade 20, 22, 24, 30, 35, 62
Bentham, Jeremy 117
Berindeasa, Maria 51
Berlin 104, 120
Berlin, Treaty of 97
Bessarabia 87, 104
Bethlen, Miklós, Count 113–14
Bibescu, Dumitrachi 53
Bibescu, Gheorghe, Prince of Wallachia (1842–1848) 53
Bielski, Marcin 124n52
Bihor county, Romania 136, 139n34
Birecik (Bir), Turkey 16
Bismarck, Otto von 103
Bistreţu, Dolj county 65
blackthorn (*prunus spinosa*) 156

Blahniţa de Sus, Gorj county, Wallachia 72
Bleibtreu, Karl 131
Bleichröder, S. (bank) 104n39
Blejoiu de Sus, Prahova county 39
bœuf à la mode (bou di modă) 122
Bogdana Monastery, Moldavia 41
Bohemia 17, 54
Boian *see* Boyany
Boiangi, Evanghelie, merchant 51–52
Bolkunov, I. F., Russian consul-general 57n60
Bologna 17
Born, Ignaz von 116
Borundean, Ioan 40–41
Borusul, Prahova county, Wallachia 50
Bosnia 17
Bosnian language 150
Botoşani county 106, 136n28
Botoşeşti, Mehedinţi county 107n64
Bounin, French consul in Bucharest 80n52
Bourdain, Anthony 147
boyars (nobles) 2, 23, 25, 27, 36–37, 40–43, 50–55, 58–62, 69, 71, 73, 76–77, 80–83, 87, 91, 97, 102, 104, 117, 119–21, 133–34, 141–42
Boyany (Boian), Ukraine 41
boza 117n22
bragă 117n22
Bragadiru, Ilfov county 99
Brăila 60n83, 85, 88, 90–91
Brăiloiu, Ioniţa, boyar 50
Brâncoveanu, Constantin, Prince of Wallachia (1688–1714) 29
Brâncoveanu, Grigore, boyar 61, 76n38
Brănişca (Branyicska), Hunedoara county 46n70
Braniştea, Mehedinţi county 107n64
Braşov (Kronstadt) 22, 23, 50, 69, 72, 79, 114, 154
Brastavăţu, Romanaţi county (today Olt county) 107n66
Brătăşanu, Ionică 107n66
Brătianu, Iane 39
Brătianu, Ion I. 102
Brătianu, Iordache 39
Brătianu, Oancea 39
Braudel, Fernand 7, 152

202

Brazil 98, 101
bread 9, 46, 50, 55, 64, 114, 121, 125–26, 128, 132, 138–39, 145; mămăligă as, 22, 27, 80, 114–19, 127, 136; bread cubes, added to mămăligă 129
Breaza, Prahova county, Wallachia 50
Brognard, Francisco Antonio von, Habsburg internuncio 44n61
Buburuz, Lazor 158
Buburuzeni, Moldavia 158
Bucium, Iași county 41
buckwheat (*fagopyrum esculentum*) 16, 27n82, 36, 63, 150n3, 154n37; mămăligă made with, 121
Bucovina *see* Bukovina
Bucșănescu, Moldavian boyar 82n70
Bucșănescu, Hera, *postelnicel* 51
Buda 20, 63–65, 121
Budai-Deleanu, Ion 132–33, 152n17
Budinszky, Johan 117
Buftea, Ilfov county 99–100
Bukovina 37, 57, 59, 67–68, 117, 152; mămăligă dumplings *à la*, 128n77
Bulgaria 17, 30n98, 53, 58, 83, 91, 99, 145n10
Bulgarians 78, 87, 89, 121; Bulgarian language 152–55
bulrushes 114
Bulz (Csarnóháza), Bihor county, 25n64
Burgberg *see* Vurpăr
Burger, Dr. Johann 65
Burtsov, Ivan Grigor'evich, Captain 82n69
Burzenland *see* Țara Bârsei
Butculescu, Marin 72n6
butter 2–3, 117, 124, 127, 132, 134, 138–39
Buzău county 49
Buzducu, Romanați county (today Buzduc, com. Drăgotești, Dolj county) 107n66
cabbage 25, 41; pickled, 61, 126; potted, 114, 140; soup, 119
Căcărăzeni, Cârligătura county (today com. Dumești, Iași county) 151n7, 158
Căcărăzeni, Orhei county, Moldavia (today Cucuruzeni, Rep. Moldova) 151n7, 158
Căcărează, Giurgea 158
Cairo 14–15
Călărași county 136

Călărași, Botoșani county 136n28
Călărași, Călărași county 121
Călinești, Teleorman county 108n69
Callimachi, Alexandru, Prince of Moldavia (1795–1799) 59–60
Callimachi, Gavriil *see* Gavriil, Metropolitan of Moldavia
Callimachi, Grigore, Prince of Moldavia (1761–1764) 42n46
Callimachi, Ioan Theodor, Prince of Moldavia (1758–1761) 41n45, 42n46
Callimachi, Scarlat, Prince of Moldavia (1812–1818) 73n16
Campenhausen, Freiherr Pierce Balthasar von 121
Câmpeni, Romanați county (today Dolj county) 108n66
Câmpulung, Bukovina 67–68
Câmpulung, Muscel county, Wallachia 79
Canada 98
Canetzos, Constantin (Konstantinos Kanetsos) 53n34, 81n58
Cantacuzino, Constantin 25
Cantacuzino, Șerban, Prince of Wallachia 25
Caracaș, Dr. Constantin 121
capitalism 5–8, 43, 87, 96, 100, 105–6, 142–45
Caragea, Ioan, Prince of Wallachia (1812–1818) 52n28, 71–72
Caragea, Nicolae, Prince of Wallachia (1782–1783) 50n7, 51n23, 52n28, 58n64
Caragiali, Costache 2
Caransebeș 22, 64
Carinthia 17, 44
Cârligătura county, Moldavia (today Iași county) 151n7, 158
Carmen Sylva (Queen Elizabeth of Romania) 131
Carney, Judith 143
Carol I of Hohenzollern-Sigmaringen, King of Romania 103–5; eats mămăligă, 134
Carp, Moldavian boyar family 27–28
carp (fish) 41
Carpathian Mountains 13, 22, 25, 29, 40, 56–57, 59, 64, 68, 71–73, 77

Cărtărescu, Mircea 129
Catholics, see Roman Catholics
Catina, Buzău county 49
cattle 20, 41, 43, 51, 79–80, 107
Caucasus region 25–26; languages of 150
Cécke see Țețchea
Cernătești, Dolj county 134
Cernavoda 97
Cerneți River, Wallachia 74
Chazeski, H., landowner 108n69
cheese 3, 67–68, 113, 116–19, 124, 126–29, 140
Chenot, Adam 115–16
Cherali, Toma 75n30
cherries, lack of, in mountainous districts 68
Cherniwchan, Jevan 69
chickpea (*cicer aretinum*) 63
China 31, 67n111
Chioar (Kővár) fortress, com. Remetea Chioarului, Maramureș county 22
Chiril, monk 49
Christianity, Christians 18, 20, 22, 24, 39, 44, 60, 62, 67, 128; see also Orthodox Christians, Protestants, Roman Catholics
çiftliks 44n62
Ciocăzanu, Gligore 51
Clocociov Monastery, Olt county 61n86
Cluj county 136
Cluj-Napoca (Kolozsvár), 22
Cocores, Vasile 70
coffee 30, 114, 117, 144
Colibași, Romanați county (today Olt county) 107n66
Columbia 144
Columbus, Christopher 14
Comana, Giurgiu county 39
Comșa, Ecaterina 129
Conachi, Costachi, Moldavian boyar 76n36
Congolese 144
colonialism see empires
Conservative Party of Romania 105
Constanța 97
Constante, Lena 127
Constantinescu, Gheorghe 106
Constantinople, see Istanbul

cookbooks 13, 124, 126–29, 146–47
Copăceni (Kapocsány), Bihor county 25n64
Corcova, Mehedinți county 107n64
Corlățel, Mehedinți county 81
Corlățești, Prahova county 50
Cossacks 54n43
Costinescu, Emil, minister of finance 104n41
cotton 100, 135, 143, 145n10
Covurlui county, Moldavia 69
Creangă, Ion 133, 135
Cretan War (1645–1669) 22
Crețeni, Vâlcea county 50
Crețu, Vintilă 70
Criciova, Timiș county 136n28
Crimea 26, 43
Crimean War 95, 142
Cristian (Grossau), Sibiu county 118
Croatia 18, 35
Croatian language 150
Croats 35, 67
Csarnoháza see Bulz
Cucureasa Mountain (Bistrița-Năsăud county)
Cucurezi, Cucuruzi, Vlașca county (today Cucuruzu, Giurgiu county) 151, 153, 158
Cucurruz, slave 151n6
cucuruz, history and meaning of word 150–54, 158
Cucuruzeni see Căcărăzeni
Cuieșd, Bihor county 25n64
Cunningham, Charles, British consul at Galați 92n48
Czartoryski, Prince Adam 57n60
Czech language 17, 150
Dacians 128
Dalmatia 17, 22
Dâmbovița county, Wallachia 39–40, 51, 59, 80, 103n32
damson (*prunus institia*) 55, 68
Dănciulescu, Constantin 74n23
Dancu Monastery, Iași 41
Danube river 20, 22, 25, 29, 35, 39, 44, 49, 55, 56, 58, 62, 73–77, 81–82, 85–86, 88–93, 97, 122, 151
Darwinism 124

Dârzeanu, Ioan 80, 119
Dascălul-Creață, Ilfov county 102
Davidescu, Haralambie, landowner 108n68
de Feller, François-Xavier, Abbot 67
Dej (Dés), Cluj county 22
Delani (Gyalan), Bihor county 25
Delureni 25n64
Dés *see* Dej
Dimitrie, printer, Wallachia 63
Dionisie Eclesiarhul 60
Dionisie, hegumen 50–51
Disconto-Gesellschaft (bank) 104n39
Disraeli, Benjamin 90
Dobre a Vladi 59
Dobriceni, Romanați county (today Olt county) 106n59, 108n66
Dobrogeanu-Gherea, Constantin 96, 103
Dobrun, Romanați county (today Olt county) 107
doctors *see* medics
Dolj county 53, 107, 136
Dombó *see* Delureni
Dorna Candreni, Bukovina 67
Dositei Filitti, Metropolitan of Ungrovlachia 61
Douglass, Frederick 144
Drăgoești, Moldavia 41
Drăgoești, Olt county (today Vâlcea county) 108n67
Drăgoi, Sabin V. 138
Dragoș Vodă, Călărași County 136n28
Drănic, Dolj county 107n65
Drexler, Austrian agent in Craiova 80n52
Drogheda Argus and Leinster Journal 90
drought 66, 114; *see also* famine
Dubrovnik (Ragusa) 17
Duca, Constantin, Prince of Moldavia (1693–1695) 28–29
Dudești, Dâmbovița county 103n32
Dufile, Equatoria (today Uganda) 100
Durnești, Botoșani county 136n28
Edirne 24, 114; Treaty of 85, 88
eggplant 131
eggs 127, 129
Egypt 14–16, 26, 35, 43, 75, 99
Ehrler, Johann Jakob 45
Élesdlok *see* Luncșoara

Elizabeth, Queen of Romania (Carmen Sylva) 131
Eliza-Stoenești 102
Emin Pasha 100
Eminescu, Mihai 96
empires, imperialism 4–5, 8–10, 36–39, 42, 44–46, 58, 73, 89, 100–1, 114–15, 125–26, 141–43; *see also* Brazil, France, Germany, Great Britain, Habsburg Empire, Italy, Ottoman Empire, Portuguese Empire, Russian Empire, Spain
England, 30, 35 *see also* Great Britain
English language 27, 127–28, 146; people 35, 37n15, 54, 56, 61, 117, 131
Enzenberg, General 37n17
Equatoria 100
erotica 135
Ethiopia 16n10
European Commission of the Danube 97
European Union 145
export 36–37, 43–46, 51, 54n43, 59, 62, 72–76, 81, 87–99, 103–5, 108–10, 142, 145
famines, 46, 66, 71–75, 87, 89–91, 114, 142
fasting 68, 126
Fântânele, Botoșani county 106
Fărăgău, Mureș County 136n28
Fierbinți, Ialomița county (formely Ilfov county) 55, 103
Filimon, Nicolae 134–35
First World War 109
fish 20, 36, 41, 116–17, 133
Flămânzi, Botoșani county 106–7
Fleischhackl von Hackenau, Franz, Austrian consul in Bucharest 53, 71, 72
Flești Monastery, Argeș county 53
Focșani, Moldavia 59, 67, 82n70, 87
folklore 126, 132–33, 136–40
forests 28–29, 39, 42–43, 49, 74, 98–99, 109, 119, 157; alleged cradle of Romanian language, 152
Formont, Guillem de, French vice-consul in Bucharest 74–75
Fornetty, French consular official 73n15
Fotoaia, Vlașca county (today Giurgiu county) 39

France, French people, language 15, 37, 43, 53, 61, 72, 74, 80n52, 88, 92–93, 116–18, 122, 127, 131
Francis II, Emperor 72
Frank Johnson, Alison 4–5
Franz Joseph, Emperor 95
Friedrich Wilhelm II, King of Prussia 59n71
frontiers, borders 18, 20, 25, 31, 33, 35–40, 43–44, 50–51, 62, 73–74, 75, 77, 86–86, 104, 115–16, 120, 150–151; moral/social 36–37, 135, 139–40
Frumoasa, Teleorman county 136n28
Fuchs, Leonhart 17
Fussell, Betty 6
Gabaccia, Donna A. 5
Găgești, Putna county (today com. Bolotești, Vrancea county) 29
Galata Monastery, Moldavia 154n37
Galați 57, 76, 88, 90–93
Galicea Mare, Dolj county 107
Gângiova, Dolj county 109
García, Maria Elena 5–6
gardens, gardening 17–18, 28, 30, 40–41, 47, 100, 157
Gârla Mare, Mehedinți county 107
garlic 61, 117, 156
Gavriil (Callimachi), Metropolitan of Moldavia (1760–1786) 43, 55
Gemeni, com. Dârvari, Mehedinți county 107n64
Genoa 14, 88n18, 98
Georgescu, Irina 129, 147
Georgia 3
German East Africa 101
Germans 16, 18, 28, 29, 35, 54, 64, 89, 91, 95, 115, 118, 120, 131; see also Austrians, Saxons
German language 15, 17, 23, 121, 150–51, 154, 157
Germany: Empire (*Kaiserreich*), 99, 101; Federal Republic, 140; see also Bavaria, Habsburg Empire, Prussia
Gheorghe, Hagi 74n22
Gheorghița, Moldavian man 41
Ghercuț, Iojă 73n18
Gherghița, Prahova county 50
Gherla 22

Ghica, Costache, Moldavian boyar 73n16
Ghica, Dumitrachi, Great Ban of Wallachia 55
Ghica, Grigore II, Prince of Moldavia (1735–1739) and Wallachia (1748–1752) 40
Ghica, Grigore III, Prince of Moldavia (1774–1777) 55
Ghica, Grigore V, Prince of Wallachia (1822–1828) 82n65
Ghica, Matei, Prince of Moldavia (1753–1756) 41, 54
Ghica, Scarlat, Prince of Moldavia (1757–1758) 42
Ghinia, Moldavian woman 40
Giers, Mikhail Nikolaevich, Russian Ambassador to Romania 104n39
Giurescu, Constantin C. 6–7
Giurgiu (Giurgevo, Yergöğü), Wallachia 39, 75, 83n77, 85–86, 91, 97
Giurgiu county 151, 158–59; see also Vlașca county
Glodeani, Cârligatura county (today Glodenii-Gândului, Iași county) 28n83
Glogova, Mehedinți county 75
Glogoveanu, Nicolae 51, 53n34, 73–74, 81
Golescu, Constantin 'Dinicu' 66, 120
Golescu, Iordache 137
Golescu, Radu 51, 61, 120
Golești, Argeș county, Wallachia 51
Golfin, Romanați county (today Dolj county) 107n66
Gorizia 18
Gorj County, Wallachia 72, 76, 106
Gorovei, Petrache 72n14
grapes 52, 68, 152–53, 155; pressings, 55; see also vinyards, wine
Graz 120n36
Great Britain 51, 74, 88–93, 97–101, 104, 109, 142
Grecianu, Costandin 51
Grecianu, Zmaranda 51
Greeks 3, 28, 60, 77–80, 89, 120n36, 133
Greek language, 15, 60, 82, 85, 121, 151n11, 153; national dances, 76
Grigore, Constantin 102
Grigorescu, Nicolae 133

Grigorie II, Metropolitan of Ungrovlachia (1760–1787) 53
Griselini, Francesco 116
Grossau *see* Cristian
Gubandru, Romanați county (today Olt county) 107n66
Gyalan *see* Delani
Gypsies *see* Roma
Habsburg Empire 4, 9, 17–18, 24–25, 30–31, 33, 35–39, 44–46, 49, 56–69, 71–74, 80, 113–15, 117, 120, 125, 132, 141–42, 150–51; *see also* Banat, Bohemia, Bukovina, Carinthia, Carniola, Croatia, Hungary, Slavonia, Transylvania
Hagi Emin Aga, Ottoman official 80
Hagi Gheorge of Cerneți, Wallachian merchant 74n22
Hagi Ianuș, Wallachian merchant 81n58
Hagi Pop, Transylvanian merchant 50–52, 54, 60
haiducs 39, 108–9
Hamilton, General Joseph Andreas von 37
Hangerli, Constantin, Prince of Wallachia 52
Háromszék (Trei Scaune) county, Transylvania 114
Hărtiești, Argeș county 61n86
Hațeg county, Transylvania 72
hawthorns 114
d'Hauterive, Alexandre Maurice Blanc de Lanautte, Comte 116–17
Hebrides 100
Hédervár, Hungary 22
hemp 25
Hermannstadt *see* Sibiu
Heydendorff, Johann von 118
honey 20, 39, 116
Horezu Monastery, *see* Hurez
Horezu Poenari, Dolj county 107n65, 109
horse chestnut (*aesculus hippocastrum*) 30
horses 30, 36, 43, 64, 79–80, 92
Hottentots (*sic*; Khoekhoen people) 125
Hucău, river, Moldavia 41
Humboldt, Alexander von 120
Hunedoara county 138, 158
Hungary, Hungarians 7, 18, 20–24, 30, 35, 43–44, 68, 71, 90, 120, 131–32, 141, 157; *see also* Banat, Croatia, Habsburg Empire, Slavonia, Transylvania
Hungarian language *see* Magyar
Hurez Monastery, Wallachia 29, 39, 43, 49
Huși, Moldavia 59
Iacov Stamati, Metropolitan of Moldavia 118
Iane, priest at Vălenii, Prahova county 49
Iași 27, 29, 41–42, 46, 59–60, 72, 76, 79, 82, 91, 100, 121n40, 122, 134–36; University of, 1; National Theatre, 95
Iași county 28n83
Ileana, Moldavian woman 40
Ilfov county, Wallachia 40, 55, 80, 102–3
imperialism *see* empires
imports 45, 81–2, 87, 89 104
Indian Ocean 14
Ioana, Moldavian woman 40
Ionescu de la Brad, Ion 69, 89
Iorga, Nicolae 6–7, 25
Ipsilanti, Alexandru, Prince of Wallachia 52, 58–59
Ipsilanti, Alexandru, Greek revolutionary 77–80
Ipsilanti, Constantin, Prince of Wallachia (1802–1806) 73n21
Iraq 16
Ireland 89–93, 133n17, 142
Isabel, Princess Imperial of Brazil 101
Isar, Wallachian man 49–50
Islam, Islamic law 42; *see also* Ottoman Empire
Ismail 91
Ismail Gedikli of Brăila 60n83
Istanbul 16, 20, 28, 30, 39, 55–56, 58–60, 62, 72, 74–76, 81–83, 85–86, 89–90, 116, 118, 133
Italy 14, 30, 98, 125n55
Italian language, people 15–16, 25, 27n78, 29, 154, 156
Iuliena, nun 51
Izimșa, Mehedinți county 107n64
Izvoarele, Mehedinți county 107n64
Izvorul de Jos, Vlașca (today Giurgiu) county 40
Jakobson, Roman 151
janissaries 24

Java 100, 101n23
Jegalia, Călărași county 136n28
Jerusalem, Orthodox Patriarchate of 48
Jews 54, 100
Jianu, Angela 8
Jieni, Romanați county (today com. Rusănești, Olt county) 108n66
Jiu county 109
Jiu river 66
Joseph II, Emperor 45–46
Jósika family 46n50
Kanetsos *see* Canetsos
Kantakouzenos *see* Cantacuzino
Kapocsány *see* Copăceni
Kara Mustafa Pasha, Grand Vezir 30
Karlowitz, Treaty of 35
Karlsbad (Karlovy Vary) 54
Kaunitz, Wenzel Anton, Prince of Kaunitz-Rietberg, Habsburg Chancellor 58–59
kebabs, food of princes 134
Kephala, Dionisios, Prussian agent in Focșani 82n70
Khrushchev, Nikita 7
Kiselev, General Count Pavel Dmitrieveich 85–87
Kisősi *see* Aușeu
Klein Dikman *see* Ticvaniu Mic
Kogălniceanu, Enache 50n10
Kogălniceanu, Mihail 95, 103, 122
Kolozsvár *see* Cluj
Koronelli, A. I. 87
Kotor (Montenegro), 151
Kővár *see* Chioar
Kövesd *see* Cuieșd
Kreuchely von Schwerdtberg, Baron Ludwig, Prussian consul in Bucharest 77, 80n52, 81n62
Kronstadt *see* Brașov
Kućanja, Serbia 25n73
Küçük Kaynarca, Treaty of 49
Kukuitz, fabled Mexican goddess 151n11
Kukur, personal name 151n6
kukuruz see *cucuruz*
Kule *see* Turnu
kvass 117n22
La Plata, Argentina 104n39
Lăculețe skete, Dâmbovița county 51

Lăcusteanu, Mihai 81n57
ladybirds 151, 154n36
Lahovary, General Iacob N. 102n27
Laloșu, Vâlcea county 108n68
lamb, spit-roasted 134; mămăligă with, 127
Latin 15, 23, 36, 113, 121, 150–51, 153–57
Laudan, Rachel 5, 125
Lăunele de Jos, Argeș county (today Vâlcea county) 108n70
Laz people 26
Lebanon 16
Lemberg *see* L'viv
lentils 61, 68, 117, 140
Leorind, Giurgi 73
Lévi-Strauss, Claude 10
Liberal Party of Romania 102–3, 106, 136
Liiceanu, Gabriel 129
linseed 114
Lipan, Costache, merchant 81
Lipia-Bojdani, Ilfov county 102–3
Lippa, Austrian agent in Sibiu 80n52
Lippmann, Edmund von 151n11
Livezi, com. Podari, Dolj county 107n65
Liverpool 91
Lloyd's List 104
Lombards, Lombardy 118, 120n36
Long Turkish War (1593–1606) 18
lovage 128
Lucchesini, Girolamo, Marquis 59n71
Luchian, Ștefan 136
Luncșoara (Élesdlok), Bihor county 25n64
Lupescu, Mihai 126
Luță, Nicolae 107n66
L'viv (Lemberg) 132
Macedonia 17, 145n10
Mád, Hungary 22
Madrid 18
Magheru, Romulus, Major 103n35
Magyar (language) 24, 26, 114, 121, 150, 157; *see also* Hungary, Hungarians
Mahmud II, Ottoman Sultan 72, 75, 82
Maior, Petru 65
Majdanpek, Serbia 25n63
Mălăești, Iași 158
Mălăești (Malajesd), Hunedoara county 158
mălai, etymology of, 154; meanings of, 27, 63, 116, 127–28; in literature and folk-

lore, 132–33, 137–39; as personal name, 158; as nickname, 23
Malaya 144
Malta 90
Mămălată 27, 159
mămăligă, *passim*; history of word, 154–55; as personal/place name, 27, 68–69, 159; historical recipes, 113–29
Mămăligă, Chiril 69
Mămăligă, Ianeș 69
Mămăligă, Neculai 159
Mămăligă, Ștefan 69
Mămăligă, Toader 159
Mămăligă, Vlad 69
Mămăligani (*Mameliganÿ*), Alba county 159
Manea, Wallachian man 49
Manning, Anne 131
maple 65
Manu, Mihalache, caimacam 81n60
Mărăcinii Lungi, Prahova county 50
Maramureș county 22
Margire a lui Malai 158
Maria Theresa, Empress 45, 115
Marie, Queen of Romania 109
Marin, Sanda 126–27
Marincu, Ioniță 107n64
Maros county (historical), Transylvania 23
Mârsan, Dolj county 107n65
Marta, abbess 51
Mary (saint) *see* Virgin Mary
Maryland, United States 144
Mârzăști, Iași county 41
Mattioli, Pietro Andrea 17
Mátyus, István 67
Maurer, Maria 122–24
Mavrocordat, Constantin, Prince of Moldavia (1741–1743) and Wallachia (1735–1741, 1744–1748) 41, 67, 120n36
Mavrocordat, Nicolae, Prince of Moldavia (1711–1716) 29n88
Mavrogheni, Nicolae, Prince of Wallachia (1786–1790) 52n28, 56n56, 58–59
McCann, James C. 6, 31
McNeill, William H. 67–68
Mediaș (Mediasch), Sibiu county 113
medicine, medics, medical discourse 30, 46, 65, 67, 115–16, 118, 121, 124–26, 145

Mediterranean Sea 13–15, 19, 22, 26, 44
Mehmed Emin Rauf Pasha, Grand Vezir 72n12
Mehmet Ağa Hacı Alişoğlu, merchant 89n23
Mehmet Tabak 75
merchants, traders 22, 25–26, 36, 43–44, 53–54, 58–61, 64, 73–76, 80–83, 85–93, 120, 133, 142, 145, 151n11
Meri Goala, Teleorman county 108n69
Merișescu, Tache 121
Merkelius, Michael, Austrian consul in Bucharest 57n59, 59–61
Messer, Ellen 6
Metternich, Clemens, Chancellor 72
Metzberg, Austrian agent 58–59
Mexico 3, 13, 104n40, 105n49, 125, 151; Revolution of 1810–1821, 73
Michael the Brave, Prince of Wallachia 18–19, 23
Michael I, King of Romania 127
Miciu, Dumitru, landowner 108n70
Mihai, Roma student 1
Mihalache, bailiff, Prahova county 56n54
Mihalache, landowner, Vlașca county 40
Mikes, Kelemen 114
Miklouho-Maclay, Nikolai 150
millet 13, 16–17, 23, 24n60, 26n70, 27–29, 36, 40–42, 50, 58, 61, 63, 75, 81, 83, 154–55; mămăligă made with, 113–17, 121–22
mills 42, 74, 79, 90
Mocarelli, Luca 6
Mocenigo, Alvise III 36n5
Mohács, Battle of 20
Moldavia (principality, later region of Romania) 20, 22–23, 25–30, 39–51, 54–55, 58–62, 66–69, 71–72, 74–77, 81–83, 87–89, 91–93, 95, 97, 99, 106–7, 113, 117–19, 121–22, 124, 126–27, 129, 134, 141–44; Moldavian regional words, 104, 149
Moldova, Republic of 3; *see also* Bessarabia; Moldavia
monasteries 29, 39, 40–43, 49–51, 53, 58–62, 79–80, 87, 123, 141, 154
Montmorency, Mathieu Jean Felicité, duc de, French Minister for Foreign Affairs 80n52, 81n62

Morea (Peloponnese) 15n9
Moreno-Cruz, Juan 69
Morocco 16n10
Morțun, Vasile 136
Moruzi, Alexandru, Prince of Wallachia (1793–1796) and Moldavia (1802–1806) 60–63
Moruzi, Constantin, Prince of Moldavia (1777–1782) 55
Moșoiu, landowner 108n67
Mozambique 3, 136
Mungiu, Cristian 2
Munich 120n36
Mureș county 136; *see also* Maros
Muslims 85, 100–1; *see also* Turks
Mustafa III, Ottoman Sultan 44n62
Mustafa-Aga, *beșli-aga* 58–59
Musteață, Theodor 60
Nădejde, Sofia 125, 133
Nagysáros *see* Vel'ky Šariš
Nagyvárad *see* Oradea
national identity, nationalism 1–6, 9–10, 60, 63–65, 78, 95, 120–27, 131–33; national dances 76
Naum Râmniceanu, chronicler 79
Neagu, Wallachian man 49
Neculce, Ion 28–29
Negoiești, Dolj county 107n65
Negre (Negri), Constantin, caimacam of Wallachia 60
Negruzzi, Constantin 122
Neofit, Metropolitan of Ungrovlachia (1738–1753) 39
neoserfdom 96
Netherlands 16, 30, 35
nettles 71, 128
Nicholas I, Emperor of Russia 85
Nicolantin, Antonie 50n9
nobles, nobility *see* boyars
nuns 51–52
nuts, beech 50; nut oil, 118
oats 17, 36, 42, 63–64, 110, 154n37
Obedeanca, Prahova county, Wallachia 50
Obedeanu Monastery, Craiova, Wallachia 50
Obislavele, Dâmbovița county 39
Obogeanu, landowner 108n68

Obradović, Dositej 43, 64
Obradovici, Grigore 64–65
Odessa 92
Oișteanu, Andrei 132
Oliphant, Laurence 93
Olt county, Wallachia 76, 108, 136
Oltenia (Little Wallachia) 35–36, 38, 40, 50–54, 73–74, 108–9, 114–15, 133, 154
Omer, Pasha of Vidin 24
Onceni, village, Siret valley, Moldavia 27, 68
Onești, Bacău county 106
onions 61, 117, 134, 140
Oprea, man 49
orache (*atriplex*) 114
Oradea (Nagyvárad) 25, 63
Orășani, com. Ostroveni, Dolj county 109
Organic Statutes 85, 87–88
Orhei county, Moldavia 15n7, 158
Orthodox Christians 22, 39, 42, 69, 72, 155; *see also* Christianity, monasteries, Romanian Orthodox Church
Ortiteag (Ürgeteg), Bihor county 25n64
Örvend *see* Urvind
Osman of Kule 29
Osman Pasvanoğlu, Pasha of Vidin 62
Osterhammel, Jürgen 37
Ostrovu Mare, com. Gogoșu, Mehedinți county 107n64
Ottoman Empire 4, 9–10, 14–31, 35–45, 49, 53, 58–62, 66–67, 72, 74–83, 85–89, 99, 114, 119–20, 141–43, 150–52; *see also* Turkish, Turks
oxen 28, 64, 79, 133
Padina Mare, Mehedinți county 107n64
Padua 25, 120n36
Paisie, hegumen 53
Palade, Teodor, Moldavian boyar 41
Panaiteanu-Bardasare, Emanuel 100
pandurs 73, 75, 81
Panjek, Aleksandar 6
paprika 30, 131
Papua New Guinea 150
păpușoi (Moldavian term for maize), 27n83, 59, 63, 82n73, 104, 155–56, 159
Păpușoi, Roma slave 69
Părăianu, Ion 49n3

Parapeanu, Captain 102
Parfene Bârzul, monk 40
Paris, Treaty of (1856) 95–97; World Exhibition (1889), 134; World Fair (1937), 127
Pârvu, Ștefan 29
Pascu, George 151
Pătrășcu, Axente 42n50
Pătru, logofăt 81n61
Pavlović, Velija, merchant 80
Paz Sanchez, Miguel de 37n20
pears 68
peasants, peasant culture 2, 45, 51, 53, 55, 58, 61, 69, 73–74, 86–89, 95, 98, 100–9, 117–19, 124–27, 133–36, 142, 144
Peel, Sir Robert 90
Peicăneanu, Dimtru Radu 83n76
pellagra 4, 104, 124–25
pepper (capsicum), Romanian word for explained 156n57; *see also* paprika
Peregu Mare, Arad county 136n28
Petraru *see* Pietrari
Petőfi, Sándor 131–32
Phanariots, Phanariot regime 39, 70–71, 77, 85, 134
Philadelphia 136
Philip II, King of Spain 18
Philippides, Dimitris (Daniil) 120n36
Pietrari (Petraru), Vâlcea county 49
pigs, swine 23, 50, 52–55, 64; *see also* pork
pineapples 54
pine cones 152
Pintea, Ilie 49n4
Pisani, Andrei, Russian consul in Moldavia 76n36
plague 44, 71, 116
plantations 69, 143–44
Pleșoianu, Vasile, boyar 52
plums 55, 61, 64, 68, 126, 153; plum sauce, 119
Podu Grosului, com. Bâcleș, Mehedinți county 107n64
Poiana-Lungă, Botoșani county 106
Poienari, *see* Horezu Poienari
Poland 3, 26, 41, 43, 54–55
Polish language, 150
polenta 3, 117–19, 121–22, 124, 131n2; antiquity of word, 27n78

Polynesians 125
Popescu, a leaseholder 107n68
pork meat 2; bacon, 50; fat, 199; *ragoût de porc* with mămăligă, 127; *see also* pigs
Porte *see* Ottoman Empire
Poromb, scribe 159
Portuguese Empire 14
porumb (maize), word history 27, 63, 156–57
Porumb, Armenian merchant 69
Porumb, seller of land 159
Porumb, Stanciu 159
Porumbacu (Porumbok), Sibiu county 159
Porumbarul, Vasile 159
Porumbreni, Wallachia 159
Porumbriu, buys land 159
Porumbu, Radu 159
Porumbul Vornic 159
Porumbul, serf 159
Porumbul, Wallachia 159
Porumbul, witness 159
potatoes 4, 31n108, 46, 62, 67, 89, 108n69; mămăligă made with, 126
Požarevac, Serbia 24
Požega, Croatia 19
Prague 17–19
Protestants 114
Prussia 76–77, 80n52, 97
pumpkins 23, 25
Punjabi language 151n11
Putna county, Moldavia 41
Putna Monastery 41
Putna river 29
quarantines 44, 71, 115–16
Raab, Austrian agent in Iași 72–73
Răcășdia (Rakasdia), Caraș-Severin county 115
Racoviță, Constantin, Prince of Moldavia (1756–1757) 42n46
Racoviță, Mihai, Prince of Moldavia (1716–1726) 29
Racovița, Romanați county (today com. Voineasa, Olt county) 108n66
Radislavov, Tsviatko, merchant 89n23
Rădoiești, Teleorman county 108n69
Rădulești, Ialomița County 136n28
Raeț, Dolj county 76
Rafail, hegumen 43n54

Ragusa *see* Dubrovnik
Raicevich, Ignaz Stefan 49, 58n61, 116
Rakasdia *see* Răcășdia
raki 75, 81, 83
Rákoczi family, estates of 23–24
Rămești, Vâlcea county 108n68
Raosaljić, Radonja 'Chuchuruz' 151n6
rape (oilseed) 108n69
Raspe, Rudolph 116n15
Rauwolf, Leonhart 16, 18
Red Sea 14, 90
Reid, Thomas Wemyss 99
Reinhard, Charles 43n59
Ressu, Camil 136
rhubarb 30
rice 4, 30, 61; rice porridge, 24
Rodna, Transylvania 27
Roma (Gypsies) 10, 43, 64, 122, 132–33, 138–40, 158–59
Roman, Radu Anton 127–28
Roman Catholics 29, 41, 58–59, 67, 69
Roman county, Moldavia 73, 158
Romanați county, Wallachia 53, 106–8
Romanian Academy 95
Romanian language 22, 27, 29, 42n48, 59, 63–65, 72, 86, 113–14, 121–22, 127, 131–40, 149–59
Romanian Orthodox Church 95
Rome 14
Ropcea, Traian V. V. 108n70
Roset, Dracache, Grand Spathar of Moldavia 73
Rosetti-Roznovanu, Nicolae 62n92
Rothenthurm *see* Turnu Roșu
Rotopan, Ion 59
Routh, Sir Randolph 90n30
Rudolf II, Emperor 18–19
Rumyantsev-Zadunaisky, General Count Pyotr Alexandrovich 43n58
Rural Law of 1864 95–96
Rusănestii de Sus, Romanați county (today Olt county) 108n66
Ruse (Rusçuk), Bulgaria 81n63, 86
Russian Empire 40, 45–46, 49, 59–60, 62, 66, 73, 75–77, 80, 85–87, 89, 92–93, 97, 104, 141; Federation, 146; Russian people, language 54, 150

Russo-Turkish Wars: (1768–1774) 45–56; (1787–1792) 58–59; (1806–1812) 73–75; (1828–1834) 85; (1877–1878) 101; *see also* Crimean War
rye 46, 55, 63, 110, 117n22, 154n37
Sacher-Masoch, Leopold von 131
Sadeler, Aegidius 19
Sadova, Dolj county 66
Sadova Monastery 53
St. Maria Monastery, Zadar, Croatia 151
St. Mary *see* Virgin Mary
St. Pantelimon Monastery, Bucharest 61
St. Peter 135
St. Spiridon Monastery, Iași 42
Salaberry, Charles-Marie d'Irumberry, Comte de 9, 53–54
salami 54
Sălătrucu, Argeș county, Wallachia 77
salt 20, 56, 116, 118–19, 137–38
Sampson, Steven 146
sanitary cordons 44, 86
Santoni, Pietro, Sardinian merchant 92n49
Satu Mare county, Romania 136
sausages 126
Saxons, Transylvanian 23, 50, 113, 118, 126
Scărișoara, Romanați county (today com. Băbiciu, Olt county) 107n66
Schäser, Christian 113
Șchei district, Brașov, Transylvania 69
Scheia, Roman county, Moldavia 73
Schilling, Leopold, Austrian agent in Iași 60n80
Schladen, Count Friedrich Leopold von, Prussian Minister to Porte 76–77
Schwantz von Springfels, Friedrich 36, 38, 115
Scotland 100; *see also* Great Britain
Scottish governess, fictional, advises against mămăligă 133
Scott, James 5
Selim III, Ottoman Sultan 44n62, 56, 60
Semlin *see* Zemun
Serbia 25, 67, 145; Habsburg Kingdom of, 35–36
Serbs 35, 56, 62, 64, 78–80, 115
Serbian language 150–51
serfs, serfdom, enserfment 69, 96, 145, 159; 'neoserfdom', 96

sesame 16
Sestini, Domenico 116–17
Severin, Ivan Ivanovich, Russian consul in Wallachia 58n63
Seville 14
sheep 20, 43, 56, 80; milk, 113; droppings, 154n36
shepherds 10, 31, 56, 101, 133, 134n18
Shvishtov (Zistovi, Şiştova), Bulgaria 89n23
Sibiu (Hermannstadt), 22, 52n30, 60n80, 80n52, 118; salami of, 54
Sibiu county 136n28, 159
Siguranța (Security Services) 106
Silahdar Fındıkhlı Mehmed Aga, Ottoman historian 25
Siliștea-Gumești, Teleorman county 108n69
Silistra 81
Simnicea, Suceava County 136n28
Sion, Iordachi 72n14
Siret river, Moldavia 27
Skye, Isle of 100
Slatina, Wallachia 58, 76
slaves, slavery 10, 43, 69, 90, 101, 123, 143–44, 151n6
Slavic languages 15, 150–51, 153, 156
Slavici, Ioan 133
Slavonia 19, 25
Slobozia-Mândra, Teleorman county 108n69
Slovak language 150
Smederevo, Serbia 24–25
socialism, socialists 96, 103, 125, 127, 136, 146
Socola Monastery, Moldavia 51
Sohod, Bacău county 40
Șoldești, Putna county, Moldavia (today com. Fitionești, Vrancea county) 27
songs, ballads 108, 138–39, 151n11
Soranzo, Jacopo 17
sorghum 16–17
Soviet Union *see* Union of Soviet Socialist Republics
soya beans 125
Spanish Empire, people, language 14, 18, 37, 54; 151n11
Sperber, Galia 13

Speteni, Ialomița county 102
Spinești, Putna county (today Vrancea county) 41
Sremski Karlovci (Karlowitz), Serbia 35
Stachowski, Kamil 152
Steter, General Ivan Ivanovich 66
Stainville, Etienne (Graf Stefan Steinville), Habsburg commander in Transylvania 36n8
Stan, brother of Ilie and son of Mihai 49
Stana, abbess 151n6
Stânișoara, mountain, Neamț county 134n18
Stanley, Henry Morton 101
Ștefan clucer 72n6
Ștefania, Moldavian woman 40
Stephen the Great, Prince of Moldavia 134
Stignița, Mehedinți county 107n64
Știrbei, Barbu, Wallachian boyar (18th century) 53–54
Știrbei, Barbu Dimitrie, Prince of Wallachia (1849–1856) 54
Știrbei (Știrbey), Prince Barbu (1872–1945), 99, 107n65
Știrbei, Romanați county (today com. Iancu Jianu, Olt county) 108n66
Stoianovich, Traian 143
Stoker, Bram 131
Strejeștii de Jos, Romanați county (today Olt county) 108n66
Sturdza, Ion Sandu, Prince of Moldavia (1822–1828) 83n76, 87n9
Styria 17–18, 44
Suceava county 136n28
sugar 54, 65–66, 118, 144
sugar beet 62
Sulzer, Franz Joseph 116
Summerers, Francis British consul in Bucharest 51
Susana, mother superior 51
Suțu, Alexandru, Prince of Wallachia (1818–1821) 76–77
Suțu, Mihai, Prince of Wallachia (1783–1786, 1791–1793), of Moldavia (1793–1795) 52, 55–56, 58–59, 83; nicknamed *Păpușoi Vodă*, 59
Suțu, Mihai, Prince of Moldavia (1819–1821) 75–76, 83

213

swine *see* pigs
Switzerland 17, 140
Syria 16
Szamosújvár *see* Gherla
Tallar, Johann Georg 115–16
Tâmna, Mehedinți county 107n64
Tănase Turcul 49
Tancoigne, J. M. 81n62
Țara Bârsei (Burzenland) 72
Târgoviște, Wallachia 59, 79
Târgșor Monastery, Wallachia 39, 50
Tatars 26–27
tax, taxation, tithes 23, 25, 28–29, 36–37, 40–43, 51–52, 61, 68, 71, 76, 82, 87, 106, 108, 141–42; *see also* tribute
Teasc, Dolj county 107n65
Teișani, Prahova county 49
Teișanu, Băluță 51
Teleajen river, Wallachia 49
Telechiu (Telegd), Bihor county 25n64
Teleorman county, Wallachia 29, 59, 81, 106n59, 108n69, 136
Tempea, Radu 72
Țețchea (Cécke), Bihor county 25n64
The Land is Waiting (documentary) 1–2
theatre 2–3, 93–94
Thévenin, Léon 127
Thököly, Imre 24
Thrace 16
Ticvaniu Mic (Klein Dikman), Caraș-Severin county 115
Țimburești, com. Murta, Dolj county
Timișoara (Temeșvar), Ottoman fortress 22n47, 25, 35; *see also* Banat of Temesvar
tithes *see* tax
Tinăud (Tinód), Bihor county 25n64
tobacco 28, 30, 79, 145
tomato seeds 23–24
tortillas 128
Transylvania 20–30, 35, 44–46, 50–51, 54, 56–57, 59–60, 63, 65–67, 69, 71–72, 75, 79, 81–82, 87, 89, 113–14, 118, 120, 121, 126, 131–32, 141, 149, 154, 157–59; German dialects of, 151
Trei Scaune *see* Háromszék
Trestieni, Prahova county 50
Trevelyan, Charles 90

tribute 20, 49, 55–61, 73–75, 79, 86; *see also* tax
Trieste 44, 88, 90
Trinidad 100
Trocan, Ion 75n30
Tudoran, Mihail 50
Tulcea 91
tulips 30
Țumbru, Vasile, merchant 50
Tunis 16
Turkey *see* Ottoman Empire
Turkic peoples 101
'Turkish corn' (name for maize) 15–16, 22–23
Turkish, Ottoman Turkish 15, 59, 82, 117, 151–52
Turks 40, 49, 53, 75, 81, 89
Turnu, Wallachia (today Turnu Măgurele) 29
Turnu Roșu (Rothenthurm), Sibiu county 115–16
Uganda 100
Ukraine 3, 41, 132, 146
Ukrainian language 150, 152n19, 155n51
Ungrovlahia, Metropolitanate, estates of 39, 50, 53
Union of Soviet Socialist Republics 7
United States of America 3, 5, 7 69, 88–90, 96, 104n40, 125n55; *see also* America
Ürgeteg *see* Ortiteag
Urlați, Saac county (today Prahova county), Wallachia 50
Urvind (Örvend), Bihor county 25n64
Urzicuța, Dolj county 107n65
Văcărescu, Ianache (Ienăchiță) 58, 59
vaccination 86
vakıf 42
Vâlcea county, Wallachia 29, 36, 49–50, 108
Valea Stanciului, Dolj county 107n65
Văleni, Olt county 136n28
Văleni, Prahova county 49
vampires 115
Varaždin, Croatia 18–19
Vârciorog (Vércsorog), Bihor county 25n64
Varna 91
Vârnav, Constantin 121
Vaslui county 89
Vatican 14
Vel'ky Šariš (Nagysáros), Slovakia 24

Venice 14, 16–17, 22, 36, 88, 116
Verbița, Dolj county 107n65
Vércsorog *see* Vârciorog
Verne, Jules 131
Vertumnus, Roman god of gardening 18–19
Veteranyi, Aglaja 129, 140
Victoria, Queen 95
Vienna 17, 22n47, 24, 30, 36–37, 113, 115–6, 118, 120n36
vineyards 43, 68
Vinidicta, nun 51–52
Virgin Mary, Feast of 126
Visser, Margaret 6
Vistireasa, Prahova county 39
Vlachs *see* Aromanians
Vladimirescu, Tudor 73–75, 77–80
Vlașca county (today Giurgiu county) 40, 80
Voineasa, Romanați county (today Olt county) 108n66
Voroneț Monastery, Moldavia 41
Vrata, Mehedinți county 107n64
Vulturești, Olt county 108n67
Vurpăr (Burgberg), Sibiu county 136n28
Wallachia 20, 23–30, 35–45, 47, 49–63, 66, 68, 71–83, 85–88, 91–93, 95, 97, 102, 107–8, 115–16, 118–22, 132–34, 141–44, 149, 152, 154, 158–59; national dances, 76; Little Wallachia, *see* Oltenia
von Wallis, General Count Franz-Paul 37
wars, warfare 18, 22, 24, 29–30, 42–46, 58–59, 73–75, 77–80, 85–88, 93, 101, 116, 132, 142, 147

Warasdiner-St. Georger (Gjurgevatz) frontier regiment 18n31
Warman, Arturo 6
Wathay, Ferenc 21
wax 20, 43
wheat 13, 17, 23, 29, 36, 40, 42, 46, 49–50, 52, 55, 58, 60–61, 63–64, 67, 74, 76, 79, 87–88, 92–93, 95, 99, 105, 107–11, 114, 118, 121n40, 125, 128, 136, 145, 154n37
whey 138–39
Wilkinson, Wiliam 74
willow 128
wine 36, 40, 50, 54–55, 79, 91, 116, 134, 140; *see also* grapes, vineyards
Wolf, Andreas 118–19
women 51–52, 128–29, 133, 135; admiring gaze of, 77; accused of theft, 64
wormwood 128
Yergöğü *see* Giurgiu
Xenopol, A. D. 124–25
Ypsilantis *see* Ipsilanti
Zadar 151
Zamfirescu, Duiliu 133
Zanne, Iuliu A. 136
Zemun (Semlin) 45n67
Zen, Caterin 16–17
Zimnicea, Teleorman county 108n69
Zlătari Monastery, Bucharest 43, 121
Zöld, Péter 41n39
Zrjenanin (Becicherec Mare), Serbia 67
Zvorsca, Romanați county (today Dolj county) 107n66

CPSIA information can be obtained
at www.ICGtesting.com
Printed in the USA
BVHW061353090922
646649BV00004B/458